TONI MORRISON AND THE NATURAL WORLD

TONI MORRISON AND THE NATURAL WORLD

An Ecology of Color

Anissa Janine Wardi

University Press of Mississippi / Jackson

The University Press of Mississippi is the scholarly publishing agency of the Mississippi Institutions of Higher Learning: Alcorn State University, Delta State University, Jackson State University, Mississippi State University, Mississippi University for Women, Mississippi Valley State University, University of Mississippi, and University of Southern Mississippi.

www.upress.state.ms.us

The University Press of Mississippi is a member of the Association of University Presses.

First printing 2021
∞

Portions of the following appear in this book and are reprinted with permission of the University Press of Florida:

"Cotton Fields and Cane Stalks: Labor and Death in *Of Love and Dust* and *Song of Solomon*," by Anissa Janine Wardi, in *Death and the Arc of Mourning in African American Literature* (Gainesville: University Press of Florida, 2003), selected excerpts.

"Wetlands, Swamps, and Bayous: Bodies of Resistance in Kasi Lemmons's *Eve's Bayou* and Toni Morrison's *Tar Baby*," by Anissa Janine Wardi, in *Water and African American Memory: An Ecocritical Perspective* (Gainesville: University Press of Florida, 2003), 83–114, selected excerpts.

Library of Congress Cataloging-in-Publication Data

Names: Wardi, Anissa Janine, 1969– author.
Title: Toni Morrison and the natural world : an ecology of color / Anissa Janine Wardi.
Description: Jackson : University Press of Mississippi, 2021. | Includes bibliographical references and index.
Identifiers: LCCN 2021007221 (print) | LCCN 2021007222 (ebook) | ISBN 9781496834164 (hardback) | ISBN 9781496834171 (trade paperback) | ISBN 9781496834188 (epub) | ISBN 9781496834195 (epub) | ISBN 9781496834201 (pdf) | ISBN 9781496834218 (pdf)
Subjects: LCSH: Morrison, Toni—Criticism and interpretation. | African American authors—History and criticism. | American literature—20th century—History and criticism. | LCGFT: Literary criticism.
Classification: LCC PS3563.O8749 Z944 2021 (print) | LCC PS3563.O8749 (ebook) | DDC 813/.54—dc23
LC record available at https://lccn.loc.gov/2021007221
LC ebook record available at https://lccn.loc.gov/2021007222

British Library Cataloging-in-Publication Data available

CONTENTS

PREFACE

It is September, and the colors of the garden are still vibrant. Outside with my children, my enjoyment of the yellow snapdragons, purple zinnias, and dusky hydrangeas is mitigated, for this "riot of color" is another reminder of my unfinished book. I have not returned to my work since Toni Morrison's death, which has been a little over a month ago now. The announcement of Morrison's death coincided with my birthday, and thus celebratory wishes were punctuated with condolences, an uncomfortable juxtaposition that is strangely apt for the work that I do in African American ecocriticism, an orientation to the natural world that is, by turns, beautiful and traumatic. In the days and weeks that followed, I received messages of sympathy from family, friends, colleagues, and students. These gestures were touching but gave me pause. Do I deserve to receive these words of concern? I met Morrison a couple of times, attended a handful of her public readings, and presented at Toni Morrison Society conferences. I have spent more than twenty years writing about Morrison's work, presenting my research at conferences, evaluating Morrison scholarship for academic journals and presses, and teaching her novels in introductory courses and upper-level seminars. Yes, I am affected by her death, deeply so, but this loss should not be personal, right? She is, after all, not "mine."

As I struggle to understand this peculiar feeling of being intimately connected to the work of a writer with whom I had no personal relationship, I turn to emails I received from former students. Their eloquence clarifies my emotional response and offers me permission to mourn:

"I wanted to thank you for exposing me to Ms. Morrison's work during my three extraordinary years as your student. Her death hit me much harder than I expected, and that has everything to do with how deeply and intimately you helped me (and so many others) connect with her work. That depth of connection between student, professor, author and text is so magical. I'm certain that, in the wake of her passing, that magic will only grow stronger for your students."[1]

"I don't think I have ever or will ever read a better writer and I'm so grateful to you for incentivizing me to read all of her books and to then lecture on them so eloquently. The ending of *Jazz* is still my absolute favorite page in any book and I'll never forget your reading of it, as the book speaking to the reader: 'Talking to you & hearing you answer—that's the kick.' Anyways, we're all so lucky to have been alive at the same time as her. And I'm thankful you led me to her."[2]

Thankful to my students, I now acknowledge that I am in mourning, a "crooked kind of mourning" for a writer whose work I have studied my entire adult life, whose writing compelled me to abandon law school and enter a life in the academy, and whose words, spoken and written, echo in my ears. While this book is dedicated to my loving husband, Casey, and my beautiful children, Malcolm and Penelope, who remind me to notice the splendor of the living world—brightly hued butterflies, blossoming trees, birdsong, and moss peeking out from stones—it is also my tribute to Toni Morrison, a gesture of gratitude for a writer who has offered the gift of truth and beauty to the world. Her words will live on, and so, as my dear friend reminded me, "Toni Morrison can never really die."

TONI MORRISON AND THE NATURAL WORLD

Introduction

"ALL OF THEM COLORS WAS IN ME"

Embodiment and Material Ecocriticism

In *Beloved*, Toni Morrison deftly turns to color as a signifying system of loss, sorrow, and joy. After her granddaughter's murder and the subsequent familial dissolution, Baby Suggs retreats to her bed to ponder color. Though Sethe obliges her mother-in-law's request, bringing her everything from "fabric to her own tongue" (*Beloved*, 4), it is not until Sethe's dead daughter returns to 124 Bluestone Road that Sethe reaches for color:

> Now I can look at things again because she's here to see them too. After the shed, I stopped. Now, in the morning, when I light the fire I mean to look out the window to see what the sun is doing to the day. Does it hit the pump handle first or the spigot? See if the grass is gray-green or brown or what. Now I know why Baby Suggs pondered color her last years. She never had time to see, let alone enjoy it before. . . . Now I'll be on the lookout. Think what spring will be for us! I'll plant carrots just so she can see them, and turnips. Have you ever seen one, baby? A prettier thing God never made. White and purple with a tender tail and a hard head. Feels good when you hold it in your hand and smells like the creek when it floods, bitter but happy. (*Beloved*, 201)

Sethe arrives at a nuanced understanding of Baby Suggs's dissolve into color, regarding it not only as an act of mourning but as a sensory indulgence, a purposeful engagement with the material world. Filled with thoughts of her daughter returned, Sethe revels in the splendidness of color. In Morrison's fictional universe, colorscapes are tied to elements of the natural world—grass, turnips, and creeks—and thus characters' intimacy with place is articulated through chromatics.

Toni Morrison and the Natural World: An Ecology of Color uses an ecocritical approach to examine the biophysical environment in Toni Morrison's body of work. Key moments in Morrison's fiction are communicated through the living world. For example, in her inaugural novel, *The Bluest Eye*, the fate of the protagonist, Pecola, is linked to the outcome of marigold seeds. Morrison voices the gentrification of a Caribbean island in *Tar Baby* through the consciousness of two-thousand-year-old daisy trees. In her Pulitzer Prize–winning novel *Beloved*, the protagonist, Sethe, is imprinted with a "chokecherry tree," and the slain child at the center of the novel emerges from a stream. And in *Home*, white terrorists violently claim ownership over a Black neighborhood, and all but one elderly man, Crawford, flee the scene. Crawford sits on his porch, gazing at his land, and for this attachment to place, he is murdered, his eyes brutally wrenched from their sockets. Morrison provides no information about Crawford's connection to his house, the built environment, but explains that he refused to leave the magnolia tree his great-grandmother planted, which later serves as his burial site. This study provides insight into the natural world as a recurrent and significant topic in Morrison's fiction, of which the author herself was keenly aware: "I must confess, though, that I sometimes lose interest in the characters and get much more interested in the trees and animals. I think I exercise tremendous restraint in this, but my editor says, 'Would you stop all this *beauty* business.' And I say, 'Wait, wait until I tell you about these ants'" ("The Language Must Not Sweat," 120). Here Morrison explains that her interest in the biophysical world at times rivals—if not supersedes—her attention to her characters. Following Morrison's lead, this book pivots on the axis of the nature-culture interaction, the mesh, for the physical environment can never be divorced from human society. I borrow the concept of the "mesh" from Timothy Morton, who argues in *The Ecological Thought*, "The ecological thought imagines interconnectedness, which I call *the mesh*. Who or what is interconnected with what or whom? The mesh of interconnected things is vast, perhaps immeasurably so" (15).

Morrison's ecological consciousness holds that human geographies are always enmeshed or intertwined with nonhuman nature. It follows, then, that ecology, the branch of biology that studies how people relate to one another and their environment, is an apt framework for this book. The interrelationships and interactions between individuals and community, and between organisms and their natural world, are central to this analysis because they highlight that the human and nonhuman are part of a larger ecosystem of interfacings and transformations.

This study of Morrison and the biophysical world provides new insights into Morrison's fiction and participates in the recent materialist turn in ecocritical theory that recognizes the human as embroiled with the nonhuman. Matter is not inert but dynamic, agentic, and part of the assemblage of the living world. Serenella Iovino and Serpil Oppermann, in *Material Ecocriticism*, argue that the living world is endowed with narratives, and this "storied matter" is transmitted through interchanges of organic and inorganic matter, human and nonhuman forms. Stacy Alaimo, in *Bodily Natures*, maintains that human materiality is inseparable from other physical bodies, a concept that she refers to as transcorporeality. Alaimo's work illustrates the entanglement between body and place and "accounts for the ways in which nature, the environment, and the material world itself signify, act upon, or otherwise affect human bodies, knowledges and practices" (7–8). In her interdisciplinary study on the transcorporeal understanding of matter, Alaimo stresses the need for a theoretical rearticulation of the contact zones between human corporeality and the more-than-human worlds. Natural environments are not distinct from society; that is, "culture" is not outside of "nature," which opens up the ecocritical conversation to include issues of race.

It is reasonable to conclude that Morrison scholars have shied away from applying the terms of ecocritical analysis to her body of work because of the uneasy relationship between African American literature and ecocriticism. Paul Outka, in *Race and Nature*, provides insight into the "terrible historical legacy of making people of color signify the natural as a prelude to exploiting both" (3), which "makes the possibility of an uncomplicated union with the natural world less readily available to African Americans than it has been to whites who, by and large, have not suffered from such a history" (3). Therefore it follows that writers and critics may be reticent to label African American literature as environmental in recognition of a national history that debased African American humanity through the rhetoric of "nature." Moreover, ecocritical discourse has historically privileged and romanticized the natural world and set it apart from social landscapes. Such a bifurcation of the human from the nonhuman refuses to recognize the layered, nuanced, and fraught relationship that exists between people of color and the natural world. The fusion of history onto the natural world is the very bedrock of African American ecocritical thought.

The Toni Morrison Society's Bench by the Road Project illuminates the conflation of history and geography. The project was inspired by Morrison's own words regarding the absence of markers and memorials to commemorate enslaved African peoples. Morrison employs the discourse of place to speak of this national erasure:

> There is no place you or I can go, to think about or not think about, to summon the presences of, or recollect the absences of slaves. . . . There is no suitable memorial, or plaque, or wreath, or wall, or park, or skyscraper lobby. There's no 300-foot tower, there's no small bench by the road. There is not even a tree scored, an initial that I can visit or you can visit in Charleston or Savannah or New York or Providence or better still on the banks of the Mississippi. And because such a place doesn't exist . . . the book [*Beloved*] had to. ("A Bench by the Road," 1)

The society answered Morrison's call; since 2006, it has commissioned benches to be placed in areas significant to African American history, including Sullivan's Island, South Carolina, and Oberlin, Ohio, in recognition that geography is imprinted and consecrated. The Bench by the Road Project deliberately encourages dwelling in place, a contemplative act that situates people in imbued geographic spaces. The benches create narrative maps accompanied by bronze plaques whose inscriptions are notably terse, holding no more than thirty-five words. In this way, the narratives emerge from the biophysical world, a gesture resonant with the earth historian Lauret Savoy's *Trace: Memory, History, Race, and the American Landscape*, a study that theorizes terrains of memory. Lauret maintains that "we make our lives among relics and ruins of former times, former worlds. Each of us is, too, a landscape inscribed by memory and loss" (2), an elision of place and personhood that is in keeping with Morrison's creative vision.

What often emerges in African American literature is "nature" as a politically charged, racialized topography, imprinted with a history of slavery, racism, and barbaric Jim Crow practices, where the woods are not merely unspoiled sites of wilderness but "a place where one might be dragged, beaten, or lynched" (Savoy and Deming, 12). Evelyn White in "Black Women and the Wilderness" gives voice to the physical world as a repository for racial terror: "I wanted to sit outside and listen to the roar of the ocean, but I was afraid. I wanted to walk through the redwoods, but I was afraid. I wanted to glide in a kayak and feel the cool water splash in my face, but I was afraid" (377). Heeding these words, this book recognizes that "'nature' is not a pristine external scene but the marriage of a place with the lives that have lived in it" (Savoy and Deming, 4). Hence, in the African American expressive tradition, the material world is alternately presented as a sympathetic ally and an entity that was forced to collude with oppressive systems. In "Widening the Frame," Savoy and Deming consider the complex ecocritical vision of writers of color, arguing that "for some, the land has been origin and continuity for millennia; for others the land holds the memory of those who worked it under a

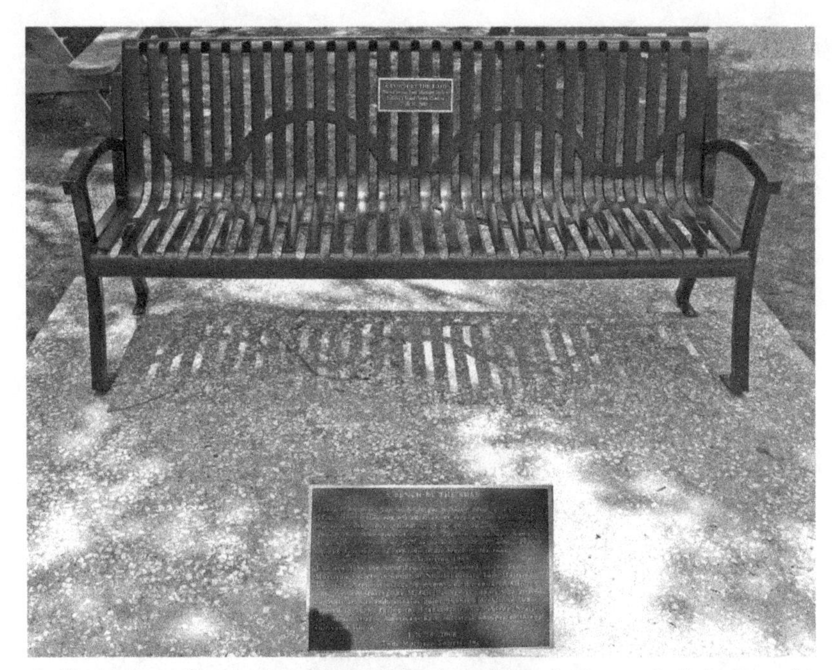

Toni Morrison Society Bench by the Road Project, Sullivan's Island, South Carolina, 2012. Credit: Ron Cogswell / Flickr.com, https://www.flickr.com/photos/22711505@N05/7759487838.

system of bondage; and for many, this is a place migrated to in search of new beginnings or a place of refuge from intolerable oppression" (7).

The environmental historian Dianne D. Glave, in *Rooted in the Earth*, complicates the ideological assumption that an antienvironmental stance prevails in African American culture, going so far as to label it a stereotype. She instead argues persuasively that a robust African American environmentalism exists in both life and art: "African Americans have long envisioned the environment in luminous and evocative ways, while at the same time remaining pragmatic and realistic about the wilderness" (6). Glave illuminates the distinct conceptualization of the "wilderness" for African Americans: "The woods and swamps were fearsome places populated by even more fearsome whites and not tranquil retreats akin to the idyllic refuge later described in Henry David Thoreau's *Walden*. African Americans did not 'find themselves' in the wilderness; instead they found, potentially, deliverance from lives of servitude" (Glave, 33). Moreover, as Carl Anthony argues in "Reflections on African American Environmental History," "We need a new story about race and place in America. This new story is not only about toxic waste dumps and hazardous materials; it is about the fundamental right of a people to have a relationship with all of creation" (206).

The second barrier that has precluded African American literature from ecocritical investigation has been the constricted scope placed on environmental writing. Bernd Herzogenrath, in his chapter "White" in *Prismatic Ecology*, voices the implicit assumptions in the field of ecocriticism: "In a way, is not a white ecology—at least in the political, racial sense—what has been there, always, what is silently (or not so silently) practiced as the default mode of ecology? Is not green the new white?" (1). The ready association of environmentalism with whiteness underscores ecocritics' exclusion of African American texts from analysis, the assumption being that ecocriticism is an orientation best suited to a narrow conceptualization of "nature writing"; however, such a presumption relies on a limited notion of what constitutes environmental literature.[1] Carolyn Finney, in *Black Faces, White Spaces*, a study that considers the ways in which the American environment is racialized, sheds light on the racial othering of African Americans in environmental discourses:

> The dominant environmental narrative in the United States is primarily constructed and informed by white, Western European or Euro-American voices. This narrative not only shapes the way the natural environment is represented, constructed, and perceived in our everyday lives, but informs our national identity as well. Missing from the narrative is an African American perspective, a nonessentialized black environmental identity that is grounded in the legacy of African American experiences in the United States. (3)

An engagement with African American experiences in the United States is necessarily an environmental one, whether, for example, in the transatlantic crossing, plantation labor, or the Great Migration, although critics often do not bring an ecocritical lens to such historical events.

Further, punctuating the African American expressive tradition are moments of pure communion with the natural world. Morrison, after all, explains that her editor characterizes her rendering of nature as "beautiful." Important for this analysis is that Morrison does not solely engage with elements of the biophysical world that are aesthetically rich, for the author's response to her editor's caution ("Would you stop all this *beauty* business") is "Wait, wait until I tell you about these ants." Morrison's assertion underscores that ants should be regarded as a thing of beauty, and indicates that they—and by extension other elements of the living world—are important to her characters, the story line, and the novels themselves. As I will explicate throughout the book, many of Morrison's characters experience epiphanic moments in nature, where they revel in the beauty of the natural world and find succor there.

Toni Morrison and the Natural World marks the first full-length ecocritical study of the Nobel laureate's work, and although it is not intended to be an exhaustive study, it offers an archetype for reading Morrison's fiction ecocritically. This is important work, for as Glave explains, "only recently have African Americans been considered in the study of environmental history—a history traditionally defined as by and for white men" (6). Camille Dungy, in the introduction to *Black Nature: Four Centuries of African American Nature Poetry*, likewise explains that her collection provides "a new way of thinking about nature writing and writing by black Americans" (xxi). Indeed, Dungy's statement is twofold: not only is it incumbent on critics to reconsider the genre of environmental writing, but we must also rethink the African American expressive tradition through the lens of the natural world. *Toni Morrison and the Natural World* attempts to do just that.

MORRISON'S VISION OF SUSTAINABILITY

Sustainability is perhaps the key term in modern environmental thought. Chatham University, where I am a professor, has a School of Sustainability and Environment. The definition of sustainability our website proffers is illustrative of the term: "Sustainability has grown from a niche field to an increasingly crucial lens through which all aspects of society are being considered." Often we limit our notion of sustainability to that which lies outside the human realm, relying on a binary that bifurcates the human from the more-than-human world. Yet if we return to the second part of the definition, it is "all aspects of society" that should be reconsidered through the lens of sustainability, a line of inquiry that the cultural geographer Carolyn Finney explores:

> When people ask me about sustainability, the first question I ask is, "What are we trying to sustain?" Sustainability for me, partially, is about relationship—that human beings have to the Earth and the land, as well as the relationships we have to each other. And both of those—we can't have one without the other in terms of living well. In order to talk about what kind of relationships we want to sustain, we have to be critical about [them]. There's a lot that's problematic in the existing ones that we have. If we're talking about issues of the difference between the rich and the poor, and understanding that there are

> some problems. . . . I don't want to sustain that relationship the way that it is now. It doesn't support everybody. I'm interested in sustainability in that before we sustain something, we first get real with what we have. . . . Are we willing to . . . change things? We don't necessarily throw everything out. But maybe some of that stuff has to look different. (Chen, "Professor Spotlight")

An ecocritical examination of Morrison's work is in keeping with Finney's large-scale questioning of sustainability as a concept that goes beyond what is conventionally understood under the rubric of "nature." The idea that human relationships are at the crux of Finney's capacious definition of sustainability is central to an African American ecological agenda; the natural world never supersedes the human. Finney's reasoning that we—as a people, a society, a nation—must be thoughtful of what we *choose* to sustain, and by implication what we *deliberately* disregard, speaks to a rigorous engagement not only with the natural world but also with the history that has occurred in those geographic spaces. Throughout Morrison's canon, she provides various models of sustainability. Principally, what is sustaining to her characters is the memory and acknowledgment of ancestral history. In that way, the geographic spaces where people toiled, lived, and created family and culture are sacred ground for Morrison's characters, allowing for an engagement with a home space outside of dominant society. That Morrison consistently mines her people's heritage speaks to Glave's work of unearthing ancestral connections to the natural world: "Enslaved people did not stumble upon or discover wilderness. Instead, African Americans actively sought healing, kinship, resources, escape, refuge, and salvation in the land. The environment held social meaning for enslaved people" (8). In Morrison's work, her characters' intimacy with—and attachment to—the natural world allows for a reclamation of national identity and a reintegration into the biocultural landscape.

COLOR THEORY

Color is the cord that anchors this book's exploration of Morrison's environmental vision and is explored, first, as a concrete semiotic marker of skin tone and its attendant network of meanings in a hierarchized, racialized society. Heather Sullivan, in "The Ecology of Colors," theorizes the relationship between nature and color: "The goal here is to overcome the spatial distinction between ourselves and the rest of the biosphere. Rather than locating nature elsewhere or in the wild or outdoors, nature appears—visually, sensually—all around us in its most energized forms of light and colors. Nature is, to reiterate, the process of emergence of material reality of which we are a part" (90). Color, then, is a primary way in which we experience the natural world. In *The Secret Language of Color* Joann and Arielle Eckstut argue that "one can use the lens of color to explore the very nature of our universe" (33):

> The elements of our universe are filled with color. Color tells us when to rise and when to go to sleep, when to go outdoors, and when to seek shelter. Color has helped us answer questions about what might be on planets we have yet to visit and whether these planets might be hospitable to humans. It's even helped us answer possibly the biggest question we've ever thought to ask: How was our universe created. (49)

Color is an epistemology that humans use to navigate environmental landscapes, and my engagement here with color is a recognition of the intractable relationship between chromatics and ecology. Indeed, as Oppermann posits in "Nature's Colors: A Prismatic Materiality in the Natural/Cultural Realms," "Color is a constitutive part of human and non-human interactions with the more-than-human environment" (159).

Color is also limited by the human brain. As Victoria Finlay, in the *Brilliant History of Color in Art*, explains: "Colors exist only because our minds create them. The universe is pulsating with energy we call electromagnetic waves. These range hugely in size. Cosmic waves move in wavelengths of about a billion a millimeter, while long-range radio waves are sometimes several miles wide. Between them is a whole gamut of waves—infrared and TV and gamma and X-rays. But although we've developed scientific instruments to pick up all of these, human eyes can detect only a tiny portion" (91). Or as Eckstut and Eckstut argue: "Without the eye and brain, there's no such thing as color" (20). Further, the colors that we see are not the colors adhered to an object but the colors that the object does *not* absorb. Kassia St. Clair in *The Secret Lives of Color* describes this process—known as subtractive color—thus:

> Different things are different colors because they absorb some wavelengths of the visible light spectrum, while others bounce off. So, the tomato's skin is soaking up most of the short and medium wavelengths—blues and violets, greens, yellows and oranges. The remainder, the reds, hit our eyes and are processed by our brains. So, in a way, the color we perceive an object to be is precisely the color it *isn't*: that is, the segment of the spectrum that is being reflected away. (13)

Color is an unstable epistemology; we are seeing, naming, and assigning meaning to what is not absorbed by that material entity; in short, we are ascribing color meaning to an object that is, in fact, not that color. Extending this paradigm to racialized bodies, where the color of pigmentation has come to define personhood, reveals, in a material and political context, the faux reasoning attached to color and meaning.

Beyond our optical limitations of sight and the processing of visible light, the linguistic environment of color varies greatly from culture to culture; thus this book recognizes that the "language of color reveals much about the way we conceptualize the world" (Ball, 15), or as the linguist John Lyons suggests, colors "are the product of language under the influence of culture" (quoted in Ball, 18). Language actually influences what and how we see. After all, if "we trace our languages all the way back to antiquity—to a time before the written word—the world appears virtually colorless, at least in terms of language" (Eckstut and Eckstut, 36). This is surprising, given that the natural world is saturated with color and the average human can see a surprising "ten million colors" (199). Paul Cezanne remarks: "Colour is the place where our brain and the universe meet" (quoted in Hitchcock, 60). Cezanne's meditation on color suggests that color is physical, or "placed," and we can only experience the world, the "universe," as inundated with hues.

Humans have gone to great lengths to "mine, gather, harvest, and process colors" (Adler, 28), for color, after all, is intrinsic to nature *and* to art. In fact, the word "pigment" comes from the Latin word *pingere*, "to paint." Cohen, in *Prismatic Ecology*, astutely argues that "color is not some intangible quality that arrives belatedly to the composition but a material impress, an agency and partner, a thing made of other things through which worlds arrive" (xvi). Cohen lists some of these environmental compounds: "pulverized minerals, juice pressed from harvested berries, oak gall boiled in water and mixed with powdered eggshells, common ash, rare pollen, acidic urine" (xvi). To this list, I would add twigs, blood, animal fat, bark, and bugs.

The triadic relationship of color, the biotic world, and art is particularly apt for an ecocritical analysis of Morrison's writing, for not only does Morrison's literature contain a chromatic intensity, but the author threads theoretical treatises on color and nature throughout her work. For example, in *Paradise*, Morrison describes autumn, when "gourds were swelling in the places where radishes had been," with color-saturated diction: "September marched through smearing everything with oil paint: acres of cardamom yellow, burnt orange, miles of sienna, blue ravines both cerulean and midnight, along with heartbreaking violet skies" (232). This explosion of color is couched in a discourse of visual art. Morrison names standard colors of paint and calls attention to the medium of oil paint, which, as opposed to acrylics, contains more pigment and thus offers vivid coloring. Further, when painting with oils, artists can apply additional layers of paint, which deepens and enriches their color palettes. What is especially significant here is Morrison's recognition of the intractable relationship between color, the natural world, and artistry. After all, it is "September" that paints the biosphere, in recognition of the natural world's aesthetic agency. In *Song of Solomon*, Pilate's evocative discourse on blackness exemplifies Morrison's handling of color, but importantly, in the following passage, she highlights racial pigmentation:

> You think dark is just one color, but it ain't. There are five or six kinds of black. Some silky, some wooley. Some just empty. Some like fingers. And it don't stay still. It moves and changes from one kind of black to another. Saying something is pitch black is like saying something is green. What kind of green? Green like my bottles? Green like a grasshopper? Green like a cucumber, lettuce, or green like the sky is just before it breaks loose to storm? Well, night black is the same way. May as well be a rainbow. (40)

Here Morrison showcases color as embodied. We do not encounter color in the abstract; it is mapped onto and inheres in material beings. Further, Pilate's color ontology is politicized, as she undermines the notion that blackness is monolithic. In Morrison's body of work, blackness is not static darkness, an aspectral hue, an absence of color, but as prismatic as a rainbow and conflated with the night sky.

Environmental systems are not rigidly demarcated and bounded, and thus my work in this book, heeding the philosophy of ecology and following Morrison's complex rendering of blackness, traffics in shading, blending, and the interconnectivity of chromatic hues. Color, after all, is not stationary; according to Jude Stewart in *Roy G. Biv*, "color is a shivering, glorious, active thing" (xiii). In fact, even the colors of the rainbow "merge seamlessly from one to the other [and] any judgment on where one color ends and the other begins is arbitrary. Even Newton waffled on this point. At the beginning of his experiment, his spectrum included eleven colors" (Eckstut and Eckstut, 13). He later reduced the number of spectral colors to seven so that they would accord with the main tones in the musical scale (13). Moreover, "indigo dwells between blue and violet because Isaac Newton liked the color of an imported dye" (Cohen, *Prismatic Ecology*, xxix). The colors we see, how and where we see and experience them, and the names and attributes we give to them, are culturally imposed, and thus using color as a thread throughout this ecocritical study of Morrison's literature reminds us of the interrelationship between human and natural geographies. The book is organized by color, but it problematizes those demarcated color palettes as the hues—and their corresponding topics—mix and bleed into one another.

This book is indebted to Jeffrey Cohen's ecotheory of color insofar as I borrow heavily from his chromatic organization in *Prismatic Ecology*. While Cohen speaks back to the predominance of green in environmental discourses, my application of a multihued response to Morrison's work is to first and foremost insert race, bodies of color, into the ecocritical conversation, a concept that is only cursorily mentioned in Cohen's edited collection. Brown, black, and white are preeminent signifiers of meaning in a racially hierarchized society, and therefore my aim is to recompose Cohen's theory in the service of African American ecocriticism. A more-than-green ecology is materialized in the book's organization. Using brown as both a material and metaphoric starting place foregrounds the impossibility of removing race from ecotheory when applied to the work of Toni Morrison, specifically, and African American literature more broadly.

While color is at times and in certain cultures celebrated, it is also a site of loathing in the West, associated, as it is, with primitivism, infantilism, and vulgarity. Philip Ball in *Bright Earth: Art and the Invention of Color* explains that, for centuries, colors were associated with a kind of Eastern "decadent orientalism" that is "suited to simple races, peasants, and savages" (13). Indeed, reason was linked to cooler tones, whereas unseemly passion was supposedly reflected in brighter hues. Morrison's work challenges this Orientalist ideology in recognition that such a view of color is inevitably and implicitly linked to corporeal hues. Morrison's inaugural novel, *The Bluest Eye*, is a powerful treatise on the color caste system, where the bluest of blue eyes is the urmetaphor for all things white and culturally valuable; and even in her final novel, *God Help the Child*, Morrison begins with a light-skinned mother's horrific response to the birth of a dark-skinned baby. While I discuss both of these novels in greater detail later in the book, I mention them here to highlight Morrison's recognition that color—its saturation and intensity—is understood as physically embodied and is powerful, bespeaking societal rankings and devaluations.

Explaining the chromatics of her work in the *Paris Review*, Morrison compares the achromatic gray tones of *Beloved* to the brightly hued *Song of Solomon*:

> Part of that has to do with the visual images that I got being aware that in historical terms women, black people in general, were very

> attracted to very bright-colored clothing. Most people are frightened by color anyway. . . . They just are. In this culture quiet colors are considered elegant. . . . But the slave population had no access even to what color there was, because they wore slave clothes, hand-me-downs, work clothes made out of burlap and sacking. For them a colored dress would be luxurious; it wouldn't matter whether it was rich or poor cloth . . . just to have a red or a yellow dress. I stripped *Beloved* of color so that there are only the small moments when Sethe runs amok buying ribbons and bows, enjoying herself the way children enjoy that kind of color. The whole business of color was why slavery was able to last such a long time. It wasn't as though you had a class of convicts who could dress themselves up and pass themselves off. No, these were people marked because of their skin color, as well as other features. So color is a signifying mark. Baby Suggs dreams of color and says, "Bring me a little lavender." It is a kind of luxury. We are so inundated with color and visuals. I just wanted to pull it back so that one could feel that hunger and that delight. I couldn't do that if I had made it the painterly book *Song of Solomon* was. ("The Art of Fiction")

Morrison's language here moves effortlessly from color in the abstract to an exigency of chattel slavery and finally to skin color, and thus an attentive reading of color in Morrison's work is always already steeped in a lexicon of race, offering a textured, multilayered presentation of chromatics.

BODIES OF COLOR

Bodies of color are the guiding trope throughout the book. While humans often perceive themselves as being "dramatically different" in terms of skin, hair, and eye shade, "we are relatively colorless" as compared to other species: "We have skin ranging from barely pink to an array of browns, with no bright colors to be found. Even the bluest eyes and the reddest hair, alongside a butterfly's wing or a bird's feather, look comparatively 'blah'" (Eckstut and Eckstut, 187). Despite the small range of hues, color has become a major signifier of human difference, which Morrison explores throughout her work. In this study, I begin with a body infused with rainbow colors, a multilayered metaphor culled from *The Bluest Eye*. In this passage, Pauline Breedlove, whose race is the source of her victimization by society, is enchanted by the elision of her body with elements of the natural world:

> When I first seed Cholly, I want you to know it was like all the bits of color from that time down home when all us chil'ren went berry picking after a funeral and I put some in the pocket of my Sunday dress, and they mashed up and stained my hips. My whole dress was messed with purple, and it never did wash out. Not the dress nor me. I could feel that purple deep inside me. And that lemonade Mama used to make when Pap came in out the fields. It be cool and yellowish, with seeds floating near the bottom. And that streak of green them june bugs made on the trees the night we left from down home. All of them colors was in me. Just sitting there. So when Cholly come up and tickled my foot, it was like them berries, that lemonade, them streaks of green the june bugs made, all come together. (91)

Pauline's body is prismatic, imprinted with purple, green, and yellow. Reliving her connection to her southern agrarian roots, Pauline experiences a sensuous engagement with the natural world that is not outside the self but infused throughout the body. Importantly, this color-saturated passage is not sanitized, predicated, as it is, on agricultural labor and death and encoded as a long-ago memory. It is nonetheless a refutation of her marginalized status as a southern migrant in Lorain, Ohio. In conceptualizing herself in terms of a multihued interiority, Pauline, in this instance, questions society's mapping of identity solely through the binary of black and white, colors that are absent in the passage. Pauline's musing on pigment and its enmeshment with berries and bugs introduces Morrison's evocative handling of color and the natural world. Morrison's ecopolitics merge with race and color. Although the natural world is a generally overlooked area of analysis, this study demonstrates its pervasiveness in Morrison's fiction, and the politics associated with reading her novels from an ecocritical perspective.

In Morrison's oeuvre, color is a multilayered signifier, with a major referent being skin pigmentation, a pairing that held particular currency in the eighteenth century, when race was theorized quite differently than it is today. Rather than regarding race as a fixed, biological category, Americans of that time understood race as a dye of the skin that was subject to change largely due to environmental factors. Katy Chiles in *Transformable Race* argues that "the dye metaphor tells us much about the way race was conceptualized in this period: that it was external, that it was something that happened to the surface of the body, that it developed over time, that it was related to the place where one lived, and that it could possibly change" (1). In the context of an ecocritical reading, it is salient to consider the role that the natural world was thought to play in one's bodily condition. Chiles further explains:

"As the term *dye* demonstrates, the late eighteenth-century discourses of literature and natural history were tightly interwoven" (2). In fact, the supposed mutability of the physical body was at the nexus of multiple discourses, including "natural-historical, nativist, environmentalist, and theories of social influence" (6). Eschewing strict racial categories suggested that somatic differences were not located—as people would come to believe—in the blood; rather, they were recognized as skin deep and, importantly, could and did change owing to environmental factors, including climate, landscape, air, geography, soil, and food. These external forces that acted on the body resulted in the changing of corporeal hue.[2] The most famous of these cases was an African American man by the name of Henry Moss from Virginia, who, in developing white patches on his skin, appeared to be turning white. Chiles explains that Moss became a site of fascination for the general public, scientists, and politicians alike.

While this history is captivating in its own right, the configuration of color, the natural world, and human identity sheds light on this study insofar as bodies are perceived as part of the living world; each boundary is porous to the other. This environmental explanation of color difference often pivoted on the axis of racial hierarchy with a belief that the sunny climate of Africa not only accounted for darker pigmentation but created an inferior—even uncivilized—race of people. While this faux reasoning of racial epistemologies gave way to later, equally irrational notions of race as a fixed, internal category, my interest in this eighteenth-century thinking is twofold: one, that geography was considered a prime indicator of one's chromatic appearance; and two, that the dye metaphor was so readily used, which unmistakably pairs the production of color with corporeal hues.

CHAPTER BREAKDOWNS

Chapter 1, "Brown Ecology and Fertility: Skin, Dirt, and Compost in *Paradise* and *The Bluest Eye*," offers a treatise on brown, the color of soil, compost, and rot. Though seemingly a hue consigned to decay, brown matter, the very substance that allows for growth and fertility, is life. Dirt, according to William Bryant Logan's treatise on the subject, is "the skin of the earth." I use this corporeal metaphor to tie brown's ecological significance intimately to Morrison's work. Brown is the color adhered to people who, in an American context, have long been treated as "other." The skin's epidermal pigmentation was stigmatized and culturally denoted as unclean and polluted. Therefore, in prioritizing brown as the book's first chapter, I begin, as Morrison does, by centering African Americans. In that way, the universe of color in Morrison's fiction is always already inside a palette of browns. From an ecocritical perspective, dirt is closely tied to artistry: "The first paint was mud; the first pigment brown ocher. Hands dipped in dirt and water, fingers pressed on stone. . . . In those ancient paintings, the color palette runs from iron oxide orange to burnt wood charcoal, a universe of color within the range of brown" (Hitchcock, 259).

Not only was the earth used as an early paint, but brown pigmentation is intimately linked to the human body. According to St. Clair in *The Secret Lives of Color*, the color "mummy brown" actually consisted of ground-up mummies: "Mummy, also known as Egyptian brown and *Caput mortum* ("dead man's head"), was used as paint—usually mixed with a drying oil and amber varnish—from the twelfth until the twentieth centuries" (254). In fact, mummies had been exhumed and used for medicinal purposes for centuries, and since apothecaries were also responsible for creating color, it is not surprising that the rich brown powder was used to manufacture brown pigment. Lest the story of mummy brown be relegated to an obscure chapter of art history, this practice continued until well into the twentieth century. The owner of a London art shop, which has been in existence since the early nineteenth century, confessed in 1964 that "we might have a few odd limbs lying around somewhere but not enough to make any more paint" (255). A brown ecology, then, is inextricable from its association with dirt and skin.

It is in these racial, artistic, and environmental contexts that I apply a brown ecology to *The Bluest Eye*, a novel framed by a discourse on soil. Claudia, the narrator, turns to the soil to mediate Pecola's abuse: "We had dropped our seeds in our own little plot of black dirt just as Pecola's father had dropped his seeds in his own plot of black dirt" (1). The dirt, the ground on which these acts of violence occur, is a metonym of the neighborhood, the nation, and its ecosystems. Chapter 1 examines moments of transcorporeal exchange, including marigold seeds and embryos, and racist ideology and dirt.

In *Paradise*, Morrison again returns to dirt as she explores a multigenerational group of women who lead unorthodox lives and are perceived by the community as "detritus." The elements of compost are marked throughout the women's story. Not only are they conflated with rich soil, but their behaviors and aesthetics bespeak the features of compost heaps and gardens, which they tend throughout the novel. In Morrison's fictional universe, a brown ecology is materially and politically centralized. All other hues in Morrison's canon exist in relationship to brown, a loaded signifier in social and natural landscapes.

Chapter 2, "Green Ecology and Healing: Botanical Life in *Beloved*, *Home*, and *Song of Solomon*," considers green as the preeminent color of ecological thought, environmental discourse, and conservation movements. Cross-culturally, green is associated with the natural world. The papyrus stalk was the ancient Egyptian hieroglyph for the color green, and the Latin word for green is *viridis*, "which is related to a large group of words that suggest growth and even life itself" (St. Clair, 209). Most importantly, green is the color of chlorophyll, which produces the oxygen necessary to sustain life on Earth. This chapter will pay attention to those characters in Morrison's fiction who find respite, that is, breathing space, in the green world. Morrison's green ecology traffics in a secular reenchantment that Landy and Saler, in the introduction to *The Re-enchantment of the World*, define as "everyday miracles, exceptional events which go against (and perhaps even alter) the accepted order of things; and . . . epiphanies, moments of being in which, for a brief instant, the center appears to hold, and the promise is held out of a quasi-mystical union with something larger than oneself" (27). What emerges in Morrison's fiction are moments of enchantment with the plant world that provide a contrast to the unrelenting and ubiquitous social networks of racism in which the community is enmeshed.

Even in *Beloved*, Morrison's treatise on the brutality of chattel slavery, characters experience notable moments of enchantment with the vegetal world. Baby Suggs, holy, the spiritual center of the novel, preaches to the newly emancipated in a forest. She exhorts the community to reject the entrenched racism that is imbricated in the mind and body. From a materialist framework, racist ideology does not exist outside of flesh but transcorporeally bodies forth its virulence on other entities. The members of the community, for the time they inhabit the wooded landscape, "go against the order of things" and experience epiphanic moments of healing. Likewise, the isolated Denver, Sethe's youngest daughter, who is traumatized by her mother's act of infanticide and the community's subsequent shunning of her family, retreats to the bower, a circle of boxwood bushes. Here Denver's "imagination produced its own hunger and its own food" (*Beloved*, 29), suggesting her elision with plant life as she begins to adopt autotrophic attributes. Like plant organisms that can make their own food, Denver's imaginative state in these "green walls" is self-sustaining and provides "salvation." Morrison does not merely turn to metaphor in describing Denver; rather, her language highlights the material interrelationship between flora and humans, for there is "little difference between hemoglobin—blood—and chlorophyll. The two are one microscopic atom away from each other, sharing another 136 atoms in common" (Oladipo, 263).

In *Song of Solomon*, Pilate's home is a living green space, with a moss-colored sack hanging from the ceiling and the odor of pine pervading the air. Pilate, the moral center of the novel, chews on fresh twigs and is repeatedly described as a tall, black tree. Yet the text contains quiet moments that likewise illustrate Morrison's arboreal ecology. Critics have paid much attention to Ruth Dead's prolonged breast-feeding of her only son, and this chapter theorizes how a green ecology sheds new light on Ruth's relationship to Milkman and her relationship to the natural world.

In *Home*, Morrison chronicles the trauma that the adult siblings Frank and Cee suffer: Frank is a war veteran struggling with post-traumatic stress disorder, and Cee has been abandoned by her husband and medically abused at the hands of a eugenicist. It is only through a return to their hometown, the rural hamlet of Lotus, Georgia, that they begin to heal. In Lotus, Frank and Cee are met by color, immersed in the sensory world of flowers, vegetables, and quilt patches. Frank's earlier disparaging remark that there is nothing to do but breathe in Lotus can be reread as an acknowledgment of the breathing space that he is afforded there. After all, Morrison begins chapter 2 of *Home* with a one-word sentence: "Breathing" (7). These examples illustrate the manifold ways in which a green ecology unearths Morrison's rendering of the plant world as cathartic.

Chapter 3, "Orange Ecology, Death, and Renewal: Fire, Ash, and Immolation in *God Help the Child* and *Sula*," examines orange's manifestation in fire, which, from an anthropocentric perspective, is regarded as dangerous and deadly, a punishing element, uncontainable and random. Fire is also evocative of post-Reconstruction torture that white supremacists unleashed against newly freed African Americans in the form of the Ku Klux Klan's burning crosses, or race riot conflagrations in Tulsa, Detroit, and Washington, DC. Fire is a material and symbolic element of violence, yet from an ecological prism, it is more complicated. While it is an act of destruction, forest fires, in particular, are necessary for healthy ecosystems. In fact, fire is an essential contributor to habitat vitality and replenishment, a catalyst for healthy change known as succession.

In this chapter, I examine Morrison's complex handling of fire in *Sula*, where Eva, the maternal figure in the text, immolates her beloved son, Plum, who returns from war a drug addict. Later Eva tries in vain to extinguish the flames that take the life of her adult daughter, Hannah. In Morrison's final novel, *God Help the Child*, Queen is killed by fire, a death that heals the relationship of Bride and Booker, the couple at the center of the novel. Both *Sula* and *God Help the Child* pivot on the axis of destruction, violence, and renewal.

Chapter 4, "Blue Ecology and Resistance: Islands, Swamps, and Ecotones in *Tar Baby* and *Love*," addresses water and its indelible relationship to life. After all, Earth is a blue planet. Not only does water make up more than two-thirds of the earth's surface, and our body mass, but as Wallace Nichols in *Blue Mind* reminds us, "ocean plankton provides more than half of our planet's oxygen" (8). Water is an element necessary for life. In considering whether other planets in our solar system have water, the marine biologist Sylvia Earle succinctly remarks: "No blue, no life" (quoted in Hitchcock, 98). Rainwater, in particular, enhances our polychromatic world. As the environmental journalist Cynthia Barnett explains in *Rain: A Natural and Cultural History*:

> Rain is Earth's great brightener, beginning with the sky. As fine dust, pollution, and other tiny particles build up in the atmosphere, our celestial sphere grows paler and paler, from blue to milky white. A good rain washes the particles away. . . . On the land, spring rains are the primitive artists, greening hills and valleys and coaxing flowers to vivid bud and bloom. Summer rains are the long-lived masters of color—the steadier they fall on hardwood trees in June, July, and August, the richer reds and yellows ignite the autumn foliage. . . . Dearth of rain often means dearth of color—dry prairie, dusty sand, desert animals with pale skins to reflect the sun's heat. Many tropical rain forest creatures evolved bright pigments and sharp markings so those of the same kind could find them in the rain-blurred jungle. The vibrancy and patterns of an African butterfly called the squinting bush brown depend entirely on whether it emerges from its pupae in rainy or dry times. (15–16)

Barnett deftly explores the constellation of water, flora, fauna, and color. In short, rain gives life and then illuminates it with color, so much so that Barnett identifies "color-giving rain" (33) as the basis of human civilization (38). Of course, "too much rain for too long settles with grim darkness: mold, rot and floodwaters that never seem to drain" (38). The sense that rain can "turn to terror and the deepest grief" is also in keeping with African American ecocritical thought insofar as blue, for all its water and life-giving associations, is a melancholy color, a hue of sadness. Reading blue, then, in terms of a blues ecology provides a nuanced framework for considering an African diasporic perspective. In that way, I employ a blue/blues ecology as a framework for theorizing survival and trauma, and physical and psychological dislocations. Specific attention will be paid to islands, swamps, and shorelines as sites of resistance in *Tar Baby* and *Love*. These ecotones are liminal spaces where aquatic and terrestrial frontiers meet, and where past and present and human and nonhuman ecosystems encounter and integrate.

The book's conclusion, "A Black and White Ecology: Plantations and Race Formation in *A Mercy* and *Jazz*," considers the ways in which Morrison, in turning her attention to the colonies in *A Mercy*, examines the artifice of race and lays bare the myriad ways in which racial categorization was foundational to the building of America. Moreover, in *Jazz*, Morrison gestures to the plantation economy through references to Joe and Violet's cotton farming. This monocropping was detrimental to the physical and social landscape of the nation. In recognition of the bankruptcy of a black and white ecology, the conclusion theorizes the rainbow, a trope in Morrison's canon that complicates binaristic thinking. Morrison's characters inhabit polychromatic worlds; their ecological relationships are multifaceted and contradictory, marked by a complex interweaving of beauty and grief.

BEARING WITNESS: SOIL AND SEEDS

This book suggests that thinking more critically about the natural world enables a nuanced reading of Morrison's politics of race, gender, and nationhood. Time and time again, Morrison presents the materiality of the human body as graphically intertwined with elements of the natural world. A recent exhibit at the Legacy Museum: From Slavery to Mass Incarceration in Alabama likewise features biocultural landscapes. "Lynching in America: A Community Remembrance Project" exhibits nearly three hundred jars of soil collected from lynching sites throughout the United States. According to Bryan Stevenson, founder and executive director of the Equal Justice Initiative, "Soil is really a powerful medium for talking about this history. . . . In many ways, the sweat of enslaved people is buried in this soil. The blood of lynching victims is in this soil. The tears of people who were segregated and humiliated during the time of Jim Crow is in this soil" (quoted in Couric). The Soil Collection Project reached out to the descendants of lynched victims and community members to collect dirt from documented lynching sites. In unearthing the soil—which ranges in hue from reds to ochers to grays—the volunteers excavate and make visible buried stories of race in America. The magnitude of this display offers a stark reminder of the racial violence endemic to the nation. As spectators we bear witness to the names and stories of those able to be identified, and in the many "unidentified" jars, the soil stands in for those brutally murdered. Equally powerful is the curator's choice

The Community Soil Project Exhibit at the Legacy Museum: From Enslavement to Mass Incarceration. Credit: Equal Justice Initiative / Human Pictures.

to present the soil aesthetically. The hundreds of clear glass jars, embossed with simple white script in row upon row atop plain pine shelving, serve to illumine the deep colors of the soil. The richness of the soil—and its ability to generate new life—is part of the exhibit, for as Stevenson explicates, "We can grow something with this. . . . We can create something with this that has new meaning. That's because while soil may surround us in death, it also is the place to plant seeds of hope for a new beginning" (quoted in Couric), indicating that the soil is emblematic of this paradox, an environmental document of Black lives in America. Moreover, Stevenson's reference to seeding the soil underscores that earth is not inert matter but possesses a vital life force. Soil is both a material carrier of meaning and an enlivened entity capable of changing landscapes. Foregrounding place and personhood, the exhibit encapsulates a primary tenet of African American ecocritical thought that is echoed throughout Morrison's work, namely, that the natural world is a repository of trauma, yet has the ability to offer healing.

Toni Morrison's oeuvre illustrates the unique exigencies of African American culture that manifest the conditions of material ecocriticism. The corporeality of history and its imbrication with the soil and other elements of the living world reinforce the elision of bodies, human and nonhuman. This entanglement lays bare multilayered ancestral stories, which, for half a century, Morrison has unearthed in her fiction. Importantly, her work illustrates that terra firma, the soil beneath our feet, is imbued with narrative and thus becomes the ground on which Morrison's environmental literature is founded, a complex ecology of race and place. Not only does Morrison stand her fiction on the shoulders of her ancestors, but as material ecocriticism reveals, we are all standing on that unacknowledged and buried history.

1

BROWN ECOLOGY AND FERTILITY

Skin, Dirt, and Compost in *Paradise* and *The Bluest Eye*

Toni Morrison's voice does not begin *Paradise*; the novel's opening words come from a Gnostic text, the Nag Hammadi's *The Thunder, Perfect Mind*: "And they will find me there, and they will live, and they will not die again." These lines speak to the notion of resurrection, or that which will be born anew. Complementing the content, Morrison's act of appending an epigraph underscores transformation. That the epigraph has already been textualized, has already occurred in its own state, indicates that the material is present, and the author, in this case Toni Morrison, has reconceptualized another work, here an ancient text, in relationship to—and perhaps as a creative impulse for—her own work. The use of an epigraph, what we may call textual recycling, involves not merely re-presenting the original text but, in the context of the new work, creating a synergistic "third thing" (Morrison, "Blacks, Modernism, and the American South," 193). Morrison's epigraphic work obliquely, yet importantly, establishes the ecological cycle of birth, death, and rebirth that resonates throughout *Paradise*.[1] Effortlessly moving between life and death, *Paradise* is a novel that interrogates rebirth, or that which is born through and out of death and decay, a composting work of transformation and conversion.[2]

Compost is created from rot and decomposition. After a period of weeks or months, decayed organic material becomes a rich soil amendment, a biological process that transforms waste into healthy brown matter. It is in the context of compost and dirt that Morrison offers a brown ecology. Though seemingly a hue consigned to decay, brown material, the very substance that allows for enhanced soil, growth, and fertility, is life. Dirt, according to Logan's treatise on the subject, is "the skin of the earth." Using this corporeal metaphor, brown's ecological significance is intimately tied to Morrison's intertwining of environmental landscapes and social landscapes, soil and race. As the bedrock of life on earth, soil is elemental to Morrison's fiction

Soil. Credit: Arthon.Meekodong/Shutterstock.com.

and to artistry writ large: "The first paint was mud; the first pigment brown ocher. Hands dipped in dirt and water, fingers pressed on stone. . . . In those ancient paintings, the color palette runs from iron oxide orange to burnt wood charcoal, a universe of color within the range of brown" (Hitchcock, 259). The universe of color in Morrison's fiction exists consistently inside a palette of browns. In unearthing a brown ecology in *Paradise*, the female body is examined as a site where issues of dirt, race, and fertility converge.

Color and the natural world are sounded from the outset of *Paradise*, as the community at the center of the novel is known as the 8-Rocks, so named for the blue-black color of their skin. The 8-Rocks founded and inhabited the town of Haven and later Ruby, Oklahoma. The town of Ruby is slavish to its history, its racial purity, its exclusionary practices, and its allegiance to patriarchy. The community's provinciality is due, in large part, to the "Disallowing," the name Morrison gives to the intraracial prejudice and rejection the town's ancestors experienced generations ago. The community's newly freed forebears traveled from Louisiana and Mississippi to the Oklahoma Territory to start life anew, only to be met with rejection from light-skinned African Americans. In reaction to this unexpected hostility from fellow African Americans, the "Old Fathers" taught their descendants to be on guard not only against whites but also against other African Americans; hence the community is closed off, incestuous, and fiercely protective. The second community in *Paradise* is located seventeen miles outside of Ruby and comprises a group of multiracial, multigenerational women who occupy what is known as the Convent, which was once a colonial school for Native American girls run by nuns, and before that a gambler's mansion. The novel begins when the townsmen storm the Convent and murder these female outcasts, whom the men perceive as threats to their community.

Death begins the life of the novel proper: "They shoot the white girl first. With the rest they can take their time" (3). Morrison continues to advance this birth-death cycle, for while the men are "hunting" the women, the narrative simultaneously advances an origin story of the all-Black town and the supposed safety on which it was founded:

> From the beginning its people were free and protected. A sleepless woman could always rise from her bed, wrap a shawl around her shoulders and sit on the steps in the moonlight. And if she felt like it she could walk out the yard and on down the road. No lamp and no fear. A hiss-crackle from the side of the road would never scare her because whatever it was that made the sound, it wasn't something creeping up on her. Nothing for ninety miles around thought she was prey. (8–9)

This wandering woman might, the text continues, stop at the home of another woman, a mother, to help quiet the cries of a colicky baby. The image of the lone female walker in the moonlight, with nothing but her bedclothes and shawl for protection, who is granted unfettered mobility by a town, a place, a community of people, stands in direct contrast to the men storming the Convent, stalking the women, and gunning them down. In this passage, the town's freedom is articulated through the agency of women, implicitly mothers. The women move beyond the borders of their home and enter the biotic world—past yards, traveling on a road with only the light of the moon illuminating their way. Being in the natural world allows for female fellowship and shared mothering. The irony here is that the town's sovereignty is exemplified in the narrative of autonomous women, yet to preserve this freedom, the men murder women.

The townsmen, led by self-appointed leaders Deacon and Steward Morgan, justify their actions because they believe they are protecting Ruby by eradicating female outlaws, whom they describe as "detritus: throwaway people that sometimes blow back into the room after being swept out the door" (*Paradise*, 4). Here Morrison unmistakably advances the association of the Convent women with dirt, that which is undesirable, uncontained, and difficult to eradicate. Indeed, in reference to their supposed moral bankruptcy, the men describe the women as filthy: they are "nasty" (275) yet alluring, "drawing folks out there like flies to shit and everybody who goes near them is maimed somehow and the mess is seeping back into *our* homes, *our* families" (276). The intruders continue to employ the discourse of dirt to describe the women's dwelling: "grime," "nasty," "messy," "soiled"; in short, "things looked unclean" (12).

If the women lead dirty lives and are thus embodied dirt (sullying if not contaminating those around them), logic dictates that they should be cleansed from the pristine town of Ruby. After all, the campaign against dirt is waged over homes, bodies, buildings, and towns. Dirt is undesirable. Yet dirt is a living, vibrant substance necessary for life. That the men analogize the women to shit is surely a castigation of their lifestyle, but read from an ecocritical prism, waste can be understood in terms of fecundity. Compost is made, in part, from excrement, and thus we can read the women in terms of soil fertility, an association Morrison advances throughout the novel. The root meaning of *dirt*, according to Logan in *The Ecstatic Skin of the Earth*, is "*dritten* [which] means shit in Old Norse" (38). Logan explores the ecological and monetary value of dirt: "Until quite recently, if you sold a farm, you always got credit for the amount of compost that you'd saved. That is what I mean by dirt, the stuff of husbandry" (39). Likewise, according to David Montgomery in *Dirt: The Erosion of Civilization*: "In the mid-nineteenth century, one sixth of Paris was used to produce more than enough salad greens, fruits, and vegetables to meet the city's demand—fertilized by the million tons of horse manure produced by the city's transportation system. More productive than modern industrial farms, the labor-intensive system became so well-known that intensive compost-based horticulture is still called French gardening" (241). It is horse manure that produces, in part, sustenance for the entire city. What is undesirable is, in this instance, necessary for life.

The elements of compost are marked throughout the women's story. Not only are they elided with rich soil, but their behaviors and aesthetics return the reader to the stuff of compost heaps. The women are strongly associated with plant material (they cook large quantities of vegetables, resulting in copious peelings), hair (each woman eventually shaves her head), and later blood (they shed nutrient-rich blood in the garden). In this way, the soil surrounding the Convent is a material embodiment of women. Montgomery, in considering the organic fecundity of soil, ties the earth to the female body: "Mother earth never attempts to farm without live stock; she always raises mixed crops; great pains are taken to preserve the soil and to prevent erosion; the mixed vegetable and animal wastes are converted into humus; there is no waste; the processes of growth and the processes of decay balance one another" (202).

Morrison's novel opens itself up to an ecofeminist reading of motherhood, as each woman who enters the Convent is marked by her marred relationship with the maternal and, through her association with the other women and the more-than-human world, begins to heal, balancing, as the earth does, decay with growth. Andrea O'Reilly, in *Toni Morrison and Motherhood: A Politics of the Heart*, catalogs the many registries of broken mothering in *Paradise*: "The barrenness, abortions, miscarriages, sickly children and dead babies, as well as the maternal abandonment and neglect, motherlessness, mother loss, mother-daughter estrangement described in *Paradise* represent Haven's and later Ruby's inability to sustain community" (139). The town and the title of the first chapter are named after Ruby, sister of Deacon and Steward. The town becomes an ossified monument to their deceased sister, reduced, as she is, to text and not a living testament to her struggle as a Black woman and mother, who died because a white hospital refused to admit her. In this way, the Convent women's ability to rebuild their lives by integrating with one another and the earth is a more fitting homage to Ruby.

The death that permeates *Paradise*, from children to mothers, obliquely references compost, a biological process of decay that includes wetted organic matter, known as green waste. The relationship between fluid and brown matter marks an interesting link to the material corpus of the female body, which is also perceived as fluid filled, or "leaky":

> Within both historical and contemporary cultures women's bodies are constructed as far more dangerous than men's because of their greater propensity for the "natural" breaking of body boundaries and the subsequent potential for dirt. This potential and the fear of its pollution is rooted within their reproductive capacity, as dirt "leaks" from women's bodies in the form of menstrual blood, the "show," amniotic fluid, tears, blood during and after birth and breast milk. (Draper, 749)

In her study on the experience of men in birthing rooms, Jan Draper posits the following differentiation: "The leaky, polluting, dangerous and unbounded body of the woman comes face to face with the solid, strong, controlled and contained body of the man" (750). The men of Ruby assent to this ideology. They regard the female body as unclean and contaminated; if not checked and controlled by patriarchy, that body must be eradicated.

The elision between female bodies and dirt is made most explicit in Morrison's references to pregnant women's consumption of dirt, a practice known as geophagy. One community member, Pat, questions whether her pregnant mother and her friends ate "copper dirt in secret" (*Paradise*, 200), and later the midwife, Lone, who catalogs the many intimate services she performed for pregnant women, remarks that she "searched the county to get them the kind of dirt they wanted to eat" (271). In both of these instances, the consumption of dirt is a shared, female experience. Although hazards are associated with dirt eating, geophagy has been practiced throughout the world, especially in famine-stricken regions, and is particularly associated with people living in Central Africa. Health benefits may also come from eating the right kind of "clay, dirt or other pieces of the lithosphere" (Rosenberg), because it contains important nutrients such as phosphorus, potassium, magnesium, copper, zinc, manganese, and iron. Geophagy marks the African diaspora and can be traced from Central Africa to the Deep South, and later to the urban North. In fact, Matt Rosenberg explains: "There are good sites for nutritional clay in the Southern United States and sometimes family and friends will send 'care packages' of good earth to expectant mothers in the North." Morrison's reference to geophagy draws ecological and corporeal lines between Africa and America, earth and the female body.

Lest an ecocritical reading of *Paradise* seem far afield, the novel's title points rather directly to the Garden of Eden, which, as Jamaica Kincaid argues in *My Garden (Book)*, is "the garden to which all gardens must refer, whether they want to or not" (223). Morrison's *Paradise* is set in one of the many all-Black towns in Oklahoma that were incorporated after the Civil War. Notably, these towns were promoted as Edenic with slogans such as "Oklahoma—the future land and the paradise of Eden and the garden of the Gods. . . . Here the negro . . . can rest from mob law, here he can be secure from every ill of the southern policies" (Evans, 383). The garden, then, is not only cast as physical place but promoted as a safe space, an intertwining of social and ecological landscapes that Morrison recasts in the Convent garden but does so in terms of gender.

Initially only two women inhabit the Convent, Consolata and Mother Mary Magna, whom O'Reilly labels a "community mother" (5). Mary Magna perhaps stole, perhaps saved, a young Consolata from the impoverished streets of an unnamed South American country and brought her back to the missionary school. Eventually the school lost funding, leaving only Mary Magna and Consolata as caretakers of the home and each other. Consolata is elided with the home and garden: as a young girl, she "slept in the pantry, scrubbed tile, fed chickens, prayed, peeled, gardened, canned and laundered. . . . She got good enough to take over the kitchen as well as the garden" (225).

Years later, other women, societal castaways, find themselves at the Convent, looking for food, fuel, and directions, but staying long after. Mavis, an abused woman, whose carelessness and confusion resulted in her twin babies suffocating in a car, is the first visitor, followed by Gigi (Grace), who witnessed a boy being murdered at a rally. Next to enter the Convent is Pallas, whose mother and boyfriend engage in an affair. This young girl escapes her mother's home only to be gang raped and nearly drowned. Finally, Seneca arrives, a young woman who was abandoned by her mother, whom she thought was her sister, and ended up living in foster homes. Morrison's description of Pallas is particularly evocative in the context of a brown ecology, as she is physically aligned with the botanical world. Pallas, who arrives with "hair full of algae," is initially mute but communicates through the earth. She writes her name in the soil and quickly covers "it completely with red dirt" (*Paradise*, 175). While such an inscription may be read as an act of erasure, from an ecocritical perspective, Pallas merges with the dirt. In drawing attention to the dirt's red hue, Morrison grounds her novel in the earth of Oklahoma, which is known as port silt loam, an iron-oxide-rich soil owing to the weathering of sandstones, siltstones, and shale. Symbolically, Pallas's trauma is mapped onto the earth, and the reddish hue, signaling the earth's makeup, reveals an unmistakable link to the exigencies of Pallas's body. Pallas's interaction with the soil, albeit brief, is cathartic. All these women, under Consolata's guidance, and in their intimacy with the earth, learn to live sustainably and begin healing.

Nearly all the action in the Convent takes place in the kitchen and the garden. For example, Consolata asks Mavis, moments after her arrival, to help shell a large basket of pecans that she has just harvested. Although Mavis initially declines, Consolata remarks: "You give in too quick. Look at your nails. Strong, curved like a bird's. Fingernails like that take the meat out whole every time" (*Paradise*, 43). Though Consolata quickly leaves to see about Mother, Mavis begins shelling the pecans. Performing a domestic chore, Mavis sees her body, a synecdoche of the self, anew as she "watched her suddenly beautiful hands moving" (43). The reader first apprehends the garden outside the Convent through Mavis's eyes: "She saw flowers mixed in with or parallel to rows of vegetables. In some places staked plants grew in a circle, not in a line, in high mounds of soil. Chickens clucked out of sight. A part of the garden she originally thought gone to weed became, on closer inspection, a patch of melons. An empire of corn beyond" (41). The garden, sprawling and fecund, is tied to the female body, as both, in their unrestrained materiality, are sites of resistance in the novel and suggest something about the gardener; in fact, Kincaid avers that an overgrown garden "reveals a comforting generosity of spirit" (83). If, as ecofeminist theory holds, patriarchal power is enacted over the female body and land, the organic state of the garden suggests that the Convent women are learning to thrive outside of rigidly scripted definitions.

In the quiet of the kitchen, Mavis hears the laughing and singing of children, including her own deceased babies, Merle and Pearl, intermingling with the sounds of the natural world: "From the table where she sat admiring her busy hands, the radio absence spread out. A quiet, secret fire breathing itself and exhaling the sounds of its increase: the crack of shells, the tick of nut meat tossed in the bowl, cooking utensils in eternal adjustment, insect whisper, the argue of long grass, the faraway cough of cornstalks" (*Paradise*, 42). Gordon Hempton, an acoustic ecologist, explains that silence has a voice, and in silence we hear the musical score of life; in short, "silence is not the absence of something, but the presence of everything." Hempton's revelations shed light on Mavis's recognition of the interdependent web of existence, consisting of that which is organic and inorganic, living and dead. The Convent is a space where the larger social and biotic ecosystems are readily made apparent. Indeed, a dying Mother Superior, upon meeting Mavis, directly asks, "Where are your children?" (*Paradise*, 47), in recognition of her motherhood and her mother loss. Mother sees and hears not only Mavis's children but the girls who attended the missionary school. Her insight, Morrison indicates, is not supernatural or otherworldly but a recognition of the life–death–rebirth continuum.

Describing Mother, Consolata says to Mavis: "She is my mother. Your mother too. Whose Mother you?" (*Paradise*, 48). Notably, Morrison withholds Mavis's answer, suggesting the complex, multifaceted nature of mothering in the novel. *Paradise* pivots on the axis of mother-daughter relationships, some biological, but most surrogate, as a community of damaged women come together to create female spaces and in so doing mother one another. The Convent is by no means limned as a maternal utopia, but it is an organic space where broken women's lives are put back together largely by reconnecting to the biotic world. In this way, Logan's argument in *Dirt*, "wherever there are decay and repose, there begins to be soil" (2), holds currency here, for the women are able to transmogrify their pain into new life, a process mirrored in the Convent garden.

Each of the women, though radically different in terms of temperament, attitude, emotional stability, and former traumas, is united in the Convent through food and gardening:

> All of them, each in her turn, and like the old Mother Superior and the servant who used to, still sold produce, barbecue sauce, good bread and the hottest peppers in the world. For a pricey price you

> could buy a string of the purply black peppers or a relish made from them. Either took the cake for pure burning power. The relish lasted years with proper attention, and though many customers tried planting the seeds, the pepper grew nowhere outside the Convent's garden. (*Paradise*, 11)

One should note that the Convent women did not plant the seeds; in fact, it was Consolata "who discovered the wild bush heavy with stinging-hot peppers and who cultivated them" (*Paradise*, 225). Consolata's discovery illustrates the earth as agentic. While humans shape land, cultivate floral and vegetable gardens, fight pests, and coax nonnative plant life, it is important here that the peppers grow without a definable human hand. Their autonomy is exemplified in the customers' inability to propagate the peppers, though they planted the same seeds, and those who live in Ruby surely occupied the same growing zone, being only seventeen miles removed from the original garden. Thus we can surmise that it is the soil composition in the Convent garden that allows for the pepper's growth. The Convent women's harvesting and selling of the peppers tie them to a shared history of fertility and self-sufficiency.

Dirt is the medium through which the Convent is accessed, as the residents and community members must travel on dirt roads to enter this female space. Morrison repeatedly describes this thoroughfare in terms of its elemental composition, which indicates its distinction from the rest of Ruby. Without asphalt or concrete paving, which effectively covers the soil and plant life, dirt roads are porous to the environment. During a storm, the dirt road to the Convent "could be a tricky stretch because the earth was absorbing the rain now, swelling the roots of parched plants and forming rivulets wherever it could" (*Paradise*, 282). The Convent and its inhabitants are surrounded by soil, bordered by dirt roads, and adjacent to sprawling gardens.

In contrast to the bountiful garden surrounding the Convent, the town square contains an outdoor shrine, a monument to its history, in the form of an oven. This oven, which was once a communal working appliance, is no longer functional. Cynthia Dobbs, in "Diasporic Designs of House, Home, and Haven in Toni Morrison's *Paradise*," argues that "in Haven and then in Ruby, Morrison turns the conventionally feminine domestic space of the kitchen inside out, rendering the Oven a public icon of the town fathers' utopian plans. Private, feminine utility becomes public, masculine memorial" (116). Shari Evans, in "Programmed Space, Themed Space, and the Ethics of Home in Toni Morrison's *Paradise*," likewise claims that "no longer the site of communal food preparation or even baptisms, no longer necessary for either material or spiritual sustenance, the Oven has become simply an empty monument" (389). The men, moving from Haven to Ruby (one all-Black town to the next), carefully dismantled the oven and carried the "bricks, the hearthstone and the iron plate two hundred and forty miles west" (6), only to painstakingly reassemble and "recement" it into place. While the oven is seemingly a domestic object, that it is no longer functional but is a memorial to the Old Fathers mitigates against such a reading. The oven is encoded as a male instrument, a shrine of masonry that solidifies the elders' immovable ideologies.

The women of Ruby begrudge the oven's prominence: "The women nodded when the men took the Oven apart, packed, moved and reassembled it. But privately they resented the truck space given over to it—rather than a few more sacks of seed, rather than shoats or even a child's crib" (*Paradise*, 103). The oven is dismantled and resurrected in Ruby, but just as their ideologies are no longer tenable, so the oven is no longer practical. The women value husbandry and children over inert monuments, fecundity over a barren history. In this way, the oven becomes a grave marker, and as such it is apt that the men of Ruby hatch the plan to murder the Convent women at the oven: "Like boot camp recruits, like invaders preparing for slaughter, they were there [at the oven] to rave, to heat the blood or turn it icicle cold the better to execute the mission" (280). After the murders, the oven begins to sink back into the ground as the very foundation on which it sits falters, revealing the bankruptcy on which their town is founded. Further, this scene divulges the earth as agentic and living, capable of moving and upending a man-made artifact, even one as "flawlessly designed" as the oven-cum-tombstone.

Throughout the novel, the characters argue about the oven's fragmented inscription, which reads "the furrow of his brow." The older generation maintains that it is a religious commandment, "Beware the furrow of his brow," but the younger generation interprets it as "Be the furrow of his brow." The argument is symptomatic of the larger generational rift dividing the town: the older men hold that they should live in fear or deference to the past, while the younger wish to reimagine the town in their own image.

The reader is encouraged to sympathize with the younger generation, recognizing the dangers that befall ideologues, yet the fragment "furrow of his brow" likewise opens itself up to an ecocritical reading. Furrow, after all, refers to plowed land, specifically a narrow groove made in the ground by a plow, and a brow is the summit of a hill or the edge of a deep place. Read from this prism, to be the furrow of his brow suggests an elision between people and earth. Employing this inscription, which Anna, a community member, later feminizes as "Be the furrow of *Her* brow" (*Paradise*, 159), Morrison exhorts the community to be the land on the summit. The anthropocentric reading of this phrase—to beware or be the face of God encarnalized as man/woman—is supplanted by a reading of the divine as earth centered, a conflation of people and place. By the novel's end, graffiti that covers the hood of the oven proclaims, "We Are the Furrow of His Brow" (298), unmistakably placing humans as merely part of the larger biophysical world.

Here Morrison sounds the chord of transcorporeality, and using this paradigm, which realigns the body with the material world, it is feasible to read not only the community as the land but Ruby, the dead woman, as always already part of the eponymous town, and the inhabitants of Ruby as part of her as well. Encoding the "men of Ruby" (the town) as literally being "of Ruby" (the woman) suggests a maternal reading of the town, a material understanding that all humankind is, using Adrienne Rich's language, "of woman born." Because Ruby is synonymous with her untimely passing, the town (its birth and its life) is transcorporeally inscribed with death. To highlight this point, Ruby is buried in an ad hoc cemetery on her brother Steward's ranch (296) and thus merges with the earth in a space of life and death, outside a removed and sterile necrogeography. The irony is that the elders convince themselves that they are invincible, creating a paradise in which death is held in abeyance (recalling the biblical story of the Garden of Eden), when its very being is inscribed with death, a point Morrison highlights with the many registers of death that surround the community. Death marks the birth of the town: the women of the Convent are murdered, women abort babies, and the novel's conclusion stages a funeral for a young girl, Save Marie, all suggesting the porous boundary between one town and the next, one community and the next, and, given the logic of the novel (where Morrison signals race in the first line only to erase its significance throughout), one race and the next.

Morrison likewise illuminates a transcorporeal exchange between botanical life and social life. The organic and fecund earth surrounding the Convent directly contrasts the cultivated land of Ruby, which serves as a metonym of governance and social order: "The dirt yards, carefully swept and sprinkled in Haven, became lawns in Ruby. . . . The habit, the interest in cultivating plants that could not be eaten, spread, and so did the ground surrendered to it" (*Paradise*, 89). The plants only have ornamental purposes: no longer are the residents of Ruby growing consumable plant life, thus illustrating their removal from the biosphere. The transmogrification from the swept yards to grass lawns further bespeaks a disconnection from their cultural heritage. Richard Westmacott, in *African-American Gardens and Yards in the Rural South*, explains that "maintaining a communal dirt yard was once a routine for black families in the South, and it is also traditional in most West African villages. Even members of some of the most affluent African families . . . keep the yard completely free of grass by morning and afternoon sweepings. This smooth yard is functional on the Sea Islands as well as in Africa: keeping it grassless helps to eliminate insects and provides a place where children can play and elders can congregate" (80).

Moreover, that the lawn, the idealized American landscape, became the hegemonic plant life of Ruby speaks to rigid conformity and patriarchy; indeed, Virginia Scott Jenkins, in *The Lawn: A History of an American Obsession*, argues that "lawns in the United States are men's work" (1). She further explains that the single-family house surrounded by grass developed after the Civil War and continued throughout the twentieth century (3), becoming a status symbol for well-to-do families (27). Because the lawn aesthetic requires constant vigilance to maintain in the form of mowers, hoses, sprinklers, pesticides, herbicides, and fertilizers (9), American lawns are one of the most unsustainable landscapes. The lawn represents a monocrop where any other species are eradicated: torn out, dug up, and chemically removed. Monoculture lawns are nutrient poor and support few other species and thus mirror the community of Ruby, where the 8-Rock residents adamantly reject outsiders. The community's unhealthiness is evidenced in the Fleetwoods' four sickly children: "The reverence for the darkest of skin color [is] a logical explanation for the high levels of infant illness, if not mortality: inbreeding (in whatever culture) leads to disability of all kinds" (Wagner-Martin, 117). That the 8-Rocks intermarry, refusing to allow any diversity in their gene pool, results in weakness. Using an ecological metaphor that elides botanical seeds and seminal fluid, Morrison, in an interview with Elizabeth Farnsworth, reasons that the town "carries the seeds of its own destruction" (156). Montgomery explains the importance of ecosystem diversity: "As ecologists know, diversity conveys resilience—and resilience can help keep agriculture sustainable. . . . Monocultures generally leave the ground bare in the spring, exposing vulnerable soil to erosion for months before crops get big enough to block incoming rain" (206). By contrast, "a perennial polyculture can manage pests, provide all its own nitrogen, and produce a greater per-acre crop yield than monocultures" (Montgomery, 206–7). By purposefully including the type of plant life surrounding the dwellings of Ruby and the Convent, Morrison discloses the impossibility of segregating elements of an ecosystems. The porosity of material bodies—in this case, plants and people—is such that entities do not have stable borders and boundaries but are affected through relationships to other organic or inorganic entities. In this way, Morrison's ecological consciousness not only crosses boundaries between human and nonhuman environments but also merges the biotic and societal spheres, because "the fact is," according to Jamaica Kincaid, "the world cannot be left out of the garden" (82).

The Convent, while not a working farm, is a kind of homestead, where women live sustainable, autonomous lives, using minimal resources. According to Westmacott, "In a self-sufficient system, chickens and pigs mean far more than eggs and bacon. They are symbolic of an integrated system where scraps and crop residues are turned into manure and returned to the land. To a gardener, a manure heap is a source of satisfaction, symbolic of fertility and growth" (92). He further offers, "Self-sufficiency, self-reliance, independence, and resourcefulness are four fundamental agrarian values" (91), which the Convent women slowly adopt.

The Convent women grow and harvest vegetables, preserve fresh produce, and raise chickens for eggs and meat. Morrison does not sanitize the life cycle. Connie serves Mavis a "roast chicken supper" (*Paradise*, 48) on her first night at the Convent, and "a bit of chicken" is the only food item Connie offers to the dying Mother Magna (47). Throughout the novel, the women live in a more environmentally conscious manner that is tied to food production. Morrison showcases this point with the size and scope of the Convent kitchen, made especially poignant as it is rendered through the consciousness of the male invaders: "The kitchen is bigger than the house in which either man was born. The ceiling barn-rafter high. More shelving than Ace's Grocery store. The table is fourteen feet long if an inch. . . . Stock simmers on the stove. It is restaurant size with eight burners and on a shelf beneath the great steel hood a dozen loaves of bread swell" (5). The milk that Steward consumes unmistakably links his invasion of the Convent and his murder of the women to a violation of motherhood: "He moves to the long table and lifts the pitcher of milk. He sniffs it first and then, the pistol in his right hand, he uses his left to raise the pitcher to his mouth, taking . . . long, measured swallows" (7). During the raid, the men muse about their own childhoods, comparing the home to their own and the generous stockpot to the size of the tub in which they were bathed. Linking the Convent women to motherhood suggest that the men—with milk in one hand and pistol in the other—unconsciously perform matricide.

In this cycle of fertility and death that Morrison advances in *Paradise*, it is apt that she would include sexuality. While human relationships occur in the novel (relationships between Deacon and Consolata, Gigi and K.D., and Pallas and Carlos), Morrison locates the most erotic portraits of sexuality in the nonhuman world. Gigi's boyfriend, Mikey, relates to her a story about a fornicating rock formation:

> One hour, tops, you'll see loving to beat the sky. Sometimes tender. Other times rough. But they never stop. Not for dust storms or heat hovering at 108 degrees. And if you are patient and catch them in one of the desert's random rainfalls you will see the color of their bodies deepen. But they keep on doing it in the rare pure rain—the black couple of Wish, Arizona. . . . At sunrise, he said, they turned copper and you knew they'd been at it all night. At noon they were silvery gray. Then afternoon blue, then evening black. Moving, moving, all the time moving.[3] (63)

The overt sexuality of the rock formation is not limned as anthropocentric—a projection of human sexuality onto a supposedly inert lithic land mass—but reflects the earth's fertility, in which humans are merely a part.[4] The copulating rock couple reinforces how humans are inextricably elided with nonhuman actants. Important, too, is Morrison's employment of stone, for as Kellie Robertson reminds us in "Exemplary Rocks": "Rocks are usually synonymous with insentience . . . drained of all sensation and vitality" (91). Rejecting the belief in the "poverty of the inanimate world" (92), Robertson turns to Aristotle's *History of Animals*, wherein the philosopher describes a hierarchical chain of being from God to man and down to animals, plants, and rocks. Robertson astutely notes that "while the rock occupies the lowest rung on this ladder, it is nonetheless part of the reciprocal linkages that bound all things together in this ontological chain" (99). From a posthumanist framework, the yoking of rocks to people is apt insofar as humans are inherently entangled with organic and inorganic matter from the nonhuman world.

Robertson's explication of the vitality of medieval stones sheds particular light on Morrison's erotic stone formation in *Paradise*:

> Lapidaries and encyclopedias documented the endlessly entertaining charisma of ostensibly insensible stones: coral, for instance, was thought to make fields fertile and to drive away evil spirits, while magnetite could be used to test the fidelity of wives, since it would "repulse" an unfaithful woman. A staple of such lapidary accounts were the piroboli, the so-called "fire stones" that spontaneously burst into flame when brought together. This apparently lifelike behavior was explained as the natural attraction between a "male" and a "female" stone, a sexual dimorphism that was often allegorized as an exemplum against carnal lust. (93)

An ecocritical reading of this passage provides insight to a seemingly tangential textual moment. Morrison signifies this lithic history by portraying a rock-human relationship in such a manner as to further the fertility aspect of the cycle of renewal that punctuates the novel. Further, Morrison's stone couple showcases, in the words of Jeffrey Cohen in the introduction to *Animal, Vegetable, Mineral*, that "the human is not the world's sole meaning-maker and never has been" (7). Instead, as is evidenced throughout *Paradise*, human bodies are porous and share being—in this case, sexual being—with other material bodies.

Morrison revisits the symbol of the rock in what is perhaps the climactic healing ritual of the novel. The ceremony that the women perform, an elision of body and spirit, occurs in the basement of the Convent. Spatializing the ritual in the "good clean darkness of the cellar," the women allow Connie to draw outlines of their bodies on the stone floor:

> First they had to scrub the cellar floor until its stones were as clean as rocks on a shore. Then they ringed the place with candles. Consolata told each to undress and lie down. . . . When each found the position she could tolerate on the cold, uncompromising floor, Consolata walked around her and painted the body's silhouette. (263)

The women endure hours on the lithic floor and thus become aligned with stone. Moreover, though Consolata says very little, she relates a story of a sacred land, and this brief interlude is punctuated with reference to minerals: the fruit taste like "sapphires," the boys use "rubies" for dice, the cathedrals are made of "gold," and the little people have "diamonds" for teeth" (263–64). Valerie Allen in "Mineral Virtue" provides the Latin word for "mineral": it refers "to the underground excavation of treasures stored in the earth's bowels. So it follow that a mineral which comes from the earth, should predominantly contain earth" (128). Rocks and minerals, through physical and chemical processes, form soil, and thus Morrison's employment of stone, the parent material of soil, provides an important registry of dirt in the novel.

Charles Darwin's final scientific work sheds light on the relationship between rock and dirt. Darwin examined the role of earthworms in soil formation. This early treatise on soil bioturbation, the reworking of soils and sediments by plants and animals, examines an important factor affecting biodiversity: "Darwin noticed that in addition to grinding up leaves, worms break small rocks down into mineral soil. When dissecting worm gizzards, he almost always found small rocks and grains of sand" (Montgomery, 11).

Beyond earthworms, "burrowing animals—like gophers, termites and ants—mix broken rock into the soil. Roots pry rocks apart. Falling trees churn up rock fragments and mix them into the soil. Formed under great pressure deep within the earth, rocks expand and crack apart as they near the ground. Big rocks break down into little rocks and eventually into their constituent mineral grains owing to stresses from wetting and drying, freezing and thawing, or heating by wildfires" (17). In short, Darwin concluded that soil is a "dynamic interface between rock and life" (13), and in this way, Morrison's use of stone returns the reader to the earthiness of the women's lives. They collectively descend to the basement and perform a ritual of healing inside stone, the matrix for dirt, an organic and fertile layering that joins the earth with the women's lives.

It is in the basement where women share in the individual traumas of one another's lives and, in bearing witness, heal and mother one another. While Connie does not ritualize this healing ceremony in the outdoors, this domestic space recalls the garden in the form of a root cellar, where produce would likely have been stored, and the smell of herbs lingers. Though Morrison does not use this term per se, Connie's characterization of the basement unmistakably recalls the atmosphere of an underground storage facility: "There is a small room in the cellar. . . . It's cool and dark in the summer" (237).[5] That root cellars are dug into the earth suggests a kind of in-between place between shelter and earth. An ancient technology that grounds humans into the biosphere by using the insulative properties of the earth, root cellars have been used in many cultures. In fact, according to Peter Hatch in "African-American Gardens at Monticello," "Archaeological excavations of slave cabins at Monticello indicate the widespread presence of root cellars, which not only served as secret hiding places, but surely as repositories for root crops, and other vegetables amenable to cool, dark storage." The root cellar was adapted to the exigencies of African American life as a safe space for people and plants, a space of survival and nourishment. Morrison capitalizes on this history, as the templates of the Convent women's bodies merge with the cold stones of the cellar's floor, suggesting an elision between human and nonhuman worlds. Also evocative here is that the root cellars, in effect, bury the vegetables in the earth, creating an underground repository of prolonged fertility, staving off, for a period, the process of decay.

After the women's occupation of the basement, they move to the outdoors, where, precipitated by the rain, their healing ritual is completed:

> There are great rivers in the world and on their banks and the edges of the oceans children thrill to water. In places where rain is light

> the thrill is almost erotic. But those sensations bow to the rapture of holy women dancing in hot sweet rain. They would have laughed, had enchantment not been so deep. If there were any recollections of a recent warning or intimations of harm, the irresistible rain washed them away. Seneca embraced and finally let go of a dark morning in state housing. Grace witnessed the successful cleansing of a white shirt that never should have been stained. Mavis moved in the shudder of rose of Sharon petals tickling her skin. Pallas, delivered of a delicate son, held him close while the rain rinsed away a scary woman on an escalator and all fear of black water. Consolata, fully housed by the god who sought her out in the garden, was the more furious dancer, Mavis the most elegant. Seneca and Grace danced together, then parted to skip through fresh mud. Pallas, smoothing raindrops from her baby's head, swayed like a frond. (283)

Emerging from the literal and figurative darkness, the women are reborn by the salve that is the rain. As Morrison refers to the women as "holy," we can read this scene of renewal as baptismal in nature.[6] The women, once again, revisit the spectral presence of their former traumas, but these vestiges are washed away by rainwater. Connie, the new mother superior, facilitates the maternal healing that the natural world continues. This passage is rife with birth imagery: rainwater as amniotic, Pallas as mother, and women as botanicals. Morrison reclaims the negative association between dirt and the Convent women first proffered by the community leaders as the women skip through "fresh mud," perhaps the strongest imagery of fecundity in the passage.

Mud, nutrient rich, is a mixture of water and soil, silt, or clay. As an in-between substance, neither earth nor water, the mud foreshadows the women who will soon occupy a liminal state between death and afterlife. Sartre argued that mud is an aberrant fluid because it does not let one make a mark on it, claiming that "it is a fluidity which holds and which compromises me. . . . It clings to me like a leech . . . and leaves its trace upon me" (quoted in Giblett, 43). Refusing elemental conformity and indelibly marking whatever it touches, mud identifies the women as part of the natural and social landscape. Historically, mud has been of great interest to scientists and philosophers. Since the time of Aristotle in the fourth century BC, mud and slime, in conjunction with natural elements such as rain, air, and sunlight, had been theorized to have life-giving properties. This autochthonous theory, known as spontaneous generation, circulated for centuries and was scientifically disproved only in the mid-nineteenth century.[7] This trenchant cultural belief held that life (albeit in the form of simple organisms such as fleas, mosquitoes, and the like) arose from mud. Thus what I am interested in here is not merely that living beings emerged from inert materials but that mud, specifically, was identified as the progenitor of life.

Violence quickly follows this baptismal moment. The women, dead in spirit, arrive at the Convent and are healed and reborn by maternal and ecological connections, only to be murdered by the town's fathers. The women fight the gunmen with domestic objects—frying skillets and butcher knives—and some retreat to the garden. The women, outnumbered and overpowered, succumb to the men's gunfire. Some die in the yard, and Consolata, who dies in the home, is laid out on the kitchen table. These images disclose the fertility of the women's bodies even in death, a revival that becomes even more vivid in their disappearance.

As a symbol of compost, the Convent women continue long after their corporeal deaths. After the massacre at the Convent, their bodies are conspicuously absent. Because the corpses have vanished, the community muses on various scenarios, one of which is that "the women took other shapes and disappeared into thin air" (*Paradise*, 296). Their dead bodies are not revealed because they have in fact morphed into another form, a point that Billie Delia, a friend of the women, muses on when she considers their absence: she "was the only one in town who was not puzzled by where the women were or concerned about how they disappeared. She had another question: When will they return?" (308). Morrison answers this call in the following chapter as each woman returns to people and places that informed her life. Important to this reading, the Convent women are not apparitions but embodied, material women who continue to grow and change.[8] For example, after death, Gigi takes off her clothes and bathes in a cool lake: "This was lake country: viridian water, upright trees and—in places where no boats or fishermen came—a privacy royals would envy. She picked up a towel and dried her hair. Less than an inch had grown, but she loved how wind and water and fingers and toes rippled in it. She opened a bottle of aloe and began to rub her skin. Then, straightening the towel next to her, she looked toward the lake where her companion was just coming ashore" (310). The transcorporeal exchange between the female body, plants, and water is one in which the dead woman does not exist outside the biotic world but is sensually, materially inside it, a life that continues as something new. The scene's vividness is mirrored in all the women's postmortem vignettes. The Convent women's deaths—their bodies, bones, blood, and hair—have enriched the town, infusing new life into its decayed state. The colors that mark the afterlife narratives bespeak the growth of flora made possible by rich soil, which has given birth to a new vibrancy in Ruby.

Two residents of Ruby, Anna Flood and her fiancé the Reverend Richard Misner, return to the Convent days after the shooting and try to piece the story together, questioning how murders could have occurred without material proof of the carnage. Significantly, their conversation takes place in the garden:

> At the edge of the garden a faded red chair lay on its side. Beyond was blossom and death. Shriveled tomato plants alongside crops of leafy green reseeding themselves with gold flowers; pink hollyhocks so tall the heads leaned all the way over a trail of bright squash blossoms; lacy tops of carrots browned and lifeless next to straight green spikes of onion. Melons split their readiness showing gums of juicy red. Anna sighed at the mix of neglect and unconquerable growth. The five eggs warm umber in her hands. (304–5)

The fecundity of the vegetation is made possible by the decayed plant life. Morrison renders the garden, a space of life and death, in terms of the human body with leaning heads and red gums, suggesting, perhaps, that the women's bleeding bodies fertilized the soil and thus became part of the flora. Whether in the form of blood meal, rotting plants, or decomposing biota, death is omnipresent in the garden. Far from the bountiful and pristine grounds seared in our national imaginary, various stages of disease, decay, and death are as much a part of the biotic world as are growth and new life. Life being born from death is nowhere more apparent than in the biophysical world. After all, the most effective of fertilizers is dead organic material: "Soil organic matter is essential for sustaining soil fertility not so much as a direct source of nutrients but by supporting soil ecosystems that help promote the release and uptake of nutrients. Organic matter helps retain moisture, improves soil structure, helps liberate nutrients from clays, and is itself a source of plant nutrients. Loss of soil organic matter reduces crop yields by lowering the activity of soil biota, thereby slowing nutrient recycling" (Montgomery, 205).

Though Anna is dismayed by this mix of neglect and growth, as though incompatible, the novel suggests otherwise in the symbol of the eggs clutched in her hand. The eggs, a metonym of the five Convent women, tie the women not only to the natural world but also to maternity. The eggs are a clear metaphor for fertility and birth, which the men pathologize when they raid the Convent: "Peering out he sees an old hen, her puffed and bloody hind parts cherished, he supposes, for delivering freaks—double, triple yolks in outsize and misshapen shells" (*Paradise*, 5). Chickens also mediate the day of the shooting. An hour before the raid, Mavis shoos pullets out of the Convent's school room (49).

While chickens were once present in nearly every backyard (Squier, 13), by the 1970s, when *Paradise* is set, this would not have been the case, so Morrison's use of chickens as a motif demands critical attention. In *Poultry Science, Chicken Culture*, Susan Merrill Squier argues that historically, raising chickens, a liminal livestock, was a female-centered activity carried out in family backyards (147). She continues: "Raising chickens gave farm wives not only the power to amend the farm diet when necessary but also precious economic (and therefore at times even social) autonomy. When the rise of extension education in poultry farming destabilized this arrangement, producing a new image of the scientific male farmer in the 1930s and 1940s, women lost control over an aspect of their daily lives and crucial income as well" (129). Beyond the economic implications associated with chicken farming, Squier considers the cultural elision between women and chickens, answering the question, "Why are women like chickens and chicken like women?": "They both produce eggs, are both subject to bodily regulation and regimentation, and are both being shaped biomedically and socially to be the object of male sexual and economic desire" (155). In *Paradise*, chickens, a multilayered metaphor of gender politics, maternal disregard, and female objectification, also advance Morrison's rendering of the natural landscape of the Convent, a place that is part of the biosphere surrounded, as it is, by "corn, buffalo grass, clover and approached by a dirt track barely seen from the road" (10). And, of course, chicken manure, nitrogen rich, serves as an effective fertilizer, accounting in part for the health of the soil. For the purposes of this argument, the link between chickens and the reproductive experiences of women is not only that they both bear eggs; rather, it is the complex interweaving of life, death, and rebirth that the chicken-and-egg duality embodies: "The egg is in the chicken, and the chicken is in the egg. Chicken and egg arise in mutual dependence. Neither is independent" (Squier, 14). The chicken as metaphor for the borderland between life and death, and death and rebirth, is sounded from the outset when Mother Superior and Mavis first meet. Mother, who is on the precipice of death, instructs Mavis to step closer because of her poor eyesight: "I can't see anything unless it's right up on me. Like living in an eggshell," intimating that she is also on the cusp of rebirth (47).

Notably, Reverend Misner uses the discourse of an ecological borderland in his funeral for Save Marie, a death that follows the Convent women's: "What is sown is not alive until it dies" (*Paradise*, 305), stressing, within a religious paradigm, that corporeal death is the beginning of everlasting life. From an ecocritical point of view, the cycle of life, death, and rebirth is unending, a succession in the biotic world that continues. In this way, the window Misner senses in the Convent garden is a place that is "neither life nor death" (307), an intermediary state that eschews simple binaries. In "'Passing on' Death," Sarah Aguiar posits that most of the women may already be dead when they arrive at the Convent: "Gigi arrives at the Convent in a hearse; Mavis in the Cadillac in which her infant twins died. Pallas cannot speak at first, and Seneca engages in self-bloodletting" (514). While this bold argument is interesting its own right, it nicely supports an ecocritical reading of *Paradise* in terms of the ecological cycle of life, death, and reawakening, a natural rhythm that includes human and nonhuman actants. This theory of reincarnation is also resonant with soil, which reveals that "life depends on recycling past life" (Montgomery, 19).

Just as the opening of *Paradise* highlights the life cycle, so too does the novel's epilogue traffic in this progression, symbolized in the elision of maternity and ecology. In the final scene, Piedade, a spiritual mother figure, rocks Consolata. Though the cradled figure is not named as such, her tea-colored hair and green eyes disclose her identity. This scene, far from Oklahoma, takes place on a distant shore. Piedade's maternal rocking is prefigured in the novel: the Convent women are nightly rocked to sleep, eschewing beds in favor of hammocks, and Consolata rocks a dying Mary Magna between her breasts, "so the lady had entered death like a birthing" (223).

Morrison does not conclude *Paradise* with unblemished images of mothering, pristine gardens, or rich soil but leaves the reader on the ocean's shoreline with garbage: sea trash, discarded bottle caps, a broken sandal, and a dead radio, revealing "images of detritus redeemed" (Anderson, 98). That abiotic objects litter the shore seemingly mitigates against a reading of ecological renewal. However, Logan, in *Dirt*, reminds us that even unlikely articles have the potential to transform. He relates a story of a pickup truck bed littered with Styrofoam cups, cassette tapes, chopsticks, restaurant menus, pigeon droppings, and saw blades that sat in the elements for months. While these items are not conventionally the stuff of compost heaps, Logan observes: "Out of these leavings a forest is growing. Not on the ground. Not beside the truck. Right in the back of it. The lobes of maple leaves are sharpening as their seedlings sprout, a light and glossy green. . . . It would be hard to imagine a more improbable set of ingredients, but even a truck can become dirt" (1, 2). Heeding Logan's words, it is fair to assume that out of the waste that surrounds Piedade and Consolata, new life will eventually begin. Morrison leaves the reader with the unconventional making of compost and offers a final image of waste and renewal. Morrison's brown ecology is written on women and dirt. The ship, evocative of the slave ships of the Middle Passage, reveals a transcorporeal link between the antecessors and the generations to come. Ending with an assemblage of mothers, ancestors, water, and garbage, Morrison intertwines the living and the dead as they endlessly cycle through the biotic and cultural geographies of *Paradise*.

Garbage also forms a leitmotif in *The Bluest Eye*. In the closing moments of Morrison's inaugural novel, the adult Claudia, employing the discourse of the biophysical world—seeds, earth, marigolds, and soil—reflects on Pecola's decent into madness:

> And now when I see her searching the garbage—for what? The thing we assassinated? I talked about how I did *not* plant the seeds too deeply, how it was the fault of the earth, the land, of our town. I even think now that the land of the entire country was hostile to marigolds that year. This soil is bad for certain kinds of flowers. Certain seeds it will not nurture, certain fruit it will not bear, and when the land kills of its own volition, we acquiesce and say the victim had no right to live. (206)

While this passage has routinely been analyzed as a treatise on the ubiquity of racism throughout the nation, I suggest here another layer of meaning that Morison subtly weaves throughout the novel, namely, that the biotic world not only functions as an objective correlative of Pecola's psychological despair but is presented as an ecosphere in which the children are situated, a living world that has the possibility of being a sanctuary. Employing an ecocritical analysis where the Latin root word *eco* (*oikos* in Greek) literally translates to "home" opens up our understanding of Pecola's madness and situates it as a displacement from home. In this way, the natural world does not exist outside of—or separate from—the human sphere but is presented as a primary site of home. According to Jean Feerick and Vin Nardizzi in *The Indistinct Human*, the epistemic shift from the sixteenth century to the seventeenth gave rise to the demarcation between the human and nonhuman and inevitably positioned people at the top of that binary. *The Bluest Eye* enacts the loss that comes with the rise of what Donna Haraway labels human exceptionalism and positions the children's connection to the natural world as a form of resistance to the oppressive racial, gender, and class politics in which they are situated.[9] Moreover, the text's elision of the human and more-than-human spheres allows for a material ecocritical reading. Dana Phillips and Heather Sullivan in "Material Ecocriticism" argue: "Above all . . . human beings are 'actors' operating within material processes that include multitudes of other 'actors,' the majority of which are not human, or for that matter, conscious" (446). Further, that material ecocriticism emphasizes our "storied bodies" as well as the "agentic capacities of matter" (447) provides an ecological vision of interconnectedness that sheds light on Morrison's first novel.

In *The Bluest Eye*, Morrison explores the many registries of home—bodies, living things, houses, neighborhoods, and nations—that are inextricably part of the biophysical world. Indeed, the novel's structure highlights the relationship between dwellings and the biotic world, as Morrison begins each section with a passage from the Dick and Jane primer, a children's reader fraught with gender, race, and class politics: "Here is the house. It is green and white. It has a red door. It is very pretty. Here is the family. Mother, Father, Dick and Jane live in the green-and-white house. They are very happy" (*Bluest*, 3). The home and its aesthetic value are given prominence. Not only is the family introduced secondarily to the home, but their happiness is predicated on middle-class homeownership.

Each section of *The Bluest Eye* juxtaposes this presentation of suburban home life with the seasons.[10] The novel begins with "Autumn" and ends with "Summer," suggesting a cyclical narrative, calibrated to the rhythms of the natural world. Beginning with fall, Morrison implicitly opens on a note of loss. The beauty of autumnal trees is predicated on death. Bereft of sufficient sunlight, the leaves are incapable of producing chlorophyll, and this draining of life generates brilliant hues. While the foliage is predictable, the soil is not. We enter Pecola's "quiet as it's kept" story in the fall of 1941, a time when Lorain, Ohio, would have been ablaze in shades of crimson, orange, and gold, but curiously there were no marigolds. Lest the marigolds be relegated to mere metaphor, Morrison, writing decades hence in the novel's afterword, muses on her opening sentence, insisting on the materiality of the plant: "What, then, is the Big Secret about to be shared: The thing we (reader and I) are 'in' on? A botanical aberration. Pollution, perhaps. A skip, perhaps, in the natural order of things: a September, an autumn, a fall without marigolds. Bright, common, strong and sturdy marigolds" (*Bluest*, 213).

Marigolds, resilient flowers that bloom better and more profusely in poor soil, are long lasting, flowering from spring to fall. They are a good companion plant, with a scent that repels animals and insects. Even the underground workings of the marigolds are beneficial to the soil, repelling nematodes (microscopic worms) for years. What, then, to make of the lack of marigolds in the summer of 1941 in Lorain, Ohio? While it may seem naive that Claudia and Frieda link Pecola's baby with the marigolds—a hardy flower, a child's first garden success—it is perhaps not so. In planting seeds, children are rooting themselves, assuring themselves of belonging in an ecosystem. The children are eager for confirmation of life, the green sprouts verifying the achievement of home. Claudia, questioning whether she and Frieda failed to utter the right magic words over the seeds or planted them too deeply in the earth, finally concludes: "The seeds shriveled and died; her baby too" (*Bluest*, 1). Claudia's ritual is presented as a corrective, a recuperative act that she believed had the potential to undo the violence done to Pecola's body: "We had dropped our seeds in our own little plot of black dirt just as Pecola's father had dropped his seeds in his own plot of black dirt" (1). Claudia reasons that neither baby nor seeds had a suitable habitat, ultimately reminding the girls that the land could not tolerate even that which was destined to survive. The seed, the promise of what is to come, could not take root in unyielding earth, and thus the girls were denied the protection that the marigolds promised. Lest the reader pathologize the Breedlove family, it is useful to remember that Claudia remarks by the novel's end that the entire country was hostile to marigolds. Notably, in the late 1960s, the president of Burpee Seeds launched a campaign for marigolds to be named the national flower of the United States. Though that honor was ultimately bestowed on the rose, Burpee's gesture nonetheless showcases the national prominence and relevance of the plant. That the beloved marigold was not welcome in the nation in *The Bluest Eye*—or the nation, to paraphrase Claudia, bore hostility toward the plant—suggests the myriad ways in which racism affects and infects human and physical environments.

Claudia recognizes that human corporeality is tethered to the natural world and realigns the body with plant life and soil. The transcorporeal exchange between humans and dirt is well documented: "Foundational texts of western religions acknowledge the fundamental relationship between humanity and the soil. The Hebrew name of the first man, Adam, is derived from the word *adama*, which means earth, or soil . . . [and] the Latin word for human, *homo*, is derived from *humus*, Latin for living soil" (Montgomery, 27). The physicist and environmental activist Vandana Shiva offers a familial reading of the earth: "In traditional agriculture, the soil is the mother. . . . It is recognized as the source of all fertility. Growing up in a country like India, in the period when I did, soil literally was your cradle" (*Dirt! The Movie*). Chris Maser echoes this sentiment, maintaining that dirt is the "placenta that nurtures all of life" (quoted in Sullivan, "Dirt Theory," 517). Thus it is reasonable to conclude that Claudia and Frieda, in planting marigold seeds, are rooting themselves in a maternal body, a matrix on Earth from which life-forms generate, a first home. It is devastating, then, that this transcorporeal exchange results in death: the land is unyielding, the baby dies, and

Pecola is devoid of cognitive life. Here it is useful to consider Deborah Slicer's argument that bodies are bioregions: "The only bioregion that we can claim strict identity with is the body. . . . To be 'home' is first to inhabit one's own body. We are each, as body, a biological ecosystem" (113). Since Pecola has been, in effect, homeless from the beginning of her life, it stands to reason that her body could not house her child and that she, too, would eventually vacate the body.[11]

Morrison represents Pecola's pregnancy not as private and intimate but as enmeshed in larger environments, cultural discourses, and practices. The womb, Morrison shows, is not a closed system but is affected by the larger environment. In *Having Faith: An Ecologist's Journey to Motherhood*, Sandra Steingraber theorizes the intricate crossings between human and nonhuman spheres as she imagines the mother body as an interactive ecosystem. Steingraber's womb, an interior maternal landscape, fuses with the natural world. After amniocentesis, as she holds a vial of her amniotic fluid in her hand, she reflects on water and its flow through human and nonhuman nature:

> I drink water, and it becomes blood plasma, which infuses through the amniotic sac and surrounds the baby—who also drinks it. And what is it before that? Before it is drinking water, amniotic fluid is the creeks and rivers that fill reservoirs. It is the underground water that fills wells. And before it is creeks and rivers and groundwater. Amniotic fluid is rain. . . . The blood of cows and chickens is in this tube. The nectar gathered by bees and hummingbirds is in this tube. Whatever is inside hummingbird eggs is also inside my womb. Whatever is in the world's water is here in my hand. (66–67)

This graphic musing on transcorporeality, where the nonhuman world and its inhabitants seep through human bodies, offers a trenchant revelation of the porosity of the mother body with the biotic world. With such an awareness that humans (and, in this context, mothers) are the very stuff of the material world, alterations to the environment, however broadly or intimately conceptualized and configured, can result in profound interventions in physical, social, and political spheres, which is why Morrison contextualizes Pecola's life and pregnancy with her mother's.

Victimized throughout her life and dehumanized before she delivers Pecola, Pauline internalizes self-hatred, and moments after Pecola's birth, she exclaims: "But I knowed she was ugly. Head full of pretty hair, but Lord she was ugly" (*Bluest*, 126). Pecola is immediately thrown out of a maternal shelter and becomes an orphan, an exile, desperately seeking home. One of the most dramatic examples of Pecola's displacement takes place in her mother's workplace. Pauline finds refuge in the shelter of the Fishers' well-to-do home, where she is given a nickname, an identity, and a power that she cannot wield in her own life:

> She looked at their houses, smelled their linen, touched their silk draperies, and loved all of it. . . . When she bathed the little Fisher girl, it was in a porcelain tub with silvery taps running infinite quantities of hot, clear water. She dried her in fluffy towels and put her in cuddly night clothes. Then she brushed her yellow hair, enjoying the roll and slip of it between her fingers. No zinc tub, no buckets of stove-heated water, no flaky, stiff, graying towels washed in a kitchen sink, dried in a dusty backyard, no tangled black puffs of rough wool to comb. Soon she stopped trying to keep her own house. (*Bluest*, 127)

When Pecola, uninvited, enters the Fishers' home, she is reproached for invading the space and, in her fear, inadvertently knocks over a piping-hot blackberry cobbler Pauline baked for her charge. Pauline does not tend to her daughter's burned flesh but commands her to "get on out of here" while soothing the blonde-haired, blue-eyed girl. Once again, Pecola is devastated by her emotional and spatial separation from her mother, her maternal home. Pecola recognizes that the Fishers' home, situated next to Lake Shore Park, a segregated city park, with crocuses, roses, and fountains, is a neighborhood in which she "did not belong" (*Bluest*, 106). Instead she is relegated to the family's storefront house, where they lived "because they were poor and black and stayed there because they believed they were ugly" (38).

Pauline's notion of home hinges on material trappings and luxury items, all of which are conflated with whiteness. Class and race are inextricably linked, and Pauline, trying to avoid the dilapidated dwelling where she lives with her demoralized husband and two needy children, immerses herself in the mansion on Lake Shore Park, where home and inhabitants embody societal standards of beauty, purity, and cleanliness, all articulated through a discourse of whiteness. Note, for example, the copious amounts of water available in the Fishers' home: their white skin, already a societal sign of cleanliness, is further purified by abundant streams of water. By contrast, Pauline regards her child, with her black puffs of rough wool, and the graying stiff towels caked with backyard dust as metonyms of the "peeling box of gray" in which the family resides. Pauline's move from the undesirability of her daughter's hair to the dirt tenaciously clinging to her linens bespeaks the hegemonic association of dirt (and being dirt poor) to blackness. Indeed,

Sullivan in "Dirt Theory and Material Ecocriticism" argues that dirt is "laden with gendered, racial, and class connotations" (529), a conflation sounded throughout the novel.

Pauline accepts and internalizes the association of African Americans with dirt, which is predicated on a racist ideology that, according to Diane Roberts in *The Myth of Aunt Jemima*, positions black skin as unhygienic: "In the hierarchy of purity to pollution, blackness was dirt" (131). Roberts further maintains that "even before the sixteenth century, black denoted stain, evil, dirt," and argues that "blackness was a class, carrying degradation, dirt, savagery, stupidity and vice within it like a virus" (8). In white supremacist literature and media, African American children were caricaturized as the pickaninny, a stereotype that recycled tropes such dirty, matted hair and unkempt clothes.

Pecola inherits this toxic legacy; her body is the site on which these narratives of worthlessness, filth, and debasement are mapped. Of course, it is not just the Breedloves who absorb this colonial violence. The MacTeers' home, a drafty house where rags are stuffed into the cracks of the windows and the family routinely searches for pieces of coal near the railroad tracks, is also permeated by an ideology that implicitly prizes whiteness. Christmastime is emblematic of the family's pledge to a white, middle-class aesthetic as they buy their daughters white, plastic baby dolls: "Adults, older girls, shops, magazines, newspapers, window signs—all the world had agreed that a blue-eyed, yellow-haired, pink-skinned doll was what every girl child treasured. 'Here,' they said, 'this is beautiful, and if you are on this day "worthy" you may have it'" (20–21). Claudia, who dismembered these so-called icons of beauty, desires, instead, a sensory experience on the holiday: "I want to sit on the low stool in Big Mama's kitchen with my lap full of lilacs and listen to Big Papa play his violin for me alone. The lowness of the stool made for my body, the security and warmth of Big Mama's kitchen, the smell of the lilacs, the sound of the music, and since it would be good to have all of my senses engaged, the taste of a peach, perhaps, afterward" (*Bluest*, 22). Claudia wants to experience safety and belonging with people and elements of the natural world. She, in short, wants to feel at home, which commodified forms of whiteness mitigate against. What she receives, however, are plastic dolls with unyielding limbs, "acrid" tasting tin cups for a tea party, and new dresses that require a strict bathing regimen: "Slipping around on the zinc, no time to play or soak, for the water chilled too fast, no time to enjoy one's nakedness, only time to make curtains of soapy water careen down between the legs. Then the scratchy towels and the dreadful and humiliating absence of dirt. The irritable, unimaginative cleanliness. Gone the ink marks from legs and face, all my creations and accumulations of the day gone, and replaced by goose pimples" (*Bluest*, 22). This passage offers a multilayered metaphor of dirt not only as soil, dust, and grime but as a mark of life. "Dirt," as Patricia Yaeger offers, "is redolent with bodiliness, with the uncensored glee of childhood" (265). Morrison, in highlighting Claudia's pleasure in dirt, recognizes the transgressive potential of dirt to disrupt hegemonic social and racial norms. After all, Claudia refutes symbols of white beauty throughout her childhood. Claudia holds on to the dirt-based markings on her skin as proof that her body is unapologetically mixed with the earth. According to Nina Jablonski in *Skin: A Natural History*, "The pores and nerve endings of our skin unite us with our surroundings. Skin is the interface through which we touch one another and sense much of our environments" (1–2).

Claudia's creative energy is drained in the tub; her body, denied the sensuous pleasure of water, is scrubbed, washed, rinsed, and purified, cleansed for the holiday in which her blackness is symbolically, temporarily, erased. After the "humiliating absence of dirt," Claudia's body—the first shelter—is vulnerable, without protection. Claudia's relationship to the natural world "inspires creativity . . . by demanding visualization and the full use of the senses" (Louv, 7), which she (unsuccessfully) tries to graft onto the domestic space. This is not to suggest that the MacTeers' home is devoid of love. The parents care for and protect their girls, take in Pecola, and question the disregard that the Breedloves demonstrate for their own daughter.[12]

The MacTeers' home is rich with love, "thick and dark as Alaga syrup" (*Bluest*, 12), a stark juxtaposition to the middle-class home of Geraldine, Louis, and Junior. An African American woman who has internalized white supremacy, Geraldine employs a racist discourse that elides dirt with blackness as she distinguishes upper-class African Americans from working-class Black people. The latter, she muses, engage in behaviors that are unseemly, "dirty and loud." In *Black Rage*, William Grier and Price Cobbs argue that in a racist social economy, middle-class African Americans are encouraged "to develop disgust and contempt for bad, black . . . behavior" and to position it against the "pious, white, freshly laundered African American who is sans dirt, sans sin" (197).

Morrison dedicates pages to describing the habits and customs of these refined upper-class women—singing in church choir, attending college, and homemaking—yet key to embodying this veneer of respectability is rejection of the funk:

> Wherever it erupts, this Funk, they wipe it away; where it crusts, they dissolve it; wherever it drips, flowers, or clings, they find it and fight it

> until it does. They fight this battle all the way to the grave. The laugh that is a little too loud; the enunciation a little too round; the gesture a little too generous. They hold their behind in for fear of a sway too free; when they wear lipstick, they never cover the entire mouth for fear of lips too thick, and they worry, worry, worry about the edges of their hair. (83)

Deftly moving from descriptions of material filthiness (that which clings, crusts, and drips) to signifiers of race (lips, behinds, and hair), Morrison illustrates how disavowing one's body necessitates renouncing the exigencies of the natural world. Indeed, as Christopher Douglas argues in "What *The Bluest Eye* Knows about Them: Culture, Race, Identity," "The funk is embodied and racialized through the various phenotypic differences that mark the social construction of race and that threaten to overwhelm the whitening process" (141). He goes on to argue, "Because their bodies continually threaten to undermine the pursuit of whiteness, it is the focus of their attention" (142). The body must be controlled lest it becomes "funky," a term that Geneva Smitherman in *Talkin and Testifyin* defines as "the blue notes or blue mood created in jazz, blues, and soul music generally, down-to-earth soulfully expressed sounds; by extension, the real nitty-gritty or fundamental essence of life, soul to the max" (53). The funk, then, is by necessity body and place based. It is organic, corporeal, and unornamented. Eschewing the body, Geraldine has rejected expression, artistry, sexuality, and the living world.

Akin to Pecola's unwelcome entry into the Fishers' home, Pecola is an intruder, an interloper in Geraldine's home. For Geraldine, who reproduces rigid societal racial demarcations, Pecola embodies the funk and thus the underside of blackness. Geraldine's disgust at seeing Pecola in the home with Junior, and believing that she (and not her son) had injured her beloved cat, calls her "nasty" and "black," aspersions that imbricate blackness and dirt. Geraldine sees Pecola's matted and unkempt plaits, which she metonymically links to African Americans who are "dirty and loud," with soiled socks and shoes caked with mud. Geraldine does not see Pecola but sees the antithesis of her own tenuous class standing, which is in keeping with the societal promulgation of Black middle-class identity. According to Philip Kowalski in "No Excuses for Our Dirt: Booker T. Washington and a 'New Negro' Middle Class," Washington was preoccupied with dirt and uncleanliness (181) and used that rhetoric to identify and discursively create a new African American middle class. He routinely equated dirt and disorder with slavery and implied that filth enslaves (182). While supportive of agricultural work, he believed that dirt should remain in its "proper" place (in the ground) and be kept away from bodies and dwellings. Responding to the ideology that blackness itself was a sign of dirtiness and pollution (a reason cited for Jim Crow segregation), Washington adamantly rejected dirt and used it as a rallying cry for uplift, arguing that "people would excuse us for our poverty, for our lack of comforts and conveniences, but that they would not excuse us for our dirt" (189). Washington's rhetoric, which became a chant of sorts at Tuskegee, ties cleanliness to moral virtue. Indeed, Washington regarded oral hygiene as "bringing about a higher degree of civilization among the students" (193).

Further, the campaign to discredit southern African American midwives at the beginning of the twentieth century (to allow white male doctors in the delivery rooms) also relied on racist assumptions that positioned blackness as a trope of filth. To county health boards, the African American midwives were never seen as "clean enough" (Lee, 38). Debasing the bodies of the midwives and focusing primarily on the hands as the instrument of their work, the medical establishment created advertisements portraying the women as "too large, too ashy, too dirty" (36), a metonym of their "filthy customs and [birthing] practices" (37).

Given this cultural climate where black bodies were constructed as polluted, Geraldine and those of the newly gentrified class internalize the discourse of race and dirt and take it to its "logical" conclusion by disavowing any hint of dirtiness, lest it be connoted with an uneducated, poor, black identity, hence Junior's removal from African American children. Junior's hair is shorn, a part etched into his scalp to "avoid any suggestion of wool," and his skin has been scrubbed and lotioned so as to escape any possibility of "ash." Despite the strict borders that Geraldine tries to maintain on her son's body, Junior dreams of throwing off the mantle of racial hatred and cleanliness and does so by fantasizing about dirt: "Junior used to long to play with black boys. More than anything in the world he wanted to play King of the Mountain and have them push him down the mound of dirt and roll over him" (*Bluest*, 87). According to Yaeger, "Dirt promises an escape from bourgeoisification" (263), which, in part, drives Junior's dirt-based desire. These boys—outlaws, in Geraldine's estimation—with their "wild blackness" are permitted embodiment in their race and in the natural world. Given the ubiquitous societal reaction to blackness, it is apt that Junior desires to play with Black boys in implicit recognition that to affirm boys and dirt is to affirm the self. Sullivan argues that "there is no ultimate boundary between us and nature. We are enmeshed within dirt in its many forms" (515). Junior wants to get dirty, to reject his mother's disavowal of that which is organic. Richard Louv in *Last Child in the Woods* reasons that "we can now assume that just as children need good nutrition and adequate sleep, they may very well need contact with nature" (3). Because Junior's relationship with the natural world is thwarted and controlled by his mother, he is left isolated and enraged, turning that fury onto Pecola.

Geraldine's defensive posturing is mirrored in Soaphead Church, a mixed-race Caribbean faith healer, who promises Pecola her much-coveted blue eyes, the final catalyst for her madness. Like Geraldine, Soaphead's self-loathing crystallizes in disgust of the funk: he "abhorred flesh on flesh. Body odor, breath odor, overwhelmed him. The sight of dried matter in the corner of the eye, decayed or missing teeth, ear wax, blackheads, moles, blisters, skin crusts—all the natural excretions and protections the body was capable of—disquieted him" (167). Since dirtiness and the materiality of the body repulsed him, this "clean old man" chose to exercise his "clean and good and friendly" sexuality on the "least offensive" humans: little girls.[13] Soaphead's internal colonization—hatred of his own blackness and the exigencies of the body—results in perversion. Severely damaged by racism, Soaphead turns his hatred toward the living world. Soaphead wants to eradicate Bob, his landlady's aged dog. Too repulsed to approach the animal, Soaphead tricks Pecola into feeding the dog poison, claiming that if it reacts, she will know that she has been granted her wish of blue eyes. At this point, Morrison again aligns Pecola with nonhuman life-forms, and while the young girl recoils from the dog's agony and quickly leaves this scene of death, the dog's suffering is grafted onto her and is a precipitating cause of Pecola's emotional death. Though the dog only appears in this scene, its triangulation with Soaphead and Pecola underwrites a larger connectivity, an ecological blending that remains part of Pecola's being.

Morrison accents the porous boundary between human and nonhuman living things, an interconnected web that Frieda and Claudia enact through their relationship to the earth. Rejecting social scripts, they realize their organic connection to soil and look to the dirt to "purify and heal" (*Dirt! The Movie*). Claudia and Frieda's act of resistance to the community's loathing of Pecola and her unborn baby (and implicitly to Geraldine and Soaphead and their exaggerated disgust of all things black) is enacted through the soil. In their attempts to love Pecola's baby, they turn to dirt. Ritualizing their ceremony with song and magic words, Frieda and Claudia try for a "miracle." Louv reasons that "nature offers healing for a child living in a destructive family or neighborhood. It serves as a blank slate upon which a child draws and reinterprets the culture's fantasies. . . . In nature, a child finds freedom, fantasy, and privacy: a place distant from the adult world, a separate peace" (7). Understanding that Pecola is without home, they turn to the earth—the land—to provide her, and by extension her baby, with one.[14]

This is not the first time that the girls have turned to the earth to mediate Pecola's corporeal circumstances; earlier in the novel, Frieda and Claudia bear witness to Pecola's menarche. Pecola, shocked and frightened, is repeatedly described as making "whinnying sounds," an animallike description of her vocalization. Claudia and Frieda, equally naive, conspire to cover up Pecola's stained underclothes. Frieda commands Claudia to "bury them," conspiring with the earth to hide their shame and cleanse Pecola. That Pecola, throughout the novel, is linked to botany, dirt, and animals suggests a transcorporeal state, in which she moves beyond the borders of the body. Redrawing the boundaries of the self, the earth is thus insanguinated. For centuries there has been a fusion of blood and dirt in the garden. Blood meal—blood that has been dried to a powder form—is used as a soil amendment and acts as a quick source of nitrogen, a necessary element that supports a plant's growth. Blood meal is also used to activate compost and to repel garden pests. The stain of Pecola's blood on the earth (a vivification of growth and fertility) offers another image of human/nature hybridization that is mapped throughout the novel.

Later, when Cholly impregnates his daughter—a graphic and brutal demonstration of transcorporeality—Claudia imagines the fetus living in a soil-like habitat: "a dark, wet place, its head with great O's of wool, the black face holding, like two nickels, two clean black eyes, the flared nose, kissing thick lips, and the living, breathing silk of black skin" (*Bluest*, 148). In this powerful moment of resistance, that which is alive and full of potential is described as dark and wet, paralleling the layer of soil, rich and loamy. The baby's bodiliness, akin to the earth, refutes the pink and yellow world of Dick and Jane. Though the community disregards the baby, Claudia and Frieda see it as life—Pecola's and their own. That the epicenter of life, the embodiment of soil, did not sprout, did not verify existence, highlights Claudia, Frieda, and Pecola's exile. If we recall Steingraber's conceptualization of the womb as permeable to environmental toxins, it follows that Pecola's baby, reviled, stigmatized, and socially unwanted—that is, surrounded by social toxins—cannot thrive.

Pecola does not actively resist the social order throughout the novel, but at moments she does achieve connection to her local biosphere. One such register is Pecola's solitary walk on the aptly named Garden Avenue, where she is comforted by the familiar cracks in the sidewalks and the dandelions growing at the base of the telephone pole. At this time, Pecola resists the dominant ideology: "Why, she wonders, do people call them weeds? She thought they were pretty" (47). Pecola's alignment with the plants allows her, temporarily, to belong in her ecosystem. This small urban environment can be read as an "ecstatic place," a term employed by the environmental psychologist Louise Chawla. Using the word "ecstatic" in its original meaning, Chawla draws on the word's "ancient Greek roots—*ek stasis*—[which] as some sources have it, means 'outstanding' or 'standing outside ourselves,' which most often is experienced in the biotic world during our formative years" (quoted in Louv, 95). Chawla explains that these moments "require space, freedom, discovery and an extravagant display for all five senses. . . . These memories give us meaningful images; an internalized core of calm; a sense of integration with nature; and, for some, a creative disposition" (96). These transcendent childhood experiences do not require "spectacular scenery, but could be evoked by environments as small as a patch of weeds" (95). Losing herself in the dandelions, Pecola achieves a temporary reprieve from the social order. This moment of biophilia, which the scientist Edward O. Wilson defines as the urge to affiliate with other forms of life (quoted in Louv, 43), is ruptured when Pecola reaches her destination, the candy store owned by Mr. Yacobowski. His virulent racism toward Pecola is enacted as he refuses to acknowledge her: "At some fixed point in time and space he senses that he need not waste the effort of a glance. He does not see her, because for him there is nothing to see" (*Bluest*, 48). Pecola internalizes the store owner's unmitigated hatred and on her way home projects that hostility onto the dandelions. Filled with shame, she sees the dandelions, and a "dart of affection leaps out from her to them. But they do not look at her and do not send love back. She thinks, 'They *are* ugly. They *are* weeds'" (50). Pecola is enmeshed with nonhuman life-forms, and in this instance, the plant-human hybridity is such that her perceived unworthiness bleeds onto the dandelions, which socially are positioned as nuisances, unwanted weeds that should be torn up by their roots. Note, too, that for Pecola the biotic world is, at this moment, a repository of racism; not only does she regard the plants as ugly weeds, but the plants no longer meet her gaze; they, like society, withhold love.

By the novel's end, Pecola, mentally vacant and ruminating about her phantom blue eyes, rummages through garbage at the edge of town. Bereft of agency or home, Pecola's exilic condition is manifest in the city dump; it is the final site of her material world. In a novel structured by the seasons, it is apt that Pecola's life would mirror her father's, who, when he "was four days old, his mother wrapped him in two blankets and one newspaper and placed him on a junk heap by the railroad" (132). Throwaway people, the Breedloves were marginalized among the marginal. Pecola, like her now-deceased father, is relegated to the edge of town, perceived by society as detritus. The bodies of those who die are cast away; Morrison provides no textual details for Cholly's or the baby's deaths, and thus without funerals, these bodies are consigned to the status of waste. Yaeger provides a context for the transmogrification of people to waste: "Pollution beliefs . . . provide the rhetorical basis for acts of human disposal, for converting those who are described as dirty into rubbish, the disappeared, throwaways" (277). Morrison concludes with a transcorporeal exchange between abject bodies and waste products, which suggest a final ecological vision of interconnectedness.

As Mark Feldman offers in "Inside the Sanitation System," "Garbage is evocative metaphorically, as it raises important aesthetic questions about the movement of material objects and the shifting of meaning: What happens to the things that we cast off? Who becomes responsible for them? How does something valuable become worthless trash; and is this irreversible? How do things fragment and decay?" (44). These questions have particular currency for Pecola's life. Claudia, who criticizes society's scorn for Pecola, muses about her own complicity in Pecola's "fragmentation and decay," in implicit recognition that we are all responsible for such casting off. How does something valuable—a baby, a human being, a life—become "worthless trash"? Morrison, in critiquing consumer culture and its implicit association with promoting and commodifying a Eurocentric aesthetic, suggests that Pecola, who was bombarded by such damaging ideologies, has become, in the eyes of society, worthless trash, like Mary Jane candy wrappers, plastic Shirley Temple drinking cups, and last year's Christmas dolls. That the choking whiteness of consumer culture suffocates the black body—be it Cholly's, Pecola's, or her unborn baby's—lays bare the intertwining of society and ecology.

In recognizing that Pecola was treated as a contaminated body, an untouchable, Claudia reasons, "Cholly loved her. I'm sure he did. He, at any rate, was the one who loved her enough to touch her, envelop her, give something of himself to her. But his touch was fatal, and the something he gave her filled the matrix of her agony with death" (*Bluest*, 206). Intertwining love with agony and death symbolically echoes the refuse site where garbage and beauty coexist: "All of our waste which we dumped on her and which she absorbed. And all of our beauty, which was hers first and which she gave to us" (205). Isolated and mad, Pecola is the dumping ground, murmuring "between tire rims and the sunflowers, between Coke bottles and milkweed" (159). Just as "most people do not live in conditions rife with garbage, [and] what is cast off is both out of sight and out of mind" (Feldman, 42), Claudia and Frieda "never, never went near" Pecola again. Nevertheless, Claudia's adult voice is heard at the novel's close; hence it is reasonable to assume that she could not forget Pecola, and the "thing" they assassinated for Pecola, like the garbage she embodies, is a "pervasive social process that connects us all" (42).

Sunflower and milkweed plants. Credit: Dan4Earth/Shutterstock.com.

Just as the garbage is Pecola, and Pecola is the community, and we, the readers, are the people of Lorain, Ohio, in 1941, so it is reasonable to conclude that the marigolds could not root because Pecola's baby did not have a safe harbor. The inclusive view of the human-nature relationship that Morrison advances in *The Bluest Eye* is in keeping with Alaimo's theorizing of material interconnectivity, in which she offers: "Nature is always as close as one's skin, perhaps even closer" (2). The botanist George Washington Carver also recognized human enmeshment with living organisms, especially soil, testifying: "Unkindness to anything means an injustice done to that thing. If I am unkind to you I do you an injustice, or wrong you in some way. On the other hand, if I try to assist you in every way that I can to make a better citizen and in every way to do my very best for you I am kind. The above principles apply with equal force to the soil" (quoted in Glave, 7).

It is precisely this kind of transcorporeality, in which racism permeates and alters bodies and geographies, that permits a reading of Pecola as permeated by a toxicity that also affects society, dirt, and seeds. Pushed to the periphery of society, Pecola lives with her mother, who "still does housework" (205). Racist ideology is materialized across African American bodies: domestic workers, who clean other people's homes and children; sharecroppers and farmers, who toil in the dirt; and sanitation workers, who handled other people's trash, create an environment where Black flesh was regarded as inherently unclean, fastened, as it was, to dirt.[15] Pecola's identification with garbage—objects that have been used and discarded—is the final image in the novel, as Morrison reinforces the porous boundary between the human and nonhuman. Pecola is a transcorporeal landscape, absorbing the waste that had been dumped onto her—an amalgamated body in which social power, class, place, and racial toxicity entangle.

Here, in the waste heap, we find still life: plants that grow on roadsides and railways, plants that can root in nearly any kind of soil, adorn the garbage dump. Morrison identifies these flora as milkweeds and sunflowers. Milkweeds, perennial herbs that come in many different shapes, sizes, and colors, are found throughout Ohio, which boasts thirteen native species. The genus name of *Asclepias* was given to the milkweeds by Carl Linnaeus, the father of the modern binomial nomenclature system, after the Greek god of healing, Asclepius, because milkweed had many medicinal uses.[16] Milkweed, which attracts butterflies, can grow even in degraded soils. Sunflowers, like milkweeds, also possess healing powers, especially for the soil: "Sunflowers are hyper-accumulators, which means they uptake metals from soil in large quantities. In general, phytoremediation provides a much less invasive way to clean soil than digging it all out of the ground or using other treatments" (Jones). According to the United Nations Environment Programme, "Phytoremediation is a generic term for the group of technologies that use plants for remediating soils, sludges, sediments and water contaminated with organic and inorganic contaminants" ("Phytoremediation"). It is of note that the specific flora Morrison mentions in this passage purify the landscape. Moreover, where there is garbage, there can be compost: "The process that turns garbage into a garden is central to our survival. We depend on dirt to purify and heal the systems that sustain us" (*Dirt! The Movie*). While the final moments of *The Bluest Eye* are devastating as readers bear witness to Pecola's madness, reading the scene ecocritically, we can see at least the potential for healing. The natural landscape, positioned against the social landscape, resists by attempting to heal and detoxify the poisons engulfing the many Pecolas who walk through this world.

In both *Paradise* and *The Bluest Eye*, Morrison highlights the porosity between people and dirt: "When humans arrived two million years ago everything changed for dirt and from that moment on, the fate of dirt and humans has been intimately linked." Far from being unclean, "we depend on dirt to purify the systems that sustain us" (*Dirt! The Movie*). Without dirt, humans could not survive. Containing tens of billions of microorganisms, dirt is very much alive, and like people, it can be mistreated and malnourished. This sentiment has particular currency for African American history:

> Slave labor virtually required single-crop farming that left the ground bare and vulnerable to erosion for much of the year. Reliance on a single crop precluded both crop rotation and developing a stable source of manure. If nothing but tobacco or cotton were grown, livestock could not be supported because of the need for grain and grass to feed the animals. Once established, slavery made monoculture an economic necessity—and vice versa. In the half century leading up to the Civil War, southern agriculture's reliance on slave labor precluded the widespread adoption of soil conserving methods, virtually guaranteeing soil exhaustion. (Montgomery, 136)

The depleted state of colonial soil due to monocrop cultivation and poor farming practices offers an objective correlative to the hegemonic societies of Ruby, Oklahoma, and Lorain, Ohio. Plants, after all, feed the soil. Half of the sugar a plant creates goes toward its fruit to spread its seed, but the other half is secreted into the soil. The root system pumps sugar into the soil to feed soil biology (*Dirt! The Movie*). Therefore a diversity of plants is necessary to maintain soil health.

From an ecocritical perspective, eradicating diversity through monocrop farming is unhealthy for people and soil. In fact, Shiva, in *The Monoculture of the Mind*, argues that the key to maintaining and rejuvenating soil fertility is its "amazing biodiversity" (101). She maintains that industrial agriculture is unsustainable, as it focuses on producing a single crop that damages soil ecology, destroys the diversity of soil nutrients, and creates crop vulnerability. Shiva uses monocropping as a cultural paradigm, maintaining that diversity, writ large, is eradicated because it is deemed threatening and uncontrollable. Shiva's theory provides a framework for apprehending Pecola's status as the town pariah and the Convent women's murder. While a crop (or, metaphorically, a culture) that does not conform to a kind of uniformity may be deemed unfit, what the soil reveals is that it is diversity, first and foremost, that is sustainable, and thus Morrison turns our attention to soil. Both novels materialize Wendell Berry's conviction that "what we do to the land, we do to ourselves" (quoted in Montgomery, 1). After all, "we are made of the five basic elements that the earth is made of" (*Dirt! The Movie*). Morrison seizes on dirt, the skin of the earth, to offer a sophisticated critique of racism. In so doing, Morrison brings to the fore the tyranny of monoculture thought and the impossibility of segregating elements of an ecosystem.

2

GREEN ECOLOGY AND HEALING

Botanical Life in *Beloved, Home*, and *Song of Solomon*

Green is the preeminent color of ecological thought, environmental discourses, and conservation movements. Though the biotic world is polychromatic, green, bonded so obviously to grass, trees, and other plant life, stands for all things sustainable. In English, the word "green" is related to the Anglo-Saxon *growan*, meaning "to grow" (Finlay, *Brilliant History*, 90). Likewise, the word "chlorophyll" comes from the Greek *chloros* (green) and *phyllon* (leaf); hence the term's etymology brings to the fore the relationship between color and plant life.[1] Chlorophyll, a green pigment found in algae and plants, is essential in photosynthesis, allowing plants to absorb energy from light. Chlorophyll, moreover, produces the oxygen necessary to sustain life on Earth, which I consider in this chapter through the material and metaphorical implications of expiration.

From a biological prism, plants go through a process called cellular respiration. Plants take in the carbon dioxide that people breathe, and during cellular respiration, plants release oxygen that we use to breathe. The human and the botanical are, in effect, breathing together, inhaling and exhaling. The environmental writer Jennifer Oladipo meditates on this symbiotic relationship between humans and plants: "There is a place where that connection between people becomes sensual reality, and the oxygen that plants exhale finds its way throughout our bodies. It is inside our own beating hearts where silently, elegantly, we fully accept what plants give and begin to incorporate it in every part of us, as newly oxygenated blood flows to every limb" (268). This reciprocal relationship does not elide the physical differences between the human and the vegetal; after all, plants are devoid of a specific respiratory organ but "breathe" through leaves, stems, and roots. Rather, respiration underscores the human-plant mesh, since neither plants nor humans could survive without the other.[2]

In this chapter, I consider the characters in Morrison's *Beloved*, *Home*, and *Song of Solomon* who find respite, that is, breathing space, in the green world. What emerges in Morrison's fiction are moments of enchantment with the plant world that provide a contrast to the unrelenting and ubiquitous social networks of racism in which the community is enmeshed. bell hooks gives voice to the politics of such epiphanic experiences in the natural world: "This spiritual bond with the earth is one of the counter hegemonic beliefs that sustained exploited and oppressed black folks during the years of slavery and reconstruction" (62). This is not to suggest that Morrison's characters have solely positive interactions with the vegetal world; rather, the author's green ecology encompasses a nuanced understanding of the politics of botany, slavery, and race.

The elision of people and plants is particularly resonant in an African American context, as the plantation system relied on enslaved people's expert knowledge and field labor. Moreover, through slave ship provisions and seed and plant movement, Africa's botanical legacy is grafted onto the New World. While the trenchant story in the United States is of unskilled workers performing backbreaking field labor, many African farmers were adept horticulturalists, and throughout the slave trade, slavers stole this intellectual property and plant life alongside the lives of human beings. Thus "The African Diaspora was one of plants as well as people" (Carney, "Out of Africa," 204).

In her botanical historiography *Plants and Empire*, Londa Schiebinger convincingly argues that the geopolitics of botany are undergirded by empire building:

> Europeans have long moved plants around the world—in vast quantities and to great economic effect. . . . As time went on, plants also played a role in the political struggles surrounding slavery. . . . Expertise in bioprospecting, plant identification, transport, and acclimatization worked hand-in-hand with European colonial expansion. Early conquistadors entered the Americas looking for gold and silver. By the eighteenth century, naturalists sought "green gold." Rich vegetable organisms supplied lasting, seemingly ever renewable profits long after gold and silver ran out. (4, 7)

Plant life is not extraneous to a conversation about slavery and colonization; rather, vegetal life undergirds racial and political activity in Morrison's work.

Ubiquitous throughout the nation are plants that are not indigenous; rather, in the eighteenth century, at the zenith of territorial expansion, "the point was to bring coffee, indigo, cochineal, cassia, and sugarcane all in production within the boundaries of the empire itself" (Schiebinger, 11). At the time, botanists were "agents of empire," not only collecting plant life but laying "their own peculiar grid of reason over nature so that nomenclatures and taxonomies served as 'tools of empire'" (11). The Antiguan-born author Jamaica Kincaid in *My Garden (Book)* also theorizes botanical nomenclature as part of a larger colonial enterprise:

> One day, while looking at the things that lay at my feet, I was having an argument with myself over the names I should use when referring to the things that lay before me. These things were plants. The plants, all of them—and there were hundreds—had two names: they had a common name, that is, a name assigned to them by people for whom these plants have value, and then they had a proper name, or a Latin name, a name assigned to them by an agreed-on group of botanists. . . . The botanists are from the same part of the world as the man who sailed on the three ships, the man who started the narrative from which I trace my beginning. And in a way, too, the botanists are like that man who sailed on the ships: they emptied worlds of their names; they emptied the worlds of things, animal, vegetable, and mineral of their names and replaced these names with names pleasing to them. (160)

Kincaid deftly moves from a discourse on botanical taxonomy to chattel slavery, inviting readers to recognize the manifold ways that plants are interwoven with colonization and transatlantic slavery. Pairing Linnaeus with Columbus is apt, since many explorers throughout the seventeenth and eighteenth century became interested in botany because of the huge financial rewards associated with the cultivation of crops such as rice, tobacco, sugar, and cotton (Schell, 114).[3] In this way, plants materialize an African diasporic history.

Even without the purposeful cultivation of plants, seeds are determined to propagate through wind, water, animals, and plant explosion. Seed dispersal is evocative of the African diaspora. According to Jana Evans Braziel and Annita Mannur in "Nation, Migration, Globalization," the term "diaspora" is "etymologically derived from the Greek term *diasperien*, from *dia-*, 'across' and -sperien, 'to sow or scatter seeds' [and] can perhaps be seen as a naming of the other which has historically referred to displaced communities of people who have been dislocated from their native homeland through the movements of migration, immigration, or exile" (1). Though the etymology of the word rarely comes into play in diaspora studies, seed movement—sowing and scattering—is always already imbricated in human displacement. Likewise, Morrison's ongoing attention to flora, though not readily brought to the fore, punctuates her work.[4] In this chapter, I consider Morrison's portrayal of botany in *Beloved*, *Home*, and *Song of Solomon*, specifically examining the ways in which trees, plants, and seeds have influenced human, political, and social activity.

Sethe's mother, Ma'am, who is a site of resistance in *Beloved*, is elided with botanical life. Ma'am wrests control over her reproduction: she "threw away" all her unborn children who were conceived through coercion, and gave Sethe the name of the black man whom she put her arms around.[5] Ma'am is publicly hanged, which implies that she continued to fight against the system of slavery. Important for this analysis, Ma'am worked in the rice fields, and Sethe punctuates her scant memories of her mother with references to the crop: "By the time I woke up in the morning, she was in line. If the moon was bright, they worked by its light. Sunday she slept like a stick. She must have nursed me two or three weeks—that's the way the others did. Then she went back in rice and I sucked from another woman whose job it was" (70). Later, Sethe amplifies her lack of mothering and attributes it to the fact that "Ma'am was in the rice" (234). The evocative language of Ma'am "in the rice"—as opposed to working in the rice fields—accentuates her elision with that botanical, an Africanized botanical, according to Judith Carney in *Black Rice*, who argues: "The development of rice culture marked not simply the movement of a crop across the Atlantic but also the transfer of an entire cultural system, from production to consumption" (2). Carney continues: "Rice figured crucially among the seeds that accompanied their migration, and slaves planted the crop wherever social and environmental conditions seemed propitious. In adapting a favored dietary staple to local conditions, slaves drew upon a sophisticated knowledge system that informed cultivation and processing methods" (6). Along with human beings, seeds, plant life, and botanical knowledge were stolen from West Africa and, as a result, changed the landscape, agriculture, diet, and culture of America. Legend has it that women concealed grains of rice in their hair as they were forced out of Africa and as they were fleeing sugar plantations (154). These stories, irrespective of their veracity, are powerful and sustaining, revealing, as they do, the intimate relationship between women and rice. Rice, a material imprint of Africa on the New World through transoceanic plant movement, is not merely a foodstuff but a ubiquitous cultural symbol:

> With the dawn of each day women's pounding of rice awakens millions of African villagers, the rhythmic striking of rice grains by the

> pestle providing the steady heartbeat of community life. Rice is central to subsistence and cultural identity over a broad area of West Africa; it was to become equally so in communities of the Americas settled by enslaved persons from the rice region and their descendants.[6] (31)

It is apt that Ma'am is closely associated with rice, since she made the journey across the Atlantic and spoke in a language that Sethe can no longer understand, details that underscore her African origins. Fundamentally, Ma'am represents Sethe's origin story. Cut off from Africa, Ma'am is the matriarchal line, and in this way the plant signifies the mother body and the mother country and is emblematic of the human-vegetal interactivity in *Beloved*.

Paul D's intimacy with the plant world provides solace and eventual freedom. As an enslaved man on Sweet Home Plantation, he is only allowed short breaks from agricultural work, a respite that he takes under a tree he fittingly names "Brother." Morrison describes trees as "inviting things you could trust and be near, talk to if you wanted to as he frequently did" (21). This tableau invites a reading of human-botanical relationships: Paul D seeks not merely shade under the branches but fellowship. Paul D creates community with the nonhuman world, a necessary affiliation for his later emancipation.

While it is reasonable to read Paul D's naming of the tree as an anthropocentric act, a rigorous examination of Morrison's treatment of the vegetal in *Beloved* sheds light on his recognition of the tree's animation. His evocative naming of the tree as a sibling with whom he talks invites a reflection on plant sentience. The question of how alive plants are, and in what ways, is the subject of cutting-edge botanical research. Michael Marder, in *Plant-Thinking: A Philosophy of Vegetal Life*, argues that one of the aims of plant-thinking is to "reduce, minimize, put under erasure, bracket, or parenthesize the real and ideal barriers humans have erected between themselves and plants" (202). Researchers in botany find that plants are sensitive to light, water, and touch. Plants can learn, adapt their behaviors to stimuli, and remember.

While much research in plant biology has been conducted in the last few decades, it is important to note that Charles Darwin, best known for his groundbreaking work in evolution, spent the second half of his scientific career on botany, studying the sentience of the vegetal world. He wrote six books and more than seventy-five scholarly articles on plants. In *The Power of Movement in Plants*, Darwin made a major scientific discovery by finding that plants move volitionally. Before that, the prevailing assumption was that plants were still beings. He examined plant sensitivity and positive phototropism, the orientation of a plant to the light. As Daniel Chamovitz in

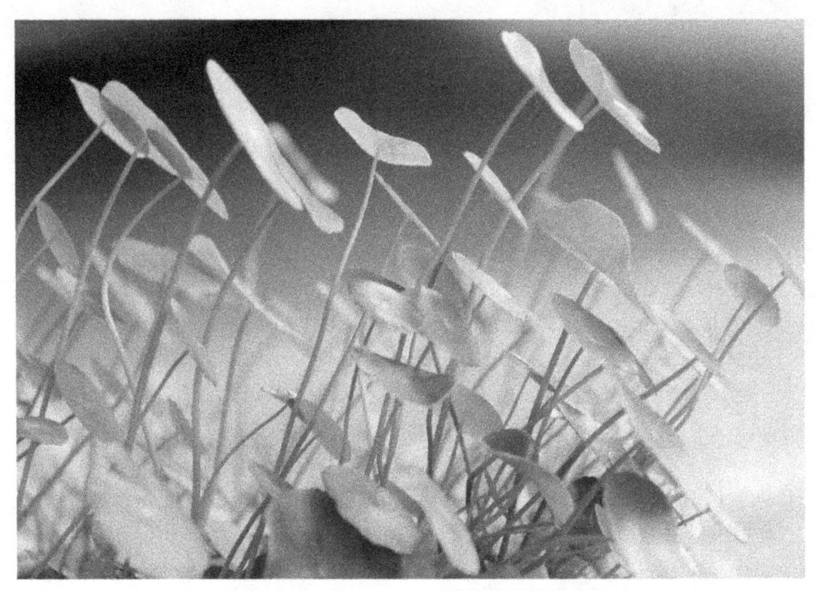

Example of positive phototropism. Credit: iamskyline/Shutterstock.com.

What a Plant Knows explains, Darwin and his son conducted experiments in which they "proved that phototropism is the result of light hitting the tip of a plants' shoot, which sees the light and transfers this information to the plant's midsection to tell it to bend in that direction. The Darwins had successfully demonstrated rudimentary sight in plants" (15).[7] Chamovitz further asserts that it is not enough that Darwin's plants saw the light in their tips; they had to absorb this light and then somehow translate it into an instruction that told the plant to bend. They needed to respond to the light. In recognition of the plants' ability to translate information about their physiological state into electrical chemical signals, Darwin posed the concept of the "root brain," which suggested that the tips of the plants' roots act as a kind of brain, and in some ways, plants exhibit traits that we associate with humanity. According to the authors of "The 'Root-Brain' Hypothesis of Charles and Francis Darwin," plants "recognize self from nonself, and roots even secrete signaling exudates which mediate kin recognition. Finally, plants are also capable of a type of plant-specific cognition, suggesting that communicative and identity re-cognition systems are used, as they are in animal and human societies, to improve the fitness of plants and so further their evolution. Moreover, both animals and plants are non-automatic, decision-based organisms" (Baluška et al.).

These findings call into question classical notions that plants are passive, automatic organisms, and specifically upend the Aristotelian dichotomy between plants and animals. According to the evolutionary ecologist Monica Gagliano in "Seeing Green,"

> The earliest Greek philosophers, such as Empedocles (495–35 BCE), Anaxagoras (500–28 BCE), and, later, Plato (427–347 BCE), believed that plants, like animals, were sensitive organisms. It was Aristotle (384–22 BCE) who first positioned plants outside of the sensitive life domain and used plant insensitivity as the key criterion to differentiate between plants and animals. Aristotle's zoocentric perspective of the sensorial world and his "default position of plant exclusion" had a profound and long-lasting influence on virtually all authors who came after him, ultimately fathering the Western paradigm of modern science. Ironically, though, the "Father of Modern Science" was no scientist himself, as he was interested in postulating rather than experimentally testing his ideas. And specifically in regards to plants, we had to wait until the seventeenth century for experimental botanists to start recognizing some of the fallacies in his fundamental assumptions. (20)

Perhaps it is because the Sweet Home men do not adhere to Western epistemology that they recognize flora outside dominant scientific discourse and Western ideology. They and the plants are subject to pseudoscience that discredits, misjudges, and misinforms. This elision between the plant world and the human community in *Beloved* speaks to Neil Evernden's questioning in "Beyond Ecology: Self, Place, and the Pathetic Fallacy": "Where do you draw the line between one creature and another? Where does one organism stop and another begin? Is there even a boundary between you and the non-living world, or will the atoms of this page be a part of your body tomorrow?" (95). This material entanglement is particularly evocative in the context of African American environmental history. As bell hooks maintains in *Belonging*: "Living close to nature, black folks were able to cultivate a spirit of wonder and reverence for life. Growing food to sustain life and flowers to please the soul, they were able to make a connection with the earth that was ongoing and life-affirming" (36).

Paul D's stolen moments of freedom under "Brother" are life-affirming and foreshadow his eventual escape, which is again mediated through an arboreal discourse. The Cherokees use tree blossoms to map Paul D's route to freedom:

> "That way . . . Follow the tree flowers . . . Only the tree flowers. As they go, you go. You will be where you want to be when they are gone." So

> he raced from dogwood to blossoming peach. When they thinned out he headed for the cherry blossoms, then magnolia, chinaberry, pecan, walnut and prickly pear. . . . When he lost them, and found himself without so much as a petal to guide him, he paused, climbed a tree on a hillock and scanned the horizon for a flash of pink or white in the leaf world that surrounded him. He did not touch them or stop to smell. He merely followed in their wake, a dark ragged figured guided by the blossoming plums. (112–13)

In *Beloved*, trees are directly tied to freedom. Morrison disrupts the conventional relationship that humans have to flora; after all, Paul D does not touch or smell the blossoms, which would suggest human agency toward the natural world. Rather, Morrison's description of Paul D "following" indicates that he is shadowing their movements, underscoring the interspecies relationship of movement for trees, which, in their growth and flowering, are also moving.[8] The fecundity represented in the blossoming trees is also of note, since these angiosperms (or flowering plants) contain the flower's ovary, which turns into the fruit, and its ovules become seeds. Blossoms, after all, initiate pollination necessary for the trees to reproduce. In this way, the trees that Paul D is searching for are maternalized. His journey symbolically comes to its logical conclusion when he reaches 124 and finds Sethe, whom Morrison constructs as a mother/tree hybrid.

From the outset, Morrison elides Sethe with plants, labeling her scarred back a chokecherry tree. Amy Denver, the white girl who serves as midwife to Sethe's delivery of Denver on her journey to freedom, christens her flesh, and Sethe adopts this botanical designation throughout her life. Amy tells Sethe: "It's a tree, Lu. A chokecherry tree. See, here's the trunk—it's red and split wide open, full of sap, and this here's the parting for the branches. You got a mighty lot of branches. Leaves, too, look like, and dern if these ain't blossoms. Tiny little cherry blossoms, just as white. Your back got a whole tree on it. In bloom" (79). That Amy Denver describes the entire tree, from trunk to berries, indicates the botanical specificity that is mapped onto Sethe. The makeup of the chokecherry tree is analogous to the scars on Sethe's back. These small trees, known as "bitter berry" shrubs, have a cluster of sour berries that span in hue from dark crimson to black, recalling Sethe's clumps of scars resulting from severe epidermal damage. While the cherries can be boiled to make preserves, the wilted leaves and seeds of the tree contain cyanide and are therefore toxic. Finally, the leaf has a serrated margin (or edge), a sawlike appearance that metaphorically signals danger. In this way, the arboreal display on Sethe's back is a complex symbol, at once a reminder

Chokecherry tree. Credit: cg-art/Shutterstock.com.

of Schoolteacher and his nephew's brutality—a metonym for the nation's violence—and at the same time a powerful association of Sethe with the natural, living world.

Sethe's scars have received a good amount of scholarly attention. Sandy Alexandre, in "From the Same Tree: Gender and Iconography in Representations of Violence in *Beloved*," contends that the scars represent "black female trauma writ large, as large as a chokecherry tree" (925), and later insightfully adds that it should be read "as a woman's rape tree and as a man's lynching tree" (936). In "Hiding Fire and Brimstone in Lacy Groves: The Twinned Trees of *Beloved*," Lorie Watkins Fulton argues that "the deadened skin of Sethe's back clearly represents feelings about the past that she refuses to give free rein" (190). Reading as an ecocritic, I maintain that this scar evidences Sethe's elision with trees. She is transcorporeally part of the arboreal world, and while Paul D is associated with trees, Sethe *is* the tree, an important gendered difference that is in keeping with Morrison's reflection on trees as maternalized plants. In "Unspeakable Things Unspoken," Morrison avers: "With all due respect to the dream landscape of Freud, trees have always seemed feminine to me" (390).

The forest scientist Suzanne Simard also feminizes trees, naming the larger, older trees in the forest "mother trees." She has conducted a good deal of research in measuring their role in maintaining the health and survival of their surrounding ecosystem. Using isotope tracers, she has found that mother trees, which can be connected to hundreds of other trees in the forest, will send their excess carbon through the mycorrhizal network to the understory seedlings. Such a move aids in the survival of the seedlings fourfold. Without hesitation, Simard argues that trees talk, arguing that there is a "massive belowground communications network where trees share information" ("How Trees Talk to Each Other"). Through a vast and complex network of root systems and fungal threads, mother trees recognize their kin and provide greater nutrients to their own saplings. They even reduce their own root competition to make elbow room for their "kids." When mother trees are injured and dying, they send what Simard characterizes as "messages of wisdom onto the next generation of seedlings" in the form of carbon and defense signals, and these two compounds increase the resistance of those trees to future stresses. While mother trees show preference for their kin, they benefit the forest in general by increasing its resilience. Removing some mother trees may not strain the system, but the balance is delicate. If you take out too many mother trees, the system collapses. Therefore, when a mother tree is cut down, the survival rate of the younger members of the forest is "substantially diminished" (Engelsiepen). The significance of the mother tree is such that the community's health and survival depend on her presence. The forester Peter Wohlleben in *The Hidden Life of Trees* further notes the maternal instinct of trees by exploring the mother trees' ongoing support for her offspring, far after the sapling stage:

> Acorns and beechnuts fall at the feet of larger "mother trees." . . . The small beech trees, which have by now been waiting for at least eighty years, are standing under mother trees that are about two hundred years old. . . . The stunted trees can probably expect another two hundred years of twiddling their thumbs before it is finally their turn. The wait time is, however, made bearable. Their mothers are in contact with them throughout their root systems, and they pass along sugar and other nutrients. You might even say they are nursing their babies. (34)

Although it would be an overstatement to suggest that Morrison explicitly references this pioneering dendrology research, it offers a striking parallel to Morrison's construction of Sethe as a plant/mother hybrid who muses on her foremother's botanical knowledge, which, owing to the slave trade, was lost to her: "I wish I had known more, but, like I say, there wasn't nobody to talk to. Women, I mean. So I tried to recollect what I'd seen before Sweet Home. How the women did there. Oh they knew all about it. How to make that thing you use to hang the babies in the trees—so you could see them out of harm's way while you worked the fields. Was a leaf thing too they gave em to chew on. Mint, I believe, or sassafrass. Comfrey, maybe" (*Beloved*, 160). The women harness elements of the botanical world to care for their babies, a description that feminizes the environment.

To this end, Sethe, throughout *Beloved*, is enmeshed with botanical life. Early in the novel, her legs are covered in sticky sap, a result of the shortcut she takes through a field of chamomile. As she washes the plant's resin from her flesh, she is haunted by rememories of lynched bodies swinging in lacy groves: "Boys hanging from the most beautiful sycamores in the world. It shamed her—remembering the wonderful soughing trees rather than the boys. Try as she might to make it otherwise, the sycamores beat out the children and she could not forgive her memory for that" (6). That Morrison specifically names the species invites reflection on the sycamore itself. The sycamore's most distinguishing feature is its thin bark, which it sheds, revealing patches of brown, gray, and white. This mottled appearance occurs because the bark is incapable of stretching to accommodate the trunk growth, and thus the tree sloughs off its outer bark. The bark of all trees accommodates trunk growth by stretching, splitting, or infilling, but in the sycamore the process is more visible, and the growth is brought to the fore in the same way that Sethe remarks that it is boys (who are, accordingly, in the midst of growing) who are hanging from the tree's branches. Further, according to Fiona Stafford in *The Long, Long, Life of Trees*, "There is probably no other tree that divides opinions so dramatically" as the sycamore, which is both lauded for its sprawling canopy, which offers much-needed shade in southern climes, and simultaneously reviled for its sap. The sycamore tree exudes a sticky substance that attracts swarming insects, and thus it is reasonable to assume that Sethe would be reminded of the sycamores as she washes chamomile sap from her legs. The unsightly oozing of the tree, along with the skin-like bark, easily conjures a wounded human body and thus offers a graphic transcorporeal exchange between the sycamore and the bodies of the lynched victims. Though Sethe chastises herself for remembering the trees, the structure and characteristics of the sycamores return her to the memory of the lynched boys.

Sethe's turn to the sycamore can also be read as a coping mechanism, obfuscating some of the racial violence and carnage that was Sweet Home.[9] This passage, though, simultaneously underscores Sethe's indelible association with the natural world, one she shares with Paul D, who arrives at 124 at this moment. To highlight the role of the vegetal in their relationship, their conversation turns immediately to sap and its adhesiveness: "Messed up my

Sycamore tree. Credit: Sunny Forest / Shutterstock.com.

legs back yonder. Chamomile. He made a face as though tasting a teaspoon of something bitter. 'I don't want to even hear bout it. Always did hate that stuff'" (7). In this way, Sethe is marked by plants as Morrison maps them onto her body and positions Paul D as recognizing the relationship of the human to the nonhuman world. After all, he has knowledge of the plant and its effects on the body. Not only is Sethe's flesh covered in chamomile sap, but her gaze is bound up in vegetal life. And in this way, her devastation that she "made the ink" is another iteration of the porosity of material bodies, for it is in this very passage that Morrison first sounds the reference to ink. While the information comes too soon for readers to understand its significance, Morrison, from the outset of the novel, presents an evocative collage of Sethe and plant life: Sethe's back, a chokecherry tree, a field of chamomile, and ink. Sethe's rememory of the dehumanizing institution of slavery through the lens of plants, while apparently incongruent, becomes, in Morrison's hands, a keen recognition of the intimate role that the botanical world played in the life of the enslaved.[10]

Ink is a key registry of plant life in *Beloved*. Sethe repeatedly decries the fact that her hands created the material that Schoolteacher used to dehumanize African Americans. Sethe claims that Schoolteacher's work linguistically dismembered her, which she describes as a dirtying: "Dirty you so bad you couldn't like yourself anymore. Dirty you so bad you forgot who you were and couldn't think it up anymore." Sethe tells Denver: "He liked the ink I made. It was her recipe, but he preferred how I mixed it and it was important to him because at night he sat down to write in his book. It was a book about us but we didn't know that right away. . . . I still think it was them questions that tore Sixo up. Tore him up for all time" (37). Underscoring its permanence, the ink Sethe made was from oak trees. While ink can be made from various plants, including huckleberry and raspberry, oak-derived ink, also known as iron gall ink, was the standard writing and drawing ink from the fifth century through the beginning of the twentieth. A well-prepared oak-derived ink was indelible because it penetrated the paper surface. The only way to remove the purple-blackish ink was by scraping a thin layer off the parchment paper. In this way, language and ideology are as corporeal as plant and human life and are materially interconnected to both. Morrison bookends her novel with references to ink and Sethe's mourning for what she deems as her complicity with Schoolteacher and his epistemological and discursive violence. "I made the ink, Paul D. He couldn't have done it if I hadn't made the ink" (271). Sethe's interaction with plants was put to nefarious use, employing the natural world for unnatural purposes. Just as Sethe's botanical scar resulted from being whipped during her late-stage pregnancy, the mother-as-tree portrait is not a pristine vegetal and human image; in fact, throughout *Beloved*, the intimate relationship the community has to plants is at times salutary and healing and, at other times, grafted with violent acts of white supremacy.

The discourse of tress is sounded again when Paul D, soon after arriving at 124, escorts Sethe and Denver to the carnival, adjacent to the lumberyard: "Up and down the old lumberyard fence, the roses were dying. The sawyer who had planted them twelve years ago to give his workplace a friendly feel—something to take the sin out of slicing trees for a living—was amazed by their abundance. . . . The closer the roses go to death, the louder their scent, and everybody who attended the carnival associated it with the stench of the rotten roses" (*Beloved*, 47).[11] Morrison unmistakably pairs death with trees. While the sawyer attempts to mitigate the scent of death by planting roses, the flower's decay, permeating the atmosphere, undermines his efforts, and in this way, the sawyer's work can fruitfully be contextualized within the environmental history of the time period.

Morrison's reference to a lumberyard gestures to the increase of large-scale logging practices in the post-Reconstruction period. Jeffrey Myers explores the exploitation of the natural world as represented in Charles Chesnutt's work, which sheds light on Morrison's ecological treatise in *Beloved*: "Both the bodies of slaves and the pine forests of the American Southeast had to be exploited in order to make the fortunes—and the culture—that cotton and tobacco plantations made possible. . . . Plantation owners literally carved this culture from both the bodies of slaves and the forests themselves" (6). Myers further offers that during this period, the Southeast was beginning "an acute phase of natural resource exploitation, despite the fact that such calls were for preserving wild lands elsewhere in the United States . . . [and] the industrial timber production or cotton and tobacco cashcrop agriculture [were] practices that created a system of debt peonage for—and in some cases virtual reenslavement of—African American farmers in the latter part of the nineteenth century" (6). In "The Louisiana Lumber Boom," Donna Fricker describes the logging in Louisiana, which characterized the practice in much of the nation: "With a policy of 'cut out and get out,' priceless natural resources were lost by the millions of acres. Large sections of the state, in a relatively short period of time, became vast 'stumpscapes' of barren cutover land as rapacious mill owners moved on to yet another stand of virgin timber elsewhere in the country. Some 4.3 million acres of Louisiana virgin timber had been clear cut—a land area roughly the size of the state of New Jersey" (1).[12] Morrison signifies this environmental history where an unsustainable number of trees were felled and reduced to logs and sawdust, and analogizes that violence to those who worked the land. This commercial logging reads as a violation, especially when read in context of the Clearing, where trees provide comfort and healing to the newly emancipated community that gathers in the grove to hear the Word preached by Baby Suggs. In this way, the smell of death, so ubiquitous in this scene, though generated from a different plant, bespeaks the violence done to the trees and to the formerly enslaved community.[13] After all, within an ecological paradigm, it is impossible to segregate elements of an ecosystem; the human community cannot be divorced from the nonhuman world, and the roses cannot be separated from the trees.[14]

Following the logic of the novel, deforestation is sinful because the trees are embodiments of sacred entities imbued with healing properties, a pairing that is nowhere more explicit than in Baby Suggs's preaching in the Clearing.[15] Baby Suggs, holy, the spiritual center of the novel, preaches to

Stumpscape. Credit: Savo Ilic / Shutterstock.com.

the newly emancipated in the forest. She exhorts the community to reject the entrenched racism that is imbricated not only in the mind but also on the body. From a materialist framework, ideology does not exist outside of flesh but transcorporeally bodies forth its virulence on other entities. The members of the community, for the time they inhabit the wooded landscape, "go against the order of things" (Landy and Saler, 27) and experience epiphanic moments of connectivity. The community's feelings of well-being do not result solely from Baby Suggs's powerful sermon but are due, in part, to the very landscape they occupy, a "wide open place cut deep in the woods" (*Beloved*, 100). *Beloved* indicates that being in the Clearing, among the trees, engenders healing.

Not only are trees healthy for the ecosystem as they absorb pollutants, protect topsoil, and prevent erosion, but recent studies have measured the physiological and psychological benefits of dwelling among trees, and these studies support the logic of Morrison's novel. The Japanese practice of *shinrin-yoku*, or forest bathing, simply refers to spending time in the forests, which is believed to be restorative, largely because of the presence of essential oils known as phytoncides (Li). Phytoncides are compounds derived from plants, wood, and some fruits and vegetables that prevent them from being eaten by insects or animals and slow the growth of harmful fungi and bacteria. Plants that produce phytoncides include onions, garlic, cedar, the tea tree, and pine. These compounds are salutary not only to plants but also to people. In fact, when humans are exposed to phytoncides, these chemicals lower blood pressure and relieve stress. Inhaling these hormones in a forest setting improves immune system functioning (Li).

Here it is useful to think of Sixo, an enslaved man on Sweet Home, who repeatedly resists bondage. He is strongly associated with the forest: he "melts into the woods before the lash could unfurl itself on his indigo behind," and "He went among the trees at night. For dancing, he said, to keep his bloodlines open" (*Beloved*, 25). He seeks physical health and mental renewal in the woods, which is apt, since forests are regarded as therapeutic: "Forest environments promote lower concentrations of cortisol, lower pulse rate, lower blood pressure, greater parasympathetic nerve activity, and lower sympathetic nerve activity than do city environments" (Li). In *Beloved*, the forest is a site of well-being and is a touchstone throughout the novel. Sethe recognizes the Clearing as a restorative landscape and thus later returns to the rock where Baby preached and remembers the "smell of leaves simmering in the sun" (111).

Not only is Sethe's life lived alongside the vegetal world, but Beloved is likewise paired with trees. After emerging from the stream, Beloved leans against a mulberry tree: "All day and all night she sat there, her head resting on the trunk in a position abandoned enough to crack the brim in her straw hat. . . . It took her the whole of the next morning to lift herself from the ground and make her way through the woods past a giant temple of boxwood to the field and then the yard of the slate gray house" (50), where she finds a stump on which to sleep. Like Paul D, who follows blossoming trees to reach his destination, Beloved moves from tree to tree to find 124 Bluestone Road. Notably, when she arrives at Sethe's home, it is a stump—and not a tree—that she inhabits. Lest we relegate the tree stump to mere setting, Morrison sounds Beloved's appearance on the tree stump six more times in the novel, with refrains such as Sethe's acknowledgment that "the minute I saw you sitting on the stump, my water broke" (202); Denver's recognition that she "had not been in the tree room once since Beloved sat on their stump" (76); and Paul D's admission that Beloved "just shot up one day sitting on a stump" (234). While all these references point to the reality of stumps dotting the landscape, that Sethe describes her water breaking when she sees her resurrected daughter highlights the stump/Beloved as symbols of death and renewed life.

While the stump is a symbol of death, a material reminder of a felled tree, stumps are not always without life. Wohlleben, in *The Hidden Life of Trees*, relates a story about the gnarled remains of an ancient tree stump, which, because the "interior had completely rotted into humus long ago [was] a clear indication that the tree must have been felled at least four or five hundred years earlier" (2). On closer inspection, though, the stump, still connected to the ground, remained green in parts, but, he reasons, "Without leaves—and therefore without photosynthesis—that's impossible. No being on our planet can maintain a centuries-long fast, not even the remains of a tree, and certainly not a stump that has had to survive on its own. It was clear that something else was happening with this stump. It must be getting assistance from neighboring trees, specifically from their roots. . . . The surrounding beeches were pumping sugar to the stump to keep it alive" (2). This was not an isolated incident: Wohlleben has observed "oak, fir, spruce, and Douglas fir stumps that were still alive long after the trees had been cut down" (5). Dendrologists affirm Wohlleben's claim, arguing that trees are social beings and, though root systems, can provide a nutrient exchange. It is beneficial for trees to work communally, for a lone tree is far more vulnerable to weather conditions, but together, many trees "create an ecosystem that moderates extremes of heat and cold, store a great deal of water and generate a great deal of humidity" (4).

The stump's liminality between life and death provides a striking analogue to Beloved, the physical reincarnation of Sethe's crawling-already baby girl, who also straddles the living and the dead. Sethe's origin story is likewise paired with a stump, not a tree stump but Nan's severed arm. Nan is Sethe's surrogate mother at Sweet Home, who nursed children, cooked food, and spoke in a language that Sethe could no longer remember: "Nan holding her with her good arm, waving the stump of the other in the air. 'Telling you. I am telling you, small girl Sethe,' . . . Your mother 'threw them all away but you . . . She gave you the name of the black man. She put her arms around him'" (62). Morrison's diction of Nan's amputated arm as a "stump" once again sounds the tree/human hybridity. Chattel slavery, according to Orlando Patterson in *Slavery and Social Death*, engendered a kind of death where the enslaved went through a process of losing identity, names, and kinship and altered the ways enslaved peoples were viewed by society and by themselves. Here it is useful to turn to Baby Suggs's recognition of slavery's attempt to negate the self as she wonders if she could have been a good singer or a good mother (*Beloved*, 140). In other words, slavery eradicated the opportunity to know and cultivate the self. Although people were alive, Morrison illustrates that parts of them were not. In fact, it is this "dirtying" of identity that Sethe would not allow to happen to her children. Once again, then, Morrison obliquely references the stump, the arboreal reminder of the life-death continuum.

In the climactic healing scene of the novel, when the women come to Sethe to exorcise Beloved from 124, Sethe experiences it as a return to the

Clearing: "For Sethe it was as though the Clearing had come to her with its heat and simmering leaves, where the voices of women searched for the right combination, the key, the code, the sound that broke the back of words" (261). Sethe's catharsis is outside of language: it is the "sound" of the women's collective voices in tandem with the memory of the forest. The women eschew words but speak in a curative language, aligning their voices with the lexicon of the trees. It is this interface between people and plants that precipitates the long road to Sethe's and Denver's healing.

An isolated Denver, Sethe's youngest daughter, traumatized by her mother's infanticide and the community's subsequent shunning, also finds solace in trees. Denver ritualistically retreats to the bower, a circle of five boxwood bushes in the back of 124 Bluestone Road. Denver returns to the trees throughout her childhood and into her adulthood, a temporal shift marked by fragrances—first wild veronica and later cologne. Denver, intoxicated by strong floral scents, bends on hands and knees to enter the "live green walls" and, once inside, is able to stand erect in the "emerald" room, which stretches seven feet into the air. Denver's "imagination produced its own hunger and its own food" (*Beloved*, 29), suggesting her elision with plant life as she begins to adopt autotrophic attributes. Like plant organisms that can make their own food, Denver's imaginative state in this "murmuring" enclosure is self-sustaining and provides "salvation" (29). This point is emphasized later in the novel when Morrison describes the giant boxwoods as a "temple," diction that sacralizes the arboreal structure and links Denver to Grandma Baby, who preaches the Word inside the embrace of trees. Denver is the inheritor of Sethe, whose flesh is imprinted with a chokecherry tree, and Baby Suggs, who "smelled like bark in the day and leaves at night" (19). Discursively constructing the arbor as a walled "tree room," Morrison shifts the terrain of the homeplace, thereby problematizing the demarcation between built and natural environments. As discussed in the previous chapter, the etymology of ecology is *oikos*, or home, and read from that prism, Morrison's ecopolitics in *Beloved* are such that the natural world functions as a place of belonging—a home—precisely because it stands outside the structures of white hegemonic society. Of course, dominant culture has used parts of the vegetal world for nefarious purposes—plantations, unsustainable agriculture, lynching—but nevertheless the natural world is incapable of being harnessed in toto. Denver boldly claims the patch of land behind 124 as her own. She is not cowed by these giant boxwoods, as she is by society, but perceives the trees as an extension of the self, and thus, in finding sanctuary in the earth, she finds refuge inside herself. These examples illustrate the manifold ways in which a green ecology unearths Morrison's rendering of the nonhuman world as cathartic.

Morrison turns to botanical life to mediate touchstone events in Sethe's life: her sexuality, freedom, and catharsis. According to Christa Sommerer, Laurent Mignonneau, and Florian Weil in "The Art of Human to Plant Interaction," "People and plants have been interacting throughout all of human history. Indeed, plants are a vital part of the human ecosystem. Recently, scientists have been developing a research framework for the exploration of this kind of interspecies communication, criticizing our overly anthropocentric terminology. Biology and the social sciences use the term 'people plant relationship' or 'ethnobotany' to describe the area of research that deals with human-plant interactions." These authors, then, propose the term "bio-interface" to describe the "interface between a cell, a biological tissue or a biomaterial and another material," which can be a human being (234). While megaflora form a leitmotif in the novel, Morrison punctuates *Beloved* with botanical life in general.

Sethe and Halle's first sexual experiences occur in the cornfield. It is reasonable that Halle turns to the natural world as his domicile, a space where he and Sethe can achieve some measure of privacy. Though bereft of legality, Sethe claims her marriage to Halle, and their consummation enacts that sacred rite, which, by implication, sanctifies the fields. Rhetorically, Morrison spends little time describing the carnality of their lovemaking but retreats quickly—and in much detail—to the corn plants. The other enslaved men on Sweet Home, desiring Sethe for themselves, sit under trees and painfully watch "corn stalks dance at noon" (27). Sethe "remembered that some of the corn stalks broke, folded down over Halle's back, and among the things her fingers clutched were husk and cornsilk hair. How loose the silk. How jailed down the juice" (27). Later the men and Sethe consume the "too young to eat" ears of corn from those broken stalks, yet "the pulling down of the tight sheath, the ripping sound always convinced [Sethe] it hurt" (27). Morrison animates the plants as they "dance" in the sunlight, and highlights Sethe's intimacy with them. Not only is this private act performed on foliage, but it is, in fact, bound up with plants. After all, Sethe does not describe touching her partner but remembers clutching the corn plants—silk and husks. Here Morrison graphically depicts the transcorporeal exchange between human and vegetal bodies. Morrison further emphasizes this interconnectivity by exploring Sethe's empathic connection to the plant, believing, in fact, that shucking it for human consumption causes the plant pain. Lest we read Sethe's empathy for the plant as merely analogical to her own loss of virginity, note that plants, though they lack nervous systems, are able to "perceive tactile sensations" (Chamovitz, 49). As Chamovitz claims, "Plants know when they are being touched and . . . plants seemingly don't like to be touched too much, as simply touching or shaking a plant can lead to growth arrest" (49–50). Plants also know when they are under attack, whether by feeding insects or by humans mowing the grass, and they react by producing chemical compounds. Some of these compounds attract the predator of the insect that is eating the plant's leaves, and other gasses emitted from the leaves warn members of the same species, thereby prompting the plant to activate defense genes to ward off the attack. Sethe's musing about the corn's response to being ripped apart has scientific merit and highlights the interconnectivity of human and nonhuman nature.

The cornfield is presented as a safe space in the novel. It is not only a sanctuary for Sethe and Halle but the locus of their escape plan. The cornfield is the first stop on their road to freedom. They were to run in the late spring when the "corn is as high as it ever got" (222). In fact, "They will go straight to the corn and not assemble in the creek. The corn stretches to their shoulders—it will never be higher" (224). Although their escape plan was botched, Sethe does manage to get her children "to the corn," which ensures their escape north. The plants, then, provide shelter and temporary safety. Their bodies, camouflaged by the plants, find respite from the hegemonic plantation society. Here the African American community claims the natural world, a place outside the realm of control by the dominant culture. Just as the flowering trees are integral to Paul D's emancipation, so the corn plants signify freedom for Sethe's children.

Morrison alternates between megaflora and micro plant life in *Beloved*. Readers inhabit large-scale wooded landscapes, where the community perches in trees to hear Baby Suggs's preaching, and shoulder-high cornfields where the children are waiting to escape. We are also called on to notice the nearly microscopic spores of the bluefern in the water. Morrison interrupts Sethe's climactic birth scene of Denver en route to Ohio with a meditation on the spores of the bluefern, ancient plants that grow along the river. This narrative, directly following Sethe's delivery of the afterbirth in the Ohio River, offers a parallel birthing.[16] Though seemingly a metaphoric interlude on the reproduction of biota, the "seeds in which the whole generation sleeps confident of a future" (84) are not likely to spawn,[17] thus mitigating the river water's life-giving potential.[18] The struggling life of the bluefern, the fertilization of which occurs in water, surrounds Sethe and Amy, creating an environment of possibility. Though the silver-blue lines of the fern's seeds are nearly invisible, Morrison calls on us to notice the evanescent life that is floating in the river, waiting and hopeful. In this way, Morrison foreshadows the dangers that await Sethe in Ohio. Owing to the Fugitive Slave Act, Sethe's new life, like the bluefern, is hopeful but not ensured. Morrison yokes together discrepant imagery in this passage. The bluefern spores are confident of their future, yet this certainty lasts no longer than a moment.

Morrison's meditation on the bluefern foreshadows Sethe's life at 124 Bluestone Road, as it, like the plant, alternates between life and death. It is not just the bluefern that hovers between existence and nonexistence, but plants, in general, "were commonly placed between dead and living things in the classical order of things, because they resisted easy assimilation to one or other realm. . . . A plant can live and die at the same time" (Read, 262). At the end of the novel, after Beloved has been exorcised, Paul D returns to 124 and sees flora, both living and dead: "First he stands in the back, near the cold house, amazed by the riot of late-summer flowers where vegetables should be growing. Sweet william, morning glory, chrysanthemums. The odd placement of cans jammed with the rotting stems of things, the blossoms shriveled like sores. Dead ivy twines around bean poles and door handles . . . and the jars and jars of dead lightning bugs" (271). Unlike seed dispersal, in which the plants ensure their chance of survival, floral cuttings are more complex; they are a symbol of death, but the cuttings, if done correctly, can also be a propagation method. While most cuttings rot in water, some plants, especially those with thick stems, can produce new shoots. Once again, Morrison uses a symbol from nature that mediates life and death.

Morrison's closing description of 124 and Sethe is couched in botanicals: "That's where she is—and she is. Lying under a quilt of merry colors. Her hair, like the dark delicate roots of good plants, spreads and curves on the pillow. Her eyes, fixed on the window, are so expressionless he is not sure she will know who he is. There is too much light in this room. Things look sold. 'Jackweed raise up high,' she sings. 'Lambswool over my shoulder, buttercup and clover fly.' She is fingering a long clump of her hair" (271). To highlight the porosity of the vegetal and human worlds, Morrison presents a final constellation of Sethe, hair, roots, plants, and color. The hues of the late summer flowers that greet Paul D are mirrored in the quilt encasing Sethe, discursively constructing her, once more, as a botanical. Not only is her hair described as the "dark delicate roots of good plants," but she is gazing outdoors and singing about plants. Although she is disconnected from society and her community, the language in this passage underscores Sethe's deep connection to the more-than-human world.

In the novel's final scenes, Morrison presents flowers as a marked memorial for the crawling-already baby, Beloved, and the sixty million and more. At the most fundamental level, plants are a metaphor for the brevity of pleasure, beauty, and life itself (Buchmann, 221). The desiccated floral cuttings in jar upon jar in 124 offer a clear analogy to Sethe's multiple losses. Floral tributes to the dead are ancient and cross-cultural. Indeed, as Stephen Buchmann explains, flowers "help us to heal and recover from losses and emotional wounds. This has always been true. Our ancestors used cut flowers as grave offerings since the time spiritual beliefs first stirred in humans. Archaeological excavations of ancient burial sites in Iraq and Israel, along with tombs of Egyptian pharaohs, such as Tutankhamen, provide us with glimpses into the burial customs of these ancient mourners, and flowers for eternity" (106). Moreover, the relationship between human death and plants is well documented: "Early humans certainly noticed that when their kin were buried in shallow graves, these sites were later colonized by blooming, opportunistic, short-lived wildflowers ecologists call ruderals," defined, generally, as plants growing on waste ground or among refuse. In this way, flowers mediate the world of the living and the dead in the novel. At the time of Sethe's daughter's death, there are no flowers and few mourners, so in this reburial of Beloved, Sethe bestows an abundance of floral grave offerings.

By the novel's end, 124 Bluestone Road, the site of murder, transmogrifies into a burial ground; the flowers growing in the yard and wilting in jars inside the home stand as a floral tribute to the slain baby and a testament to Sethe's ongoing mourning. During Beloved's brief habitation of 124, Sethe insists on providing her resurrected daughter with flowers and other material objects of beauty: bright clothing with "blue stripes and sassy prints," "fancy food," "yellow ribbons, shiny buttons and bits of black lace" (240). Sethe arranges a bounty of dandelions, violets, and forsythias and winds them throughout the house (241). This dazzling array of flowers and trinkets is resonant with Day of the Dead celebrations: "Families honor the memories of deceased loved ones around family burial plots gaily decorated with real and paper flowers, lively paper streamers, glowing candles, and offering of the decedents' favorite foods" (Buchmann, 117). The mourner's homes, altars, and graveyards are chock-full of flowers, and the strewn petals on the ground "show wandering spirits of the dead their way back home" (118). These floral maps sound a chord to Paul D's tree guide. This is not to suggest that Morrison stages a Dia de los Muertos celebration per se, but the scene points to the indelible relationship between flowers and the dead and provides a new way of reading Sethe's offering of color to Beloved. Sethe's ribbons, textiles, and flowers are a funerary tribute to the departed.

After Beloved's disappearance, Sethe is immobilized by catatonic grief, which serves as the catalyst for Denver to escape the confines of 124 Bluestone Road. She seeks help from the community and resumes her formal education. Like her mother and grandmother before her, Denver is enmeshed with the botanical world. On this journey, Denver's environmental literacy is sounded as she deciphers the lexicon of the trees: "Letters cut into beeches and oaks by giants were eye level [to her] now" (245). Although Morrison does not disclose the message of the arborglyph, or tree graffiti (Stafford, 14), that the engravings are at Denver's eye level bespeaks that her gaze, like her mother's, is bound up with the vegetal, a seeming recognition of plant intelligence and the botanical's imbrication with the human world. Further, that the plant is eye level with Denver indicates a kind of mutual gaze. While plants cannot "see" in the way that humans can, they do have photoreceptor proteins all over them, just as humans do in the back of their retinas, and they "see light in many ways and colours that we can only imagine" (Chamovitz, 9), revealing the limitations of human perception, and the multihued biosphere that is accessed by the nonhuman world. The message of the arborglyph is purposefully withheld because plant life does not have a singular message in *Beloved*. Plants provide narratives of healing and comfort while standing as a material embodiment of chattel slavery. Plants provide a canopy under which Paul D is afforded breathing space and are simultaneously harvested for the ink with which Schoolteacher wrote the crippling and distorted history of America.

Morrison's tenth novel, *Home*, likewise traffics in the botanical, an association declared by the book's cover art, depicting a tree with two birds aloft. The story of Frank "Smart" Money and his younger sister Ycidra (Cee) offers a thoughtful treatise on the politics of place and displacement. The young siblings are raised by sharecropping parents who have little time or energy to sufficiently nurture their children and thus leave them in the care of an abusive step-grandmother and an indifferent grandfather. Though only four years Cee's senior, Frank takes on a parental role with his sister, and Morrison encodes their intimate connection in botanical terms:

> She was the first person I ever took responsibility for. Down deep inside her lived my secret picture of myself—a strong good me tied to the memory of those horses and the burial of a stranger. Guarding her, finding a way through tall grass and out of that place, not being afraid of anything—snakes or wild old men. I wonder if succeeding at that was the buried seed of all the rest. (*Home*, 104)

Frank's love for—and protection of—Cee is the "buried seed" of his identity, referencing, at once, his protection of his sister as the driver in his life, and simultaneously materializing the self as the seed, an unmistakably plantlike image of the body's corpus. Frank and Cee's parents are beaten down by their tireless work in the fields, so much so that they play almost no role in their children's lives. *Home* opens with these evocative plant/human conflations.

Morrison begins *Home* with a burial that haunts the novel and is, as Frank's musing indicates, a memory that Frank and Cee repress. As children, Frank and Cee crawl in enclosed farmland, finding a fissure in the fence. Hiding in the tall grass, the children observe horses that "stand like men," a simile that unmistakably connects the animal to the human. The children are bedazzled by this spectacle of sparring horses, and as they turn to leave, they are immobilized by the intrusion of white men. Taking shelter in the tall grass, the children witness a gruesome act that reads as a live burial.

> Never lifting our heads, just peeping through the grass, we saw them pull a body from a wheelbarrow and throw it into a hole already waiting. One foot stuck up over the edge and quivered, as though it could get out, as though with a little effort it could break through the dirt being shoveled in. We could not see the faces of the men doing the burying, only their trousers; but we saw the edge of a spade drive the jerking foot down to join the rest of itself. When she saw that black foot with its creamy pink and mud-streaked sole being whacked into the grave, her whole body began to shake. I hugged her shoulders tight and tried to pull her trembling into my own bones because, as a brother four years older, I thought I could handle it. (*Home*, 4)

This entire scene highlights the elision of the human and the vegetal: the dead man is brought to the earth in a wheelbarrow, a vessel that carries plant material. Because the man's foot is still moving, his entombment reads as a live burial, a kind of "planting" into the ground. Finally, the corpse is not wrapped in a shroud or encased in a coffin but hastily interred by spades and shovels, furthering the association of his body with plant life.

Frank's admission to the reader, "Know this: I really forgot about the burial. I only remembered the horses. They were so beautiful. So brutal. And they stood like men" (5), is evocative of Sethe's confession that her memory was fixed on the sycamore trees on Sweet Home that beat out the lynched boys who were hanging from their limbs. In both of these instances, the natural world captures the memory of the protagonists, which is not to suggest that the trauma of human suffering grafted onto the natural world is erased in the novels. Rather, the biophysical world helps the characters cope with the devastation that is presented, a tableau of life and vitality that mitigates, in some small measure, the gruesome deaths that are graphically thrust onto them and, by extension, the readers. In these instances, the more-than-human world acts as a shield, a protection that helps Sethe and Frank maintain, in part, psychological distance.

Frank's nurturing of his sister—absorbing her trauma—continues throughout his life. As her only active parental figure, he teaches her how to navigate the social structures of Lotus, Georgia, as well as the biophysical world: "She followed Frank's advice always: recognized poisonous berries, shouted when in snake territory, learned the medicinal uses of spiderwebs. His instructions were specific, his cautions clear" (*Home*, 52). The living world provides a home where the children can achieve a measure of safety and belonging, feelings absent in their grandparents' home: "Often they sat by the stream, leaning on a lightning-blasted sweet bay tree whose top had been burned off, leaving it with two huge branches below that spread like arms" (52). That the tree, though injured and disfigured, continues to comfort the children, providing open arms for them to steal a moment of solace, is evocative of Paul D's respite under Brother.

With very little comfort available in Lotus, Frank disdains his hometown:

> Lotus, Georgia, is the worst place in the world, worse than any battlefield. At least on the field there is a goal, excitement, daring, and some chance of winning along with many chances of losing. Death is a sure thing but life is just as certain. Problem is you can't know in advance. In Lotus you did know in advance since there was no future, just long stretches of killing time. There was no goal other than breathing. . . . Nobody in Lotus knew anything or wanted to learn anything. It sure didn't look like anyplace you'd want to be. Maybe a hundred or so people living in some fifty spread-out rickety houses. (*Home*, 83)

Therefore it is not surprising that Frank joins the army to escape the confines of his hometown. He fights in the Korean War, and his comrades—friends from back home—die in his arms. Traumatized, Frank tries to avenge their deaths by exacting random violence, only to suffer from PTSD when he returns to the States. Frank's anxiety is unmanageable and causes temporary blackouts. On one occasion, he ends up in a psychiatric ward: "'I must have been acting up,' he said. 'Something like that.' He truly could not remember. Had he thrown himself on the ground at the sudden sound of backfire? Perhaps he started a fight with a stranger or started weeping before trees—apologize to them for acts he had never committed" (15). Interestingly, though Frank catalogs the many ways he may have been "acting up," he explains that the trees would have been the catalyst for his true atonement; after all, he would weep in their presence, offering apologies for his transgressions.

Cee likewise escapes Lotus and does so by marrying Principal, a man who exploits her (for her grandmother's car) and then abandons her. Subsequently, Cee finds work in the home of Dr. Beauregard Scott, a white physician and eugenicist, who, unbeknownst to her, is performing life-threatening reproductive experiments on her. His wife, addicted to laudanum, a potent narcotic, has given birth to daughters with disabilities, whom she seems to not engage but instead spends her days watching television and painting florals in watercolor. It is this detached, watered-down engagement with the natural world that characterizes the doctor's home. Frank's journey to healing begins only when he receives a letter from Sarah, the domestic worker in Dr. Beauregard's home, imploring him to save his sister: "Come fast. She be dead if you tarry" (*Home*, 8). Despite his emotional triggers, Frank is determined to save Cee's life. His journey, though a solo undertaking, is aided by people who feed him, clothe him, and help him to reach his destination.

Frank's journey to save his sister becomes a journey to liberate himself. He travels to Atlanta and then back "home" to Lotus. When Frank returns with Cee, he sees his hometown anew. Rather than having "no future," it is a town of "safety and goodwill" (*Home*, 119), with brightly hued flowers and trees adorned with deep green leaves. Frank experiences the town as "fresh and ancient, safe and demanding" (132). Descriptions of a color-saturated world abound in Lotus, which is particularly significant for Frank, because his psychological trauma manifests as a loss of color: "He was quiet, just sitting next to a brightly dressed woman. Her flowered skirt was a world's worth of color, her blouse a loud red. Frank watched the flowers at the hem of her skirt blackening and her red blouse draining of color until it was white as milk. Then everybody, everything. Outside the window—trees, sky, a boy on a scooter, grass, hedges. All color disappeared and the world became a black-and-white movie screen" (23). In Lotus he is met by color, immersed in the sensory world of flowers, plants, vegetables, and quilt patches. Frank's earlier disparaging remark that there is nothing to do but breathe in Lotus can be reread as an acknowledgment of the breathing space that he is afforded there. After all, Morrison begins chapter 2 of *Home* with the one-word sentence "Breathing" (7). Plants and trees improve air quality, and thus Lotus is a site of healing, providing Frank the space he needs to reconnect with his sister and his home. Frank and Cee's reclamation of home place is catalyzed by their reconnection to the natural world.

Frank takes Cee to the home of Miss Ethel, a woman known for her botanical practices. Like her enslaved forebears, Miss Ethel gardens and uses plants for healing:

> Slave knowledge of herbal medicine was akin to their knowledge of everything else in the plantation environment—discrete, detailed, and close to the ground. It was also conditioned by experience; slave women, especially, went out in the woods and wetlands to find supplies for household manufacturing and healing. They also cultivated common medicinal herbs in their garden patches. In turn they taught others what they learned, both by practice and by storytelling. (M. Stewart, 15)

Read from this prism, Miss Ethel's healing is a tribute to her foremother's earth-based knowledge. Miss Ethel immediately shoos Frank out of her home and gathers up elderly women to collectively heal Cee: "Two months surrounded by country women who loved mean had changed [Ycidra]. The women handled sickness as though it were an affront, an illegal invading braggart who needed whipping. They didn't waste their time or the patient's with sympathy and they met the tears of the suffering with resigned contempt" (*Home*, 121). Specifically, "the demanding love of Ethel Fordham soothed and strengthened her the most" (125).

After the crisis is over, Miss Ethel Fordham tells Cee that her "womb can't never bear fruit," and this news is relayed "as though she'd examined a Burpee seedling overcome by marauding rabbits" (*Home*, 128). Ostensibly, this simile advances the notion that Miss Ethel is practical, unsentimental, and resigned to Cee's barrenness. Read from an ecocritical prism, Miss Ethel associates Cee's infertile body with the seedling that, owing to the rabbit's appetite, will neither mature nor bear fruit. This material enmeshment neither exalts plant life nor reduces the human; rather, it emphasizes that living things—humans, animals, and plants—share the capacity and drive to reproduce, though that reproduction may not come to fruition. Miss Ethel's ecological insight is due, in no small measure, to her work with the earth. Her horticultural knowledge is manifest through her medicinal practice and her master gardening:

> After Miss Ethel gave her the bad news, the older woman went into the backyard and stirred coffee grounds and eggshells into the soil around her plants. Blank and unable to respond to Ethel's diagnosis, Cee watched her. . . . An aggressive gardener, Miss Ethel blocked or destroyed enemies and nurtured plants. Slugs curled and died under vinegar-seasoned water. Bold, confident raccoons cried and ran away when their tender feet touched crushed newspaper or chicken wire placed around plants. Cornstalks safe from skunks slept in peace under paper bags. Under her care pole beans curved, then straightened

> to advertise their readiness. Strawberry tendrils wandered, their royal-scarlet berries shining in the morning rain. Honeybees gathered to salute *Illicium* and drink the juice. Her garden was not Eden; it was so much more than that. For her the whole predatory world threatened her garden, competing with its nourishment, its beauty, its benefits, and its demands. And she loved it. (*Home*, 130)

Miss Ethel's gardening acumen is underscored in this scene, and the passage is important because of its location in the text: moments after Miss Ethel discloses the news to Cee that she is barren, she begins gardening. Morrison bookends Cee's infertility with references to the natural world. Of course, Cee's medical condition is anything but natural, as she was victimized by the doctor's eugenics experimentation; nonetheless her body elides with the flora in Miss Ethel's garden. Cee, emotionally numb, processes the news while watching the older woman tend to her plants. Fertility underscores the triadic relationship of Miss Ethel, the garden, and Cee. Miss Ethel serves as a maternal figure to Cee, yet Morrison does not cast her as a romanticized Mother Nature figure, living harmoniously with the biophysical world. Instead Miss Ethel confronts—and is part of—the predatory behavior that thrives in her garden. Her fierce behavior toward the raccoons, skunks, and slugs underscores that this garden is "not Eden." It is not a metaphysical landscape, but a here-and-now ecosystem that, through its rhythm of fertility, decay, and death, has the capacity to heal. Later, as Cee tries to cope with the loss of her motherhood, she tells Frank that she is visited by the little girl who was meant to be her daughter: "'You know that toothless smile babies have?' she said. 'I keep seeing it. I saw it in a green pepper once. Another time a cloud curved in such a way it look like . . .' Cee didn't finish the list. She simply went to the sofa, sat and began sorting and re-sorting quilt pieces. Every now and then she wiped her cheeks with the heel of her hand" (*Home*, 132). Her loss is mapped onto the natural world. In recognition that she is part of nature, Cee's unborn daughter is also manifest in elements of the biophysical landscape. Even the textile that Cee stitches echoes the colors and patterns surrounding her in the flowering plants and trees in her hometown.

Cee participates in the "aesthetic legacy and artistic contributions of black women" (hooks, 153). As she convalesces, the elders teach her to embroider and crochet, textile arts that piece her back together. Although the women of Lotus do not create mimetic story cloths, their quilting has a narrative quality. In fact, bell hooks discloses that her grandmother believed that each quilt "had its own narrative—a story that began from the moment she considered making a particular quilt" (159). Thus it follows that Cee's quilt stitches her wounded body and life back together; her textile work is a therapeutic response to her brokenness, since quilting, according to hooks, gives "harmony and balance to the psyche" and is an "art of stillness and concentration, a work which renews the spirit" (155). The patches can be read as a kaleidoscope representing at once those who joined to heal her (Frank and the women of Lotus), the natural world, and the personal and collective traumas of the past. After all, the quilts are made of cotton, the very crop her parents sharecropped. Historically, enslaved women "used parts of plants to dye cloth or as patterns for quilts" (M. Stewart, 13), and thus quilting is a material manifestation of artistry, history, and the natural world. Morrison's choice of a pieced quilt speaks to the various stories that are stitched together in *Home*. Using fabric for expressions of the self and surroundings, Morrison weaves together women's textile work with the garden and to the death that occurs at the outset of the novel.

Cee's quilt sutures *Home* together, for the cruel and hasty burial that begins the story is revisited in the last pages of the novel. Frank and Cee exhume the corpse, wrap it in Cee's quilt, and give the deceased a proper burial. That the siblings use Cee's "crayon colored" quilt as a shroud implies that he is part of the configuration of their own tapestry. Here Morrison stitches together past and present, and the dead man's trauma to Frank and Cee's. They later learn that the man and his son were abducted by white supremacists who gambled on the father and son to fight to death. When the father commands his son to commit patricide, the son replies, "I can't take your life." The father rejoins: "This ain't life" (*Home*, 139). Despite that being "a devil's decision-making," the son obeys the father. Frank admits that his memory of the horses was stronger than the profane burial, and moments after learning about the dead man's story, he asks about the stallions. The horses who, in their grandness, "stood like men" were sold to the slaughterhouse and used for human consumption. Violence and death haunt Lotus in the human and the more-than-human world.

Yet the biophysical landscape of Lotus, Georgia, catalyzes Frank and Cee's healing; they do not merely journey to a rural hamlet but return to a landscape of memory where they are cared for by the elders, and where their parents' home still stands. The last part of Cee's treatment requires that she lie out in the sun with her legs wide open. This "sun smacking," as Miss Ethel explains it, allows the light and heat to enter Cee's body to "rid of her of any remaining womb sickness" (*Home*, 124), a graphic transcorporeal exchange between the human and the more-than-human world. Cee is violated by her husband and Dr. Beauregard, and thus it is reasonable to conclude that the sun smacking is a recuperative act, a reclamation of her sexual and reproductive body. She opens herself up to the sun and physically absorbs part of its power in what reads as a photosynthetic process. It is shortly after conceding to what Cee perceives as a scandalous treatment that she asserts: "I ain't going nowhere. . . . This is where I belong" (126). This intimate engagement with place is mirrored in Frank's reinhabitation of their family home. Although not as corporeal as Cee's ritual with place, Frank claims the home and readies it for Cee's return. To highlight his intimacy with place, Frank unearths treasures he had buried in the recesses of his familial structure: prized marbles, Cee's baby teeth, and a broken watch found on the riverbank. The siblings each attach to place and re-create home. This is not to suggest that Morrison uncritically celebrates the agricultural South as an uncomplicated sanctuary. Morrison does not romanticize a rural homecoming but, in the closing pages, revisits the trauma that began the novel. The metaphorical burial that concludes *Beloved* transmogrifies into a physical burial in *Home*. Frank insists on a proper interment for the dead man and chooses the bay tree as his final resting place. The bay tree, where the siblings earlier found comfort, is metonymically linked to Frank and Cee's traumas: it is "split down the middle, [and] beheaded" (*Home*, 144). Yet its scars do not correlate to imminent death; the tree remains "strong," "beautiful," "alive and well." The siblings force themselves to acknowledge the dead man's bones, and we can read this refusal to turn away as their acknowledgment of the brokenness of body, home, and homeland. Morrison's turn to flora in *Home* is not exclusively a literary device that provides solace from racial violence and trauma; rather, it also provides a larger landscape for recognizing the multifaceted nature of humans' imbrication in the natural world. After all, trees become the burial sites for two Black men in the novel.

Displacement haunts *Home*. At the beginning of the novel, the Ku Klux Klan forcibly expels the Money family and their neighbors from their houses and community. The African American residents are given only twenty-four hours to pack up their belongings and flee, but one man, as mentioned in the introduction of this book, refuses to leave his home.[19] In the midst of a flurry of activity—neighbors packing and moving—Crawford calmly sits on the steps of his porch and holds vigil throughout the night, his gaze held steady on the oldest magnolia tree in the county, the one his great-grandmother had planted. Crawford's heroic refusal to move does not alter his fate; he is beaten to death and tied to that very tree. In the dark of the night, some folks hurried back to bury him, aptly, under the magnolia tree. In both of these cases, the men are not interred in a cordoned-off necrogeography but placed beneath beloved trees that are part of the community's living space. Their deaths are grafted onto place, and they become part of the trees' root systems.

That Frank and Cee's hometown is named for a plant points to home as a configuration of human and biophysical environments. Morrison's evocation of the lotus plant suggests a connection to the themes of procreation, birth, and death, which are ubiquitous in the novel. According to Jennifer Potter in *Seven Flowers and How They Shaped Our World*, "Of all the flowers that have inflamed human societies, the lotus has to come first" (3). Potter claims that studying the lotus "demonstrate[s] the fundamental power of flowers in helping early civilizations to grasp and express the world around them" (4). In ancient Egypt, this aquatic perennial was closely associated with powerful deities, including Ra, the sun god, and Osiris, the lord of the afterlife, "which gave the flower a leading role in the very mystery of creation" (5). The environment in which the lotus grows is also noteworthy; its roots are based in muddy and stagnant water. It rises from this murkiness, without being marked by it, and emerges as a showy, fragrant blossom. It retreats in the evening to opaque river water, only to reemerge from it in the daytime, again untainted by the mud. The plant's process of becoming metaphorically bespeaks spiritual enlightenment and rebirth, and thus the lotus is prevalent throughout Buddhist iconography: "The lotus is one of the eight auspicious symbols, and every important deity is shown sitting on a lotus, standing on a lotus, or holding a lotus" (Potter, 20). Morrison adopts this symbolically rich flower, freighted with spiritual meanings, as a metaphor for home. While it is possible to read the daily rise of the plant's blossom from the mud to a visage of purity as an escape from one's environment, Morrison's portrait of home is one in which the murky water not only is an integral part of the flower but is, in part, responsible for its beauty, health, and survival. In this way, Frank and Cee do not return to Lotus believing that it has transformed, ridding itself of its murky underside. Rather, they return to this space of home knowing that the beauty that is there is always already steeped in pain and hardship.

Frank reexperiences his hometown through color and nature, which soothe and comfort him. He is surrounded by yellow butterflies dancing by scarlet rosebushes, "marigolds, nasturtiums, dahlias. Crimson, purple, pink, and China blue" (*Home*, 117). Frank is astonished by the vibrancy of color, musing, "Had these trees always been this deep, deep green?" Morrison concludes that in Lotus, "color, silence, and music enveloped him" (118), providing Frank with a sensory engagement of home. However, beauty is coterminous with pain, even from the same source. Frank sees the cotton fields and intends to seek work among these "pink blossoms spread under the malevolent sun" (119). He intends to work the cotton fields that broke his parents and, by extension, his community. Cotton is synonymous with slavery, especially after Eli Whitney's invention of the cotton gin, which separates cotton fiber from its seeds. Given the international demand for cotton textile, cotton transformed the Deep South and African American life. According to Henry Louis Gates Jr., "To feed King Cotton more than a million African Americans were carried off into the Deep South." This internal migration created a second Middle Passage, a violent uprooting and dislocation of African American life. In a novel that traffics heavily in the salutary nature of the living world, it is important that Morrison includes cotton, which unmistakably materializes slavery and the many losses that were owed to plantation labor.

Plants are a major element in the configuration of home and memory for Cee, Frank, and the community of Lotus. We cannot disentangle nature from society; the plant kingdom bears the historical imprint of the community that both was forced to cultivate cash crops for the planters' wealth and also chose to nurture plants for healing, nourishment, and beauty. What we are left with in *Home* is a sense of Cee and Frank's belonging, which is reminiscent of the nature writer Scott Russell Sanders's sentiment in "Staying Put." He connects his well-being to his rootedness, claiming: "I cannot have a spiritual center without having a geographical one; I cannot live a grounded life without being grounded in a *place*" (126). Likewise, the Money siblings do not mythologize the Lotus of their past or present but choose to ground themselves in place and, in so doing, achieve a deep sense of home with their community and the living world.

In *Song of Solomon*, Morrison once again turns to the botanical to mediate the lives of the Dead family. The novel pivots between two different genealogical strands: Macon Dead II (who is married to Ruth Foster and has three children, First Corinthians, Magdalene, and Macon Dead III) and his sister Pilate Dead (who has a daughter, Reba, and a granddaughter, Hagar). Although the novel is set in mid-twentieth-century Michigan, through a discourse of nonindigenous flora, Morrison evokes slavery as a historical context for the characters' lives. Sugarcane punctuates the novel and highlights the intractable relationship of slavery to plantation work and, in the time and space of the novel, bridges the North (Michigan) with the South (Virginia). In *Song of Solomon*, sugarcane is a complex symbol of slavery, death, and imperialism.

Guitar Baines, Milkman's close friend, introduces the discourse of sugar in the novel. Guitar's hatred for sweets is perhaps the most memorable example of the motif. Guitar explains to Milkman that his inability to eat or even smell sweets is connected to his father's death at the sawmill, claiming that "it makes me think of dead people. And white people. And I start to puke" (*Song*, 61). Although at this point Guitar withholds crucial information about his father's death from Milkman (and therefore from the reader), he does explain that this aversion began when his "father got sliced up in a sawmill and his boss came by and gave us kids some candy. Divinity. A big sack of divinity. His wife made it special for us. It's sweet, divinity is. Sweeter than syrup. Real sweet. Sweeter than . . ." (61). Guitar's vomiting precludes him from finishing the story. Morrison uses Guitar—as opposed to Milkman, who "wasn't sure he trusted anybody who didn't like sweets" (61)—as an embodiment of resistance. That his body physically rejects the sweets indicates that the story of brutal labor practices embedded in the sugar is too vile to digest. Guitar realizes that the candy is intended to mask the horror of his father's brutal death. Ironically, though, the candy only reinforces the commodification of his father and forefathers. Extrapolating further, we can read Guitar's rejection of sugar as a disavowal of the larger text of slavery inscribed in sugarcane. Black (often male) bodies were equated to sugarcane production from the seventeenth to the nineteenth century, as estimates suggest that "one ton represented the lifetime sugar production of one enslaved person," and "every teaspoonful represented six days of a slave's life" (Hobhouse, 62, 63). Guitar's refusal to eat sugar reveals his inability to consume the history of human commerce that enabled the cultivation of this cash crop.

According to Hobhouse in *Seeds of Change*, "Sugar was the first food (or drug) dependence upon which led Europeans to establish tropical monoculture to satisfy their own addiction. Because sugar cane was a labor-intensive crop, the ratio of slaves/sugar always remained at least ten times greater than the ratios of slaves/tobacco or slaves/cotton, or any other crop grown in servitude. Perhaps three-quarters of all the Africans transported across the Atlantic, possibly as many as 15 million out of a total of 20 million enslaved in Africa, must be debited to sugar" (93). Morrison nods to this history throughout *Song of Solomon*, as sugarcane, "white gold" (Stuart, preface), continues to be a marker of economic exploitation and death.

Later, the story of Guitar's father's death is continued and is again framed with sugar:

> Instead of life insurance, the sawmill owner gave his mother forty dollars "to tide you and them kids over," and she took it happily and bought each of them a big peppermint stick on the very day of the funeral. Guitar's two sisters and baby brother sucked away at the bone-white and blood-red stick, but Guitar couldn't. He held it in his hand until it stuck there. All day he held it. At the graveside, at the funeral supper, all the sleepless night. The others made fun of what they believed was his miserliness, but he could not eat it or throw it

> away, until finally, in the outhouse, he let it fall into the earth's stinking hole. (*Song*, 225)

Morrison literalizes the body (blood and bones) through the peppermint stick. Refusing to be pacified with sugar, Guitar simultaneously rejects the commodification of his father and by extension those who gave their lives for the cultivation of this crop. Guitar, clutching the candy stick throughout the funeral and graveside service, bears witness to his father's death as being caused by the mill owner's greed and exploitation of Black bodies.

The horror of his father's death, a graphic depiction of violence and racism, is compounded by what Guitar sees as his mother's collusion with the forces of white supremacy:

> [Guitar] remembered anew how his mother smiled when the white man handed her the four ten-dollar bills. More than gratitude was showing in her eyes. More than that. Not love, but a willingness to love. Her husband was sliced in half and boxed backward. He'd heard the mill men tell how the two halves, not even fitted together, were placed cut side down, skin side up, in the coffin. Facing each other. Each eye looking deep into its mate. Each nostril inhaling the breath the other nostril had expelled. The right cheek facing the left. The right elbow crossed over the left elbow. . . . Even so, his mother had smiled and shown that willingness to love the man who was responsible for dividing his father up throughout eternity. (*Song*, 224)

The dismembered and fragmented body that terrorizes Guitar is symbolic of the ancestral ghosts that haunt the novel. The spectral presence of slavery and its aftermath permeates the text in the myriad references to sugarcane, slavery, and its attendant brutal agricultural practices.

This is not to suggest that in *Song of Solomon* Morrison advances the ecological world solely in terms of enslavement. In fact, Macon Dead I purchases and cultivates Lincoln's Heaven, a prosperous farm, from untamed land in spite of his illiteracy and poverty. George Washington Carver maintained that farming was an important livelihood that would "unlock the golden door of freedom to our people" (quoted in hooks, 62), and that sentiment is materialized in Macon's life as he becomes an icon of hope for the newly emancipated community. As an African American landowner in the post–Civil War South, Macon would have been an exception: out of the 6.5 million African Americans living and working on farms in the South, only 187,000 were themselves owners of farms (Clark-Lewis, 21). Therefore

Macon's exemplary life, which showed the community members that they could prosper through landownership, is cut short by angry, jealous white landowners. A young Macon and Pilate watch as their father is killed while trying to protect his land. That their father is physically displaced from the very land on which he toiled—and created an identity—suggests the interrelationship between place and personhood in the novel. As a result of their father's death, the children are taken in by Circe, a midwife, who is employed as a maid by the terrorists who were responsible for Macon's death. Although the children are understandably traumatized by their father's death and their imprisonment within the walls of the murderers, Pilate displaces her mourning for her father onto Circe's cherry preserves: "Pilate began to cry the day Circe brought her white toast and cherry jam for breakfast. She wanted her own cherries, from her own cherry tree, with stems and seeds; not some too-sweet mashed mush" (*Song*, 167). Again, the presence of sugar implies racial oppression, and thus Pilate, like Guitar, refuses to consume it. Indirectly, Morrison reveals Pilate's continued disdain for sugar through her eating and chewing habits, which are stressed throughout the novel.

Pilate, whose mouth is perpetually in motion, chews a myriad of food and nonfood items, and none of them is sugar based: "She chewed things. As a baby, as a very young girl, she kept things in her mouth—straw from brooms, gristle, buttons, seeds, leaves, string, and her favorite, when he could find some for her, rubber bands and India rubber erasers" (*Song*, 30). Later we see Pilate masticate orange seeds and peach pits. Morrison explains that the family "ate what they had or came across or had a craving for" (29). Of note is that Pilate and her family do not eat sweets produced with sugarcane (cakes, pies, cookies, candy, etc.). In fact, Pilate admits that she has "never tasted" the sweet substance right in their home, the wine that they make and sell (48).

Pilate not only ingests leaves but is associated with trees throughout her life: "Her house sat eighty feet from the sidewalk and was backed by four huge pine trees, from which she got the needles she stuck into her mattress. Seeing the pine trees started him thinking about her mouth; how she loved, as a girl, to chew pine needles and as a result smelled even then like a forest" (27). Later, when Milkman is first introduced to his aunt, he claims that she "looked like a tall black tree" (39), and remarks on the moss-green sack (39) hanging from the ceiling in what reads as the centerpiece of her living room. From her habit of chewing seeds and leaves, to sleeping on a mattress filled with evergreen needles, to the scent of pine permeating her home, Morrison constructs Pilate as a human/plant hybrid.

Major female characters in the novel are also described in terms of plant life, although the presentations are markedly different. Ruth's daughters are associated with red roses that they fashion from velvet. In fact, they labor at this activity, spending "hour after hour tracing, cutting, and stitching the costly velvet" (5). These "bright, lifeless roses" (10) were first made by Lena, who claims to have loved flowers as a child, and making these artificial replicas kept her "quiet," in the same way, she surmises, that the people in asylums "weave baskets and make rag rugs" (213). Lena's diction underscores that her engagement with the natural world was cut off and transmogrified into an activity designed to keep her and First Corinthians docile. Given their upper-class standing, the young women were encouraged to be as lovely and artificially presented as the velvet roses; they were displayed for their beauty but were kept apart from their community, both human and nonhuman. In a diatribe against her brother, Lena, a woman now in her forties, confesses that she is done making velvet roses. For Lena and First Corinthians, eschewing the velvet roses is a necessary step on their path to self-emancipation. Unlike her daughters, Ruth's relationship to the natural world is intimate and material.

Ruth is a backyard gardener, underscoring her physical engagement to plants and the living world, which her son finds distasteful. In fact, Milkman relates to Guitar an episode of seeing his mother in the garden, which, because of its disquieting nature, he safely labels a "dream." Through the kitchen window, Milkman watches his mother hand sowing tulip bulbs. As quickly as she digs holes in the dirt, the stalks begin growing: "The tubes were getting taller and taller and soon there were so many of them they were pressing up against each other and up against his mother's dress" (105). Ruth is seemingly oblivious to this rapid growth, and not until they touch her back does she acknowledge them, not with any alarm, but playfully: "They were smothering her, taking away her breath with their soft jagged lips. And she merely smiled and fought them off as though they were harmless butterflies" (105). Milkman regards the tulips, with their "bloody red heads," as suffocating his mother; the last image he describes is of the "mound of tangled tulips bent low over her body" (105). Morrison does not revisit or further develop the scene, nor does any harm appear to be done to Ruth. Guitar challenges Milkman, questioning why he did not free her from this thicket of tulips, but Milkman maintains that she was "having fun" (105). While this episode has received little critical attention, it is a significant moment insofar as the rapidly growing red tulips act as a foil to the inert red velvet flowers. Lena and First Corinthians' relationship to the natural world is severed as the women are practically imprisoned in the grand home of their late grandfather Dr. Foster. In forming floral shapes, they act on the textile, but here the tulips' animation is brought to the fore. The tulips actively seek a relationship with Ruth; after all, they propagate quickly to touch her body in an act that underscores their agency. Ruth and the tulips are co-actants; it is not merely Ruth who acts on the earth, altering the landscape, but the tulips that germinate and reach out to Ruth in what reads as an erotic and procreative gesture, a pairing that was earlier sounded in the novel. After all, plants mediate Ruth's conception of her son.

Years before, a desperate Ruth sought Pilate's assistance to help her conceive another child. Because Macon sexually avoided Ruth for years, Pilate concocts "greenish gray grassy looking stuff" (125), which Ruth slipped into Macon's food. This plant-based aphrodisiac leads to the successful conception of Milkman. Macon is furious when he realizes that he has been tricked and tries to induce a miscarriage of his son. In a similar vein, Milkman is disgusted by the earth's graphic fecundity and his mother's reveling in it. He fears the enmeshment of humans with the natural world. For both Ruth and Pilate, the porosity of the human/plant boundary is grounding, procreative, and momentarily freeing from the strictures of a racist and patriarchal society, lessons that Milkman will learn as he journeys to the South. It is only in this ancestral space that he lets go of these imposed dichotomies of the human and nonhuman spheres and grounds himself into the land and its inhabitants.

Even when Ruth is not touching the earth directly, she is still bound up with the ecological world. The centerpiece on her father's formal dining room table consisted of freshly cut flowers, twigs, and berries, a tradition that Ruth continued even as she and her new husband took over the home. One day, Ruth travels to the lakeshore to find driftwood to put on the table. She looks to Macon for approval of this presentation, maintaining, "Most people overlook things like that. They see it, but they don't see anything beautiful in it. They don't see that nature has already made it as perfect as it can be. Look at it from the side. It is pretty, isn't it?" (*Song*, 12). Macon does not acknowledge the driftwood but rather takes this moment to denigrate his wife's cooking. Ruth, thereafter, lets the driftwood covered with seaweed disintegrate on the table. She later removes the bowl, which had housed bits of the natural world and covered a water mark on the table. She never refills the bowl with plant material, and thus the boundary between the built and natural environment is fortified. However, Ruth marks the absence of the natural world in the home. Ruth's stance of resistance is in *not* obfuscating the water mark, a mark that Morrison, notably, analogizes to botanical life: "And once exposed, it behaved as though it were itself a plant and flourished into a huge suede-gray flower that throbbed like fever, and sighed like the shift of sand dunes" (*Song*, 12–13). The stain marks the place where Ruth was connected to her father, her home, and to the natural world, and thus it is a silent pronouncement of her disintegration with human and nonhuman communities.

Reading Ruth as a character who is desperate to hold on to the natural world allows for a more capacious consideration of her breast-feeding practices and nods, again, to an arboreal ecology. While critics have paid much critical attention to Ruth Dead's prolonged breast-feeding of her only son, it is important to recognize that this "bit of balm" in Ruth's life is mediated through a green space: "Part of the pleasure it gave her came from the room in which she did it. A damp greenness lived there, made by the evergreen that pressed against the window and filtered the light" (*Song*, 13). Though this "damp greenness" has not been given critical consideration, it is an exemplar of Morrison's green ecology; it is by inhabiting this space, or what Morrison christens "the green room," that Ruth permits herself to have a moment of connection with her son and the biosphere, a breathing moment that provides some measure of relief from her suffocating existence.

In an ecocritical reading of motherhood, Ruth's lactation and breast-feeding are acts that confirm her as part of the human-nature mesh while, importantly, opening up the ecofeminist conversation by exploring the history of Black women's breast milk as stolen commodity. Implicitly responding to that brutal history, Ruth claims her lactating body as her own and continues its production for her own pleasure. In that way, Ruth's continued lactation is empowering. However, just as modern-day environmentalists have reported on the carcinogens in breast milk, *Song of Solomon* likewise considers the contamination of this intimate fluid, as cultural toxins symbolically leak into the milk. Indeed, as Steingraber reminds us: "The mother's body is the first environment, the mediator between the chemicals—both nourishing and dangerous—in our food, water and air and her unborn child" (11). It follows that Ruth's despair and dejection, then, would leach into the breast milk and taint Milkman, transforming his very identity from Macon Dead III to Milkman, a name that confounds the son and the father, who receives it "coated with disgust" (*Song*, 16). Notwithstanding Ruth's motivation, Morrison highlights in this scene the maternal body as the first landscape, the original environment, and the most dramatic representative of the transcorporeal porousness of bodies and environments, both naturally and socially constructed.

Ruth's isolation is mirrored in her family's seclusion, and it is not until Milkman travels to the South in search of gold that he becomes integrated into community, ancestral history, land, and flora. In "Civilizations Underneath," Gay Wilentz discusses the African influences on the novel, contending that "when Milkman and Guitar try to rob Pilate of what they think is the gold, they encounter in the ginger-smelling air a surreal middle passage back to the western coast of Africa from whence their ancestors were stolen" (116). The recurring trope of ginger reconnects Pilate to an African diasporic cultural history. Ginger (a sweet, spicy scent) is evocative of sugarcane, as both plants mediate that brutal and buried history. Ginger, as a connective link to Africa via the Middle Passage, is historically salient, for this plant, indigenous to Southeast Asia and Africa, was transported to Europe and America:

> On autumn nights, in some parts of the city, the wind from the lake brings a sweetish smell to shore. An odor like crystallized ginger. . . . There was this heavy spice-sweet smell that made you think of the East and striped tents and the sha-sha-sha of leg bracelets. The people who lived near the lake hadn't noticed the smell for a long time now because when the air conditioners came, they shut their windows. . . . So the ginger sugar blew unnoticed through the streets, around the trees, over roofs, until, thinned out and weakened a little, it reached Southside. There, where some houses didn't even have screens, let alone air conditioners, the windows were thrown wide open to whatever the night had to offer. And there the ginger smell was sharp, sharp enough to distort dreams and make the sleeper believe the things he hungered for were right at hand. To the Southside residents who were awake on such nights, it gave all their thoughts and activity a quality of being both intimate and far away. (*Song*, 184–85)

That the lakeside residents (like Macon Dead) close their windows to prevent the ginger-scented breeze from entering the interior space of their homes suggests their refusal to honor or even acknowledge their ancestral history. By contrast, the pungent aroma permeating the Southside community, with its economically disenfranchised population, indicates a clear relationship to living history.

Morrison, who later writes that the ginger-scented air could have "come straight from a marketplace in Accra" (*Song*, 185), explores the economic relationship of Africa to the New World. Tomich's claim—that "of all the exotic spices that stimulated European overseas expansion, sugar was the most thoroughly transformed from a luxury item to an article of mass consumption through the systematic organization of production and exploitation of labor" (2)—amplifies the commodification of African bodies to the commodification of "exotic" spices. The exploitation of Africans in America is manifest in the ginger and sugarcane motifs, which dominate the southern section of the novel.

Milkman returns to the South with Pilate to bury the bones of his grandfather, the bones that Pilate had carried with her in a moss-colored sack. The long overdue burial occurs on ancestral terrain and is mediated by the scent of ginger:

> They looked a long time for an area of earth among the rock faces large enough for the interment. When they found one, Pilate squatted down and opened the sack while Milkman dug. A deep sigh escaped from the sack and the wind turned chill. Ginger, a spicy sugared ginger smell, enveloped them. Pilate laid the bones carefully into the small grave. Milkman heaped dirt over them and packed it down with the back of his shovel. (*Song*, 335)

The sigh of the bones testifies to the completion of this odyssey. Notably, Pilate and Milkman are not struck by the smell of human remains emanating from the sack but are overcome by the essence of sugar and ginger, a comforting aroma that is nonetheless the scent of death. The sugar industry's long history as a source of human misery, suffering, and death is clear: "In the service of King Sugar, men and women worked alongside one another, their bodies naked, sweating and bleeding from the lash of the overseer as they processed cane stalks into the brown muscovado sugar that was the mainstay of the industry. Sometimes laborers died where they worked, and their bodies were pushed aside. Others stepped over these stinking, fly-encrusted corpses to continue the grueling routine, uncertain they themselves would survive" (Burnside, 153). Guitar's gunshot that fatally wounds Pilate punctuates the seemingly peaceful graveside burial and ruptures this moment of holy communion with the ancestor. However, this act of violence actually regrounds the reader in the horrors of plantation labor, materializing what the scent of sugar intimates. Morrison refuses to pacify the reader with untainted narratives of homecoming and growth. While those positive elements do figure in Milkman's journey, the gothic tones of the ancestral space are unmistakable, which Milkman voices in his final blues: "Sugargirl don't leave me here / Cotton balls to choke me / Sugargirl don't leave me here / Buckra's arms to yoke me" (336). Morrison's provocative misnaming of Solomon as "Sugarman" is introduced in the opening pages of the novel. That the name "Sugarman" is encoded in Pilate's blues song—and later "Sugargirl" in Milkman's—connects the enslavement of Africans with the cultivation of sugarcane. As Pilate sings "Sugarman" to a suicidal Robert Smith at the beginning of the novel, Morrison indirectly begins a discourse of barbaric plantation labor practices tied to modern-day violence. Concluding with the death of Pilate, and the presumed death of Milkman and/or Guitar, Morrison contextualizes their deaths with ancestral trauma linked to agricultural plantations. Milkman sings, after all, of sugar and cotton.[20]

"My whole life is geography," Guitar muses, a sentiment that gestures to Morrison's green ecology, underscoring, as it does, the constellation of place, people, and plants. In Morrison's canon, plants, a dominant life-form on earth necessary for human survival, do not merely symbolize history; they are history.[21] Morrison unearths the multifaceted, contradictory, and complex narratives written on the botanical world, a living, breathing memorial to an African diasporic past.

3

ORANGE ECOLOGY, DEATH, AND RENEWAL

Fire, Ash, and Immolation in *God Help the Child* and *Sula*

Toni Morrison's orange ecology is personal. On Christmas morning, in 1993, just two weeks after she traveled to Stockholm to receive the Nobel Prize in Literature, fire consumed Morrison's home in Rockland County, New York, burning it to the ground. In an NPR interview with Terry Gross, Morrison muses on the fire and the irreplaceable belongings consumed in the blaze: her children's report cards, original papers, and a fifteen-year-old jade plant, which, according to Morrison, was "huge and beautiful, and it burnt in a snap." "Of course," she continues, "I lost manuscripts and books and some other things, but the hurt was the report cards. And the hurt was the jade bush" ("I Regret Everything"). It is not surprising that her children's mementos top her list of losses—including a photograph of one of her sons shooting a basketball into the sky—but the jade plant is of note, especially as it has priority over her manuscripts and books, which, in an interview with the *Guardian*, Morrison reveals she "couldn't care less about" ("Predicting the Past"). Given the intimate relationship between people and flora that Morrison advances in her writing, it is perhaps not surprising that in her personal life, she experiences such kinship with a jade plant and that its loss continues to haunt. Morrison's description of her house fire through plant loss is resonant with forest fire severity, calculated, as it is, in terms of vegetation mortality. In low-severity fires, the majority of plants survive, whereas in high-severity blazes, "most of the overstory trees or dominant vegetation is killed" (DellaSala and Hanson, xxviii). Read from this prism, Morrison's fire is severe, taking the plant life in her home. Morrison admits that months after this tragedy, there were days when she would only talk to people who had also experienced house fires, citing her frequent phone calls with Maxine Hong Kingston. Morrison does not recall feeling affinity with people who had suffered loss in general, but only with those who had been the victims of burnings, acknowledging the distinct nature of fire.

Fire anchors this chapter, from the devastation it causes, to its ecological benefits, to its widespread use in racial violence and terror. Although orangey flames are standard depictions of blazes, "different chemical elements cause different colored flames. From green, produced by the presence of copper, to orange, produced by sodium[,] there is no one color of fire, rather a true rainbow of flames" (Eckstut and Eckstut, 104). In fact, "The color of fire can tell you a lot about its heat and content. The base and hottest part of a forest fire will typically be white, changing to yellow, orange, and red as it cools. . . . Different matter burns off in different colors, as well, depending on the chemical composition of what is burning and what wavelengths of light it absorbs and reflects" (103). While fire is prismatic, culturally it is most closely aligned with orange, and thus orange flames are the governing metaphor and matter in this chapter.

In *The Psychoanalysis of Fire*, Gaston Bachelard argues that fire is the "ultra-living element" (7). The Greek philosopher Empedocles, who is best known for originating the theory of the four classical elements (earth, water, air, and fire), submitted that fire was the progenitor of life: "All creatures are born from and born by fire" (quoted in A. Harris, 44). If fire "is central to human civilization" (Oppermann and Iovino, 312), and "it is fire that has made humanity" (A. Harris, 47), then in this chapter I examine a broader swath of humankind. Hitchcock in *Life in Color* reflects on the color's relationship to skin tones, maintaining that "in orange all faces meet" (123). Hitchcock elaborates on this assertion: "It brings together all people of the world. If you only had one color in which to paint them, you would choose orange. Go light and you have the paler faces; go dark, and you reach the ebonies" (123). Thus skin tones are a primary manifestation of an orange ecology. The authors of *The Secret Language of Color* affirm orange's light and dark values: "When pale, it is usually identified as yellow. When dark, it is usually identified as brown" (Eckstut and Eckstut, 71). Further, the Russian abstract artist Wassily Kandinsky described orange as "red brought nearer to humanity by yellow" (quoted in St. Clair, 94), an assertion that once again encarnalizes orange. While I stressed brown skin in the book's first chapter, here orange ecology includes a broader representation of skin tones that transcend binaristic thinking. After all, skin tones tell "us about the nature of the past environments in which people lived, but skin color itself is useless as a marker of racial identity" (Jablonski, 95).

Morrison has long explored the politics of colorism, color casting, and racial othering in her work and has disclosed how these issues affected her own life. Morrison recalls first meeting her great-grandmother, Millicent MacTeer. MacTeer, an imposing, dark-complected figure, examined Morrison and

Forest fire. Credit: Peter J. Wilson / Shutterstock.com.

her sister, both of whom had lighter skin, and proclaimed them "tampered with." "'It became clear,' Morrison writes, 'that "tampered with"' meant lesser, if not completely Other" (quoted in Painter). Painter, in "Morrison's Radical Vision of Otherness," elaborates on this incident: "Deemed 'sullied, not pure' as a child, Morrison finds that Othering, as well as the racial self-loathing of colorism, begin in the family and connect to race, class, gender, and power." An orange ecology gestures toward the blending of corporeal hues that refute strict classifications and boundaries assigned to race. Orange reorients our perceptions of distinct color borders to recognize the interconnectivity of humanity's pigmentation, an ecology of many shades and hues.

Orange has been a "color without an identity. In many languages, it's one of the very last, if not the last, color named in the rainbow" (Eckstut and Eckstut, 71). Identifying as an in-between shade, straddling hues of red, yellows, and browns, orange traffics in a liminality that, for centuries, defied classification. In that way, orange offers a treatise on color as ambiguous, shifting, and morphing. Orange also underscores the ways in which chromatics are tied, most directly, to the material world, for it was not until the "eponymous fruit became widely known that the color orange was named. . . . So the fruit itself became the color" (72).

A thought-provoking line can be drawn between the ambiguity associated with orange (first recognizing it as a distinct color and thereafter naming it as such) and the complexity of fire. From an anthropocentric perspective, we routinely regard fire as dangerous and deadly, a punishing chemical reaction, uncontainable and random. From an ecological prism, however, fire is more complicated. Yes, it can result in destruction, but forest fires, in particular, are necessary for healthy ecosystems. In fact, fire is an essential contributor to habitat vitality and replenishment, a catalyst for beneficial change known as succession. As DellaSala and Hanson, in *The Ecological Importance of Mixed-Severity Fire*, maintain: "It is not just that plants and wildlife have coped with fire, but also thrive in the rich postfire environment" (xxxi).

Fire is an omnipresent ecological force. James K. Agee of the National Park Service explains that "the first plant ecology textbook to recognize fire as an ecological factor was published in 1947. Over the next quarter century, a revolution in attitudes toward fire took place, and research on fire history and fire effects on plant communities has increased exponentially" (1244). Although scholarship reveals the myriad benefits of fire, a strong cultural ideology demonizes fire and employs a strong arsenal to attack it. The authors of "Impact of Fire Suppression Activities on Natural Communities" begin their essay thus:

> Various socioeconomic, political, and ecological factors mandate suppression of most fires. A growing literature indicates that the cost of suppressing a fire nearly always includes damage to ecosystems. In a system of fire management that attempts to weigh the costs of fire suppression against potential losses due to fire, the ecological cost is often not acknowledged, despite the fact that adverse effects from suppression activities may be substantial and persistent and, in some instances, may exceed impacts attributable to the fires themselves. (Backer, Jensen, and McPherson, 937)

A disconnect exists between a cognitive recognition of fire's benefits and our automatic desire to eradicate blazes, and thus we require greater theorizing to reorient ourselves to fire's indispensable role in our ecosystem.

It is useful to remember that fire is not possible without life—plant and human. A codependency exists between plants and fire: "As a global change agent, fire has been around since the dawn of terrestrial plants, some 400 million years ago" (DellaSala and Hanson, xxv). And as Anne Harris succinctly states in "Pyromena: Fire's Doing," fire "comes a good 100 million years after the first forms of life appear; it comes, basically, when there starts to be enough oxygen in the air for things to ignite" (27). This chapter, then, builds on the themes of the previous chapter, as there can be no fire without plants, no orange without green. According to Stephen Pyne in "The Ecology of Fire," "fire is dependent on a biotic matrix to sustain it," which means that humans and other living creatures "change the way fire behaves": "Humans hold a species monopoly over the manipulation of fire: we are the keystone species for fire's ecology. We influence fire both directly, by controlling ignition, and indirectly, by changing the environment within which fires operate. This control has increased over millennia to the point where the study of fire ecology without people is a hypothetical exercise." Pyne continues: "Life created the oxygen that combustion requires, and provides the hydrocarbon fuels that feed it. Today, through the agency of humans, life also supplies most ignitions, surpassing the previously dominant source, lightning. Fire takes apart what photosynthesis has put together; its chemistry is a *bio*-chemistry. Fire is not something extraneous to life to which organisms must adapt, it is something that has emerged out of the nature of life on Earth."

The evolution of some plants illustrates the living world's ongoing relationship to fire and the many ways that plants and forests have evolved to use fire disturbances to maintain ecosystem health:

> Many tree species actually require fire to germinate their seeds, and forest fires return important nutrients to the forest soil that was previously being stored in biomass. Wildfires help to clear out dead wood and other materials that would otherwise have taken much longer to break down and provide soil nutrition for the next generation of trees and plants living in that forest. This process helps to keep a forest ecosystem healthy. ("Ecological Importance of Forest Fires")

What these varied floral adaptations reveal is the integral role of fire in the living world. Yet these benefits are not brought to the fore, which is why fire experts propose that we "abandon terms such as 'catastrophic,' 'destroyed,' 'damaged' or 'consumed' and replace them with 'restored,' 'rejuvenated' and 'recovered'" (DellaSala and Hanson, xxxv). Keeping in mind that much of what we have learned about forest fires is shaped by language, I use the lens of fire ecology to both acknowledge its deadly power and recognize its ecological benefits.

An orange ecology is profitably brought to bear in *God Help the Child*, and returning to orange as a marker of varied skin tones affords a particular lens through which to read the novel. Sweetness, whose voice begins the novel, delivers a weak apologia for her behavior toward her daughter, Lula Ann Bridewell, filled with justifications and self-righteous indignation. Her rejection of Lula Ann stems from her daughter's dark complexion, which, the light-skinned Sweetness claims, is "not [her] fault" (*God Help*, 3). Because of the baby's "midnight black, Sudanese black" skin (3), her "high yellow" (3) parents treat her as the "enemy" (5). Her mother refuses to allow her daughter, whom she refers to as a "pickaninny," to suckle "her teat" and even contemplates infanticide, holding a blanket momentarily over her newborn's face because she "wished she hadn't been born with that terrible color" (5). Her father, Louis, convinced that Sweetness had been unfaithful, never touches the baby and soon thereafter abandons his family. Sweetness, too, has very little physical contact with Lula Ann, and thus daily rituals such as bathing are a chore. In a novel that traffics so heavily in the politics of skin, it is critical to note that Bride was never held by her father and rarely touched by her mother. The parents denied their daughter this most fundamental form of social interaction, and thus her development was irreparably harmed: "Tactile satisfaction during early development is critical for healthy behavioral development in all primates, including humans, and infants who are deprived of it develop behavioral inadequacies in later life. Put simply, the absence of touch equals stress" (Jablonski, 103). While the novel enumerates the many ways in which Sweetness disdains her daughter, what is particularly noteworthy here is that Sweetness seems to apologize to humanity at large for bringing a dark-skinned child into the world. After all, the "it's not my fault" prologue is addressed to no one in particular and thus appears to be a sorrow that Sweetness extends to all who see her daughter. Although Lula Ann (now known as Bride) is an accomplished adult at the time of her mother's diatribe, Sweetness does not waver in her antipathy toward her daughter's blackness, claiming, by the prologue's end, that her "color is a cross she will always carry" (7). Sweetness's and Louis's fair coloration, paired with Lula Ann's dark complexion, embodies the range of skin pigmentation in which orange becomes the connection; however, the parents do not see this shared undertone and treat their daughter as the "other." According to Jablonski in *Skin: A Natural History*, "Skin color is one of the ways in which evolution has fine-tuned our bodies to the environment, uniting humanity through a palate of adaptation. Unfortunately, skin color has also divided humanity because of its damaging associations with concepts of race. The spurious connections made between skin color and social position have riven peoples and countries for centuries" (3).

The trauma of racial color casting and intraracism haunts the novel in expected and unexpected ways. In an attempt to curry her mother's affection, a young Bride joins with other children to falsely accuse a teacher, Sophia Huxley, of child molestation, an act that lands the teacher in jail for years and troubles Bride throughout her life. After the young girl's false testimony in the courtroom, she was rewarded with physical intimacy: "Outside the courtroom all the mothers smiled at me, and two actually touched and hugged me. Fathers gave me the thumbs-up. Best of all was Sweetness. As we walked down the courthouse steps she held my hand, my hand. She never did that before and it surprised me as much as it pleased me because I always knew she didn't like touching me" (*God Help*, 31). Color and the pain of skin tone hierarchies undergird Bride's childhood, although as an adult, Bride, who becomes a successful cosmetic executive, exploits her dark skin and uses it as an accessory by wearing "only white and all white all of the time" (33).

Whiteness and blackness are loaded signifiers in Morrison's work as she draws attention to the history of racial categorization, which was created with the aim of legitimizing chattel slavery in the Americas and promoting social hierarchies. Accepting blackness and whiteness as antithetical categories merely buys into a discourse that relies on the binary of black and white as biological—and not ideological—categories of absolute difference. In terms of pigmentation, white paint was made from natural material, including "chalk or zinc, barium or rice, or from little fossilized sea creatures in limestone graves," but the "greatest of the whites, and certainly the cruelest, is made of lead" (Finlay, *Color*, 108, 109). Though Western culture views white as pure and clean and is associated with "money and power" (St. Clair, 43), it was a pigment that was anything but pure, for the creation of white was deadly. Warnings about the poisonous nature of this element can be traced to the first century, yet lead paint was not banned in the United States until 1977. White paint was responsible for killing factory workers, children, and artists, yet it was women's search for physical "beauty" in the poisonous hue that sheds particular light on *God Help the Child*.

The fungibility of human bodies and the material world is marked most dramatically in the cosmetic industry's use of lead-based white makeup. Beauty, which, according to Morrison in *The Bluest Eye*, is one of "the most destructive ideas in the history of human thought" (122), hinged on achieving a Eurocentric visage. Women who applied the toxic paint to their face, amid warnings of the hazards of the product, would die, but first they would become physically ill, develop blue lines on their skin, and go mad. Bride, who is a cosmetic executive and sports only white, unmistakably recalls this toxic history of whiteness.

While black and white may not seem to be in keeping with an orange aesthetic, the array of skin tones presented in the novel offers a rejection of binaristic thinking and argues, implicitly, for greater interrelatedness. Given the novel's initial focus on Bride's dark skin tone—and her mother's virulent castigation of her—it is reasonable to read *God Help the Child* intertextually with *The Bluest Eye*, as Pecola, too, is deemed an untouchable by her family and most of her community.[1] However, Morrison's presentation of trauma in *God Help the Child* is far-reaching. She refuses to pander to the idea that we live in a postracial society, and continues to speak on behalf of African American girlhood, elucidating that the color caste system continues and has devastating and long-term effects. Importantly, though, the ideology of white supremacy, so readily accepted in *The Bluest Eye*, is repeatedly challenged in *God Help the Child*. As an adult, Bride is regarded as beautiful and is a leader in the cosmetic industry. Her partner, Booker, not only rejects the dogma of colorism but offers an extended treatise on the absurdity of racial preference: "It's just a color. A genetic trait—not a flaw, not a curse, not a blessing nor a sin" (*God Help*, 143). Bride offers a practical retort that while race may be a myth, the material effects of racism are anything but, and she relays that as a child she was victimized by her classmates because of her complexion: "Coon. Topsy. Clinkertop. Sambo. Ooga booga. Ape sounds and scratching of the sides, imitating zoo monkeys. . . . They treated me like a freak, strange, soiling like a spill of ink on white paper" (56). So, yes, Morrison's most recent novel may be read as a companion piece to *The Bluest Eye*, but insofar as *God Help the Child* was published forty-five years later, it is not static in its representation of race. More to the point, Pecola and Bride are positioned alongside a litany of abused children in *God Help the Child*, many of whom are not Black. As readers, for example, we bear witness to the brutal rape of a young white boy by Mr. Leigh, Sweetness's landlord. Importantly, this scene involves a triangulation with racism as a young Bride, hearing the child's whimpers, witnesses the rape, and when Mr. Leigh realizes he has been caught, he verbally attacks her with caustic gender and racist epithets. Though Bride had never heard the words, "the hate and revulsion in them didn't need definition" (56).

Bride's childhood story is paralleled to Booker's. Booker's intact family was torn apart by the inhuman rape, murder, and dismemberment of the family's eldest son, Adam. Booker, an intellectual and musician, is tormented by his brother's death and cannot, until the novel's end, convey this family tragedy to Bride; both Bride and Booker struggle with childhood traumas, internal fires that rage until the final pages of the novel. Booker and Bride have a passionate but superficial relationship, which Booker abruptly severs. Bride is stymied by Booker's harsh breakup and commences on a journey to locate him via his aunt, who lives in a rural hamlet. On the way, Bride is overcome by the natural world: the darkness of the country road, the forest in which she imagines trees watching her, and ancient dirt roads. Aptly, she crashes her car into "what must have been the world's first and biggest tree, which was circled by bushes hiding its lower trunk" (*God Help*, 82), and thus the forest is not mere backdrop but plays a significant role in shaping the second half of the novel. Bride is injured and taken in by a bohemian family: Evelyn and Steve and their "adopted" daughter Rain. Here Bride stays and convalesces until she is strong enough to resume her journey.

Evelyn and Steve found Rain, a homeless child who had been prostituted by her own mother, and took her in to raise as their daughter. When Rain, who has chalk-white skin and green eyes, first sees Bride, she is struck by her complexion and later asks her mother, "Why is her skin so black?" To which Evelyn responds, "For the same reason yours is so white." Rain then equates both herself and Bride to her kitten and comes to the realization that they were all "born that way" (*God Help*, 85). Morrison's rhetorical gesture is significant: Evelyn does not provide a scientific explanation of phenotypical differences or caution her child against racial stereotypes but offers a personal connection to Rain's own coloring, highlighting that her daughter's skin, though seemingly disparate, comes from the same source as Bride's. Further, to highlight that childhood suffering is not limited to a particular demographic, Morrison underscores that the serial murderer who killed Booker's brother Adam was "an equal opportunity killer, his victims seemed to be representative of the *We Are the World* video" (118). In this way, Morrison's vista of trauma in *God Help the Child* is broad; therefore it is appropriate to situate the novel in orange, where "all faces meet."

Bride locates Queen Olive, Booker's aunt-cum-mother, who quickly becomes Bride's confidante, continuing the healing started by the family in the woods. Although disconnected from her own children, she serves a maternal function for Bride and Booker. She sews, cooks, and provides much-needed advice. Queen, too, is associated with the arboreal world; she lives in a trailer park in the woods and is named for a tree. She explains Booker's childhood trauma to Bride, which catalyzes the couple's healing. While Booker and Bride reconcile, a fire consumes Queen's home and later is responsible for taking her life.

Morrison's description of the fire is written at the outset as a first love: "It began slowly, gently, as it often does: shy, unsure of how to proceed, fingering its way, slithering tentatively at first because who knows how it might turn out, then gaining confidence in the ecstasy of air, of sunlight, for there was neither in the weeds where it had curled" (*God Help*, 164). Morrison employs the unmistakable diction of a romantic relationship: "ecstasy," "gently," "slowly," and "shy." But by the second paragraph, Morrison elucidates the fire: Queen burned her bedsprings to destroy bedbugs, and a spark "lurking in the yard" became a house fire. Morrison's personification of the fire continues as she explains that it was joyfully "sucking delicious embroidered fabric of lace, of silk, of velvet" (164). On one hand, Morrison's description of fire is artful; she is a gifted writer known for her rhetorical flourishes. On a deeper level, though, her complex rendering of fire gestures to fire ecology, and thus it is not mere linguistic trickery that readers originally apprehend this moment as inviting. After all, "Fire has a metamorphic multiplicity; its manifestations are flame, ember, coal, ash, smoke; its states of being include ignition, conflagration, smoldering, and dying; its effects are light, warmth, and pleasure" (A. Harris, 42). The manifold incarnations of fire and its paradoxical nature are sounded throughout *God Help the Child*. Specifically, the forest—a major setting in the novel—stands as a reminder of fire as generative and necessary in maintaining a healthy ecosystem. Fire clears dead trees, leaves, and competing vegetation from the forest floor so that new plants can generate, and thins tree stands to let more sunlight in so that trees stay healthier. It improves wildlife habitats and returns nutrients to the soil. DellaSala and Hanson persuasively argue that "ecologically speaking, fire is an essential natural force greatly underappreciated in its role as one of nature's principal architects. In nature there are short-term winners and losers in any natural change event, and fire provides no exception. Some species thrive (pyrogenic or pyrophilous) in the immediate postfire environment, whereas others move on (fire avoiders), but almost all species benefit at some point in postfire succession. Thus fire is nature's way of perpetuating what has been described as 'pyrodiversity'" (xxx). Fire facilitates healing in *God Help the Child*, which, aptly, takes place in the forest. Fire's ecological benefits to the timberland are implicitly brought to bear in the novel, highlighting the transcorporeal relationship between human bodies and the nonhuman environment.

This is not to suggest that Morrison sanitizes fire's deadly effects. Queen, "seduced into unconsciousness by the smiles of smoke without heat" (*God Help*, 165), dies from complications after her severe injuries. Morrison's portrayal of Queen's bright red hair "burst[ing] into flame" illustrates the explosiveness of the event. Just as fires can be chemical agents for generation, so this fire is the catalyst for Bride and Booker's newfound commitment. As they minister to a severely injured Queen, they begin to nurture each other. In that way, the fire that takes Queen's life acts as a healing agent for Booker and Bride's relationship.

Even Queen's death is couched in a discourse of regeneration. Queen is cremated, and her burned remains are a symbol of fertility in the novel. Ash, a solid remnant of charred material, is a physical reminder of fire and thus mitigates against reading conflagrations obliterating any and all signs of life. Rather, fire transmogrifies physical material into ash. Ash is not merely detritus but can be used as a disinfectant and a fertilizer that enriches soil nutrition. In an article for the *Washington Post*, "Volcanoes Provide a Boom for Gardeners," Barbara Damrosch maintains: "The fact is, volcanic sites are among the most fertile places on the planet. Volcanoes helped form our planet—its water, air and soils—and their eruptions continue to nourish us, bringing up huge payloads of elements in the form of lava, rock and ash that eventually break down into plant-nutritive forms."

The cremated remains of Queen constitute another registry of fire and ash in the novel and signify in multiple ways. Fire, which took Queen's life, also consumes her deceased body:

> During the three days waiting until Queen's ashes were ready, they argued over the choice of an urn. Bride wanted something elegant in brass; Booker preferred something environmentally friendly that could be buried and in time enrich the soil. When they discovered there was no graveyard within thirty-five miles, or a suitable place in the trailer park for her burial, they settled for a cardboard box to hold ashes that would be strewn into the stream. (172)

Booker's impulse to return his aunt's ashes to the ground as soil amendment has currency today. Such green burial practices are gaining a foothold in the funeral industry. According to the authors of "Toxic Burials: The Final Insult," "Nature teaches us that dead organisms are recycled into the biota. Death is an inevitable part of life. Edward Abbey urged us to strive for a good death, just as we do for a good life: 'we should get the hell out of the way, with our bodies decently planted into the earth to nourish other forms of life . . . which support other forms of life'" (Stowe, Vernon-Schmidt, and Green, 1818). In fact, there are products that turn human ash into growth material for trees. One proponent of this type of interment muses: "Eventually I'd like to have a mini forest where family members can walk amongst their ancestors. . . . Not with gravestones and marble statues, but with birds chirping and a nice breeze rustling the leaves" (Stinson). While this type of interment may seem iconoclastic, "for most of human history, the dead simply returned to the earth" (Stowe, Vernon-Schmidt, and Green 1817). The handling of Queen's ashes, stored in a biodegradable cardboard box and scattered in a body of water, illustrates such an approach.[2] This is particularly apt, for even in the throes of medical treatment for her burns, Queen is described in terms of plant life: a tube with clear liquid draining into her veins looks like "a rainforest vine," and her mouth is covered by a "white clematis bloom" (166). Queen, who embodies the natural world in life, returns to it in death. While death occurs in the wake of a fire, life, too, flourishes in its aftermath.

Moments after Booker scatters Queen's ashes in the stream, Bride discloses her pregnancy. As Booker processes the news, he turns to look one last time at his aunt's ashes: "Booker gazed at her a long time before looking away toward the river where a smattering of Queen's ashes still floated" (*God Help*, 174). Here the fecundity of ash is brought to the fore. Booker's steady gaze at his aunt's ashes unmistakably pairs the burned remains with Bride's pregnancy and underscores fire's role in generating life. Postfire landscapes, after all, are biologically rich. The fire also serves as a cleansing agent for both Bride and Booker; it purifies some of the weight of their past traumas to clear the way for new growth, allowing for a healthier habitat in which to raise their child.

Cremains are also symbolically present in the novel through ash-and-ink commemorative tattoos that incorporate a small amount of charred human remains in the ink. While Booker's tattoo is not made of his brother's ashes per se, he does sport a commemorative tattoo that memorializes Adam and represents the weight of his unprocessed grief: "The last time Booker saw Adam he was skateboarding down the sidewalk in twilight, his yellow T-shirt fluorescent under the Northern Ash trees. . . . Down the sidewalk between hedges and towering trees Adam floated, a spot of gold down a shadowy tunnel toward the mouth of a living sun" (*God Help*, 115). Booker's memory of Adam's luminosity does not fade even after Booker identifies his brother's body at the morgue: "Unable to forget that final glow of yellow tunneling down the street, Booker placed a single yellow rose on the coffin lid and another, later, graveside" (116). In an attempt to capture and hold on to the light that is Adam, Booker inscribes his skin with color: "The tattoo artist didn't have the dazzling yellow of Booker's memory, so they settled for an orangish kind of red" (120–21).[3] Skin, a loaded signifier, takes on assorted meanings. From a chromatic perspective, it follows that yellow transmogrifies to orange, because Booker last saw his brother alive at dusk, and "orange best captures our attention once the sun starts to rise or set. Add a background of blue sky, sea, or ice and you're more likely to spot fluorescent orange than any other color. . . . Fluorescence glows even from a distance, especially in the ultraviolet light most abundant at dawn or dusk" (Eckstut and Eckstut, 82). Booker layers color on top of his skin pigmentation, marking his body with a luminescence that is concomitantly the color of loss. It is a color that permanently stands in for the life that is Adam's, but given the manifold skin tones associated with orange, it is a reminder of all the boys' lost lives. Candi Cann's exploration of memorial tattoos in *Virtual Afterlives* sheds light on Booker's choice to inscribe his body with a text of memory:

> The development of tattooing is one way to carry the dead around with us, while also making the status of the bereaved clearly evident to those around them. Tattooing is a visual marker that concretely indicates one's status as bereaved to the community, by memorializing the dead through the inscribing of names, images, or even replicas of body parts (such as handprints or footprints of the deceased) on living bodies. Tattoo remembrances are literally carried with us, age with us, and allow a virtual afterlife with the dead, simultaneously establishing the identity of the bereaved in a fixed and permanent way. (49)

Read from this prism, Booker, in mapping the loss of his brother onto his skin, creates a kind of permanence out of Adam's evanescent life. In a novel that traffics heavily in skin, "our personal tapestry" (Jablonski, 3), it is not surprising that Morrison turns to tattoos, as "no other creature exerts such extensive control over what its skin looks like. Humans expose it, cover it, paint it, tattoo it, scar it, and pierce it, telling a unique story about ourselves to those around us" (3). Booker uses his skin, the largest organ of the body, to memorialize his brother and to tell the story of his ongoing mourning.

Moreover, ash-infused tattoos are obliquely sounded in *God Help the Child* in the multiple references to wearing the remains of the dead. Booker contends that the death penalty is not a harsh enough punishment for the man who murdered his brother, and evokes a form of penance ostensibly practiced by "a tribe in Africa," in which "they lashed the dead body to the back of the one who had murdered it. That would certainly be justice—to carry the rotting corpse around as a physical burden as well as a public shame and damnation" (*God Help*, 120). Later, when Queen implores Booker to release himself from the burden of grieving, she, too, uses a corporeal metaphor: "You lash Adam to your shoulders so he can work day and night to fill your brain. Don't you think he's tired? He must be worn out having to die and get no rest because he has to run somebody else's life" (156). Pleading with her nephew to work through his mourning, Queen echoes Booker's diction: in both cases, Adam is "lashed" to the shoulders, the site of Booker's commemorative tattoo. Morrison's unconventional choice of "lash" to denote "carrying a burden" is evocative of chattel slavery, as the lash was routinely employed as a means of punishment. Wounds from lashing have been immortalized in pictorial iconography of enslaved people, and often these scars are on the back and shoulders, like Sethe's permanent scarring as a result of Schoolteacher's whipping. Throughout Morrison's canon, characters are called on to remember the dead, speak their names, and share their stories, but as exemplified in *Beloved*, a precarious balance exists between remembering the past and being devoured by the pain of it. Metaphorically, Booker's memorial tattoo is ash infused; part of Adam's body is forever grafted onto him. Unlike Queen's burned remains, though, the symbolic ashes that configure Booker's rose tattoo do not, in themselves, heal, regenerate, or enrich; rather, as Queen instructs just days before her own death, Booker must honor his brother by walking away from the fire.

As in *God Help the Child*, the fires that punctuate *Sula* signify in multiple directions; they are traumatic, healing, and sacrificial. Beginning with an elegy for a lost community ("there was once a neighborhood" [3]) and concluding with Nel's explicit scene of mourning in the cemetery (a despair that reverberates in "circles and circles of sorrow" [174]), *Sula* is framed with scenes of death, loss, and grief. Phillip Novak supports this reading, arguing that "death not only structures the narrative but also governs it, determines the elaboration of character and event. Death presides. And *Sula* endlessly presides over death" (185). Unlike the accidental fire that led to Queen's death, Eva, the matriarch of the novel, controls fire to take the life of her beloved son, Plum. This is not the first time that Eva performs a sacrifice. After being abandoned by her husband and left with no resources to raise her three children, Eva is rumored to have "stuck [her left leg] under a train and made them pay off" (*Sula*, 31). Though Morrison withholds the veracity of this claim, Eva returns to town eighteen months later "with two crutches, a new black pocketbook, and one leg" (34) and enough money to build a home and raise her children. Her self-sacrificing act serves as a harbinger for her infanticide of Plum.

Rhetorically, the deaths by fire in *Sula* are "aestheticized" (Bouson, 61); Morrison's prose effortlessly moves, as it does in *God Help the Child*, from the devastation of fire to its purifying properties. Plum returns from World War I a drug addict, and Eva feels powerless to mollify his desperate situation. Out of love and hopelessness, she immolates her youngest child, "who floated in a constant swaddle of love" and "to whom she hoped to bequeath everything" (*Sula*, 45), in a scene that alternates between beauty and horror. Eva's presence in Plum's bedroom and her maternal rocking comfort him. According to James Benn in "Written in the Flames," "The practice of autocremation, or 'burning the body' . . . is but one manifestation of the range of practices known as 'self-immolation' [and] is not easily reducible to a single cause, meaning or interpretation" (41). While autocremation does not occur in *Sula*, immolation is an apt descriptor for Eva's act, as it invokes a sacrificial burning and is likewise not reducible to a single cause. Given Eva's love for Plum, it is a deep personal loss as she takes his life to heal him, an act reminiscent of Sethe's infanticide in *Beloved*. For Eva, fire symbolizes her ultimate sacrifice.

In fact, Morrison's diction discloses Eva's baptism by fire:

> Now there seemed to be some kind of wet light traveling over his legs and stomach with a deeply attractive smell. It wound itself—this wet light—all about him, splashing and running into his skin. He opened his eyes and saw what he imagined was the great wing of an eagle pouring a wet lightness over him. Some kind of baptism, some kind of blessing, he thought. Everything is going to be all right, it said. Knowing that it was so he closed his eyes and sank back into the bright hole of sleep. (*Sula*, 47)

Morrison provides, at least initially, Plum's internal thoughts and physical sensations, and there is no explicit discourse of pain. Instead Plum is soothed by his mother's presence; Eva, whose physical handicap disallows her from moving about in the house, abandons her wheelchair and painfully mounts the stairs on crutches to enter Plum's room and gather him in her arms. What Plum does not know is that moments after this act of maternal devotion, he will be sacrificially set on fire. Readers fill in the ghastly reality of Plum's burning flesh that is to quickly follow, but it is noteworthy that Morrison withholds these details, for in so doing, she throws the baptismal quality of this ritual into relief. Reading the fire through an ecocritical lens, "There is beauty and ecological value in forests that may seem lifeless to many shortly after fire, but which are actually representative of ecological renewal the moment the fire occurs and for decades thereafter" (DellaSala and Hanson, xxxiv). In that way, Eva's use of fire to repair and renew her son's vitality is in keeping with the role of fire in the natural world. After all, Eva believes she is restoring his identity: "I just thought of a way he could die like a man" (*Sula*, 72). Steve Mentz in "Phlogiston" offers a paradigm of fire that resonates with Eva's immolation: "Thinking with flames outlines a twinned ecology of consuming and remaking" (61); and in this way, Eva is at once consuming the life of Plum to remake his identity. Insofar as Morrison employs religious diction in this scene, identifying the burning as a "baptism," it is logical to conclude that Eva believes that she is freeing her son's soul. It is fitting that she would turn to fire to commit infanticide: "When fire and air burn, smoke rises, and this physical movement towards the heavens fuels many allegorical interpretations" (Mentz, 70), furthering the religious overtones of Eva's immolation.

Eva does not just take life but is part of the cycle of life, death, and rebirth, and like fire, she is at once a destructive force and a "restorative agent" (DellaSala and Hanson, xxxiii). Eva gives new life to a triad of boys, neighborhood strays whose story speaks to the illogic of skin tone as a measure of selfhood. Eva takes in the boys and christens them with the same name: "Dewey one was a deeply black boy with a beautiful head and the golden eyes of chronic jaundice. Dewey two was light-skinned with freckles everywhere and a head of tight red hair. Dewey three was half Mexican with chocolate skin and black bangs" (*Sula*, 38). Although the children arrive with names of their own and are only a couple of years apart, they quickly share a singular identity, "becoming in fact as well as in name a dewey—joining with the other two to become a trinity with a plural name . . . inseparable, loving nothing and no one but themselves" (38). Even their schoolteacher "gradually found that she could not tell one from the other" (39). In her construction of the deweys, Morrison puts pressure on the outward appearance of race—pigmentation and phenotypes—as an ontological category of existence. In fact, the politics of skin tone are sounded in the main character, Sula, and her closest friend, Nel. No hierarchy is presented between Sula's "heavy brown" color and Nel's "wet sandpaper" hue; rather, their pigmentation, like other aspects of their life, is seen as complementing each other.

Beyond giving the deweys a new life, Eva tries to sacrifice her own life to save her daughter, Hannah, from an out-of-control yard fire: "Eva knew there was time for nothing in this world other than the time it took to get there and cover her daughter's body with her own. She lifted her heavy frame up on her good leg, and with fists and arms smashed the windowpane. Using her stump as a support on her window sill, her good leg as a lever, she threw herself out of the window" (*Sula*, 75–76). Morrison, who christens Eva's infanticide of Plum a "baptism," likewise uses jarring similes in Hannah's macabre death "dance" of agony, which she performs before succumbing to her injuries: Hannah was "gesturing and bobbing like a sprung jack-in-the-box" (76). Unlike Plum, Hannah is silenced in the narration of her death, yet her demise is likewise random, unexpected, and violent. Morrison yokes together discrepant imagery to lyricize death by fire. Later Eva recognizes strange occurrences—turbulent weather, unusual dreams, and lost personal items—that foreshadow her eldest child's untimely death, but at the time she merely reacted to the "familiar odor of cooked flesh" (77). An onlooker throws water on the "smoke and flame bound woman," and "the water did put out the flames, but it also made steam, which seared to sealing all that was left of the beautiful Hannah Peace" (76). In this second death by fire, the horrific conditions of the burned body are brought to the fore, and thus

Morrison positions Hannah's death alongside her brother's, recognizing the gruesomeness of his burning, which was made more traumatic because after Eva lit the fire, she walked away, leaving her son to bear his death alone.

The Peace home, then, is anything but peaceful. Eva disfigures herself to keep her children fed, and two out of three of her adult children are killed by flames at the family home. This trauma is mapped onto the remaining family members. Though Eva does not evidence remorse for taking her son's life, long after the flames have been extinguished, she continues to carry the fire: "The smoke . . . was in her hair for years" (*Sula*, 37). Sula's relationship to the deaths is more complex. Sula is an iconoclast who takes pleasure in flouting societal conventions. When Hannah is overcome by the fire, a stunned and bleeding Eva notices that Sula watches the flames consuming her mother's body with interest. Sula, on her own deathbed, affirms her maternal grandmother's suspicions, claiming: "I never meant anything. I stood there watching her burn and was thrilled. I wanted her to keep on jerking like that, to keep on dancing" (147). Sula, before ejecting Eva from her home and placing her in a retirement facility, challenges her grandmother's murder of Plum. Sula threatens Eva, arguing, "Any more fires in this house, I'm lighting them," and appends an ominous warning: "Maybe one night when you dozing in that wagon flicking flies and swallowing spit, maybe I'll just tip on up with some kerosene and—who knows—you may make the brightest flame of them all" (94). Sula uses the discourse of fire to chastise Eva for her morally questionable act and to threaten her life. According to Bachelard, "Among all phenomena, it is really the only one to which there is so definitely attributed the opposing values of good and evil. It shines in Paradise. In burns in Hell. It is gentleness and torture" (7). As readers, we are seduced into understanding Eva's immolation of Plum, but Sula's threat to wield fire sullies Eva's sacrifice, pairing it, as it does, with Sula's malevolence.

Sula's pariah status is marked on her body. She has a birthmark over her eye that functions as a Rorschach test of sorts, as it becomes a projection for her friends, family, and community. Her birthmark, which grows darker through the years, is read as a tadpole, stemmed rose, snake, and "scary black thing." The townspeople eventually speak in unison as "everybody" agrees on the meaning of the birthmark: "It was not the stemmed rose, or a snake, it was Hannah's ashes marking her from the very beginning" (*Sula*, 114). Symbolically imprinted with her mother's charred remains, Sula's birthmark is another iteration of an ash-infused tattoo. Booker chooses to mark his life with his brother's death, but Sula's ash-and-rose birthmark, while evocative of Booker's tattoo, signifies differently, serving not as a memorial tattoo but as a harbinger of death.

Rhetorically, fire becomes a place marker for death in *Sula*. Morrison associates death by fire with acts of racial hatred and violence, as does Dungy in "Tales from a Black Girl on Fire, or Why I Hate to Walk Outside and See Things Burning," who concedes: "Just as I'd grown up aware of the historical dangers of being black and discovered outside, I knew to fear fire" (31). Dungy explains that her fear of fire is metonymically linked to her dread of the forest: "Campfires and bonfires represented a conflation between the natural world and the human. The wood in those piles was innocent and yet acted out a role. Because I was afraid of what humans had done to other humans in those woods and on those tree-provided fires, I'd come to fear the forests and the trees" (30). Dungy offers a complex African American environmental perspective that is revelatory of ecological interconnectedness. Her apprehension of flames gives way to the forest in general, and in that way, as evidenced in the evocative title of her essay, she herself rhetorically becomes all those who have been the victims of burning rituals.

The deaths in *Sula* also take on greater cultural significance as Morrison moves among catastrophes plaguing the Bottomites: "floods, white people, tuberculosis, famine and ignorance" (*Sula*, 90). In emphasizing the larger narrative of midcentury African American life, Morrison turns to fire, as it carries with it the historical weight of racial terror insofar as fire has long been used as a weapon by hate groups. Plum and Hannah's death by fire unmistakably draws attention to the lynching and burning rituals executed in the decades after Emancipation and continuing throughout the twentieth century. As Chuck Jackson convincingly argues in "'A Headless Display': *Sula*, Soldiers, and Lynching," "Even though no lynchings take place in *Sula*, the novel borrows from and rearranges actions and objects typically found in lynching narratives, including bodily mutilation, the slicing off of a body part with a knife, two bodies that are burned to death (one of which is first doused with kerosene), grotesque spectacle, public rituals, and the persistence of the menacing white gaze" (375). Indeed, the racial climate of postwar America, the time period of the novel, was steeped in violence against the African American community. As John Hope Franklin and Alfred A. Moss note in *From Slavery to Freedom*:

> White citizens, in and out of the Klan, poured out wrath upon the black population shortly after the war that could hardly be viewed as fit punishment even for traitors. More than seventy blacks were lynched during the first year of the postwar period. Ten black soldiers, several still in their uniforms, were lynched. Mississippi and Georgia mobs each murdered three returned soldiers, in Arkansas two were

> lynched, while Florida and Alabama each took the life of a black soldier by mob violence. Fourteen Negroes were burned publicly, eleven of whom were burned alive. (349)

As a result of this racial violence, the NAACP published *Burning at the Stake in the United States*, a compilation of journalistic accounts of human burnings that occurred in 1919 in the South. Morrison's staging of burnings, then, plays out against a landscape of institutionalized racial brutality and killings. Jackson contextualizes Eva's immolation of Plum with this history: "The burnt flesh of his black body . . . connects him with what only could be, for Eva, a fraternity of men who have died because of the very fact of their blackness and their maleness" (384). Paired with lynching and burning rituals, cross burning, iconic of the Ku Klux Klan, is also evocative of the burnings that take place in the novel. While cross burning is a practice that predates the hate group and was not initially part of its rituals, it is strongly associated with the Klan, and thus burning takes on another valence in this novel, especially as Morrison references the myriad forms of vigilante violence that African Americans in the military faced when returning to the country.

Given this history of death and absence, the reader bears witness to a story in memoriam: "In that place, where they tore the nightshade and blackberry patches from their roots to make room for the Medallion City Golf Course, there was once a neighborhood" (*Sula*, 3). This community where people lived, played, and worked is "knock[ed] to dust," an image synonymous of ash. It is not as if the built structures are standing and the residents have left. No, their homes, businesses, and recreational centers have been obliterated in what reads as an incineration, and thus Morrison's opening words function as a eulogy, marking the space of absence. The framing of the novel, which establishes the community as a memory, is a reminder of the accumulated losses in *Sula*.

Likewise, characters such as Plum, Hannah, and Sula are pronounced absences in the narrative. Plum's body seemingly disintegrates in the fire, and Hannah is so disfigured by the flames that she has a closed-coffin funeral. Sula, without explanation, also has a closed-coffin service, an obscuring of the body that is against protocol in many African American funerals. In fact, "Nel went to the funeral parlor, but was so shocked by the closed coffin she stayed only a few minutes" (*Sula*, 173). Karla Holloway argues that "it was traditional in African American communities to leave the casket open for viewing sometime during the wake and church services. A laying-on of hands [and] touching, kissing, and expressing one's grief by viewing the remains have traditionally mattered deeply" (25). These material absences in

Sula suggest the kind of eradication associated with fire and weigh heavily on the narrative, as does the spectral presence of the unnamed, unspecified "beautiful black boys" of 1921. The elusive beautiful boys that are never fleshed out but "dotted the landscape like jewels" (56) are instead a site of narrative memory, a textual refrain that highlights the fleetingness of the past and the beauty and innocence of a generation of young men lost to war, lynching, burnings, and mob terror. The underlying melancholy for the missing boys lingers in the nation's memory, which is suggested by the geographic fusion of their bodies with the landscape, a national landscape that, in 1921, was burning in Tulsa, Oklahoma, in one of the country's most notorious race riots.[4] This race war owed its origins to an African American male's rumored assault of a white woman and an angry white mob's threat of lynching (Franklin and Moss, 352). The National Guard was called in, and Tulsa was declared under martial law. While this event nationalized and thus made visible postwar racial violence, the material evidence of the crime—the bodies—went missing, obliterated through burning or lost to drowning. As Holloway explains: "In a pattern that became morbidly consistent for post–World War I riots, including those in Rosewood and Tulsa, black mortuaries could only bury those they found. Throughout the century, survivors continued to lament the family and folk who just disappeared and could not even be funeralized" (69).

In honoring that history, Morrison's frames *Sula* with a similar semiotics of loss. Temporally beginning in 1919 and ending in 1965, Morrison brackets her novel with war, racial terror, burnings, and lynchings. The summer of 1919, which James Weldon Johnson called "the Red Summer," was, according to Franklin and Moss, "the greatest period of interracial strife the nation had ever witnessed," with race riots occurring throughout the nation (349). Likewise, in 1965 (a year that the narrator ironically claims only "seemed" better), "the U.S. war in Vietnam intensified, Malcolm X was assassinated, and the Watts riots began" (Ryan, 401). The interplay between the foreground narrative of the death of the Bottom and its background history of mob violence, race riots, and wars suggests that "peace has many tombstones" (401).

Bearing witness to such human loss, Morrison leaves readers in a graveyard, where, with Nel, we are permitted to mourn. The headstones of Beechnut Park cemetery bridge domestic tragedies with international suffering: "Each flat slab had one word carved on it. Together, they read like a chant: PEACE 1895–1921, PEACE 1890–1923, PEACE 1910–1940, PEACE 1892–1959. They were not dead people. They were words. Not even words. Wishes, longings" (171).

Sula and *God Help the Child* conclude with longings. Booker and Bride, optimistic about the birth of their child, are in the throes of mourning Queen's death. *Sula* mourns that the nation is embroiled in international wars and engaged in domestic terrorism against African Americans. Nel mourns her closest companion, Sula. Nel's grief is experienced first as a burn in her eye, a transcorporeal exchange that includes Sula's birthmark and the many fires that rage in the novel. In this final tableau, Nel, "thinking about the past," laments "gone things" (*Sula*, 174). Like the Bottom, a once thriving neighborhood, and the beautiful black boys, which the "world was full of" in 1921 (164), many things are gone in the novel, absences that linger only in memory. Nel's endless cry without a "top" or a "bottom" (174) is evocative of Morrison's own heartache for the fire that consumed her home. In an interview with Claudia Dreifus, Morrison discloses: "When I think about the fire, I think I may not ever, ever, ever get over it" ("Chloe Wofford Talks about Toni Morrison"). Bachelard's musing on the suddenness of fire may, in part, explain the lasting memory of the flames: "If all that changes slowly may be explained by life, all that changes quickly is explained by fire" (7). The shock of fire is followed by cataloging the many casualties of the flames, and those losses are where we find ourselves in the closing pages of *God Help the Child* and *Sula*. Morrison evokes and explores our human relationship to fire and the ecological benefits of fire, insisting that rejuvenation will occur in the burn area, but for now, only ash is left behind.

4

BLUE ECOLOGY AND RESISTANCE

Islands, Swamps, and Ecotones in *Tar Baby* and *Love*

Water is ubiquitous in Morrison's oeuvre; it is the transatlantic trade route, and thus it is memory. Of all the matter featured in this book, water has the most obvious link to the human body. According to the marine biologist Wallace Nichols in *Blue Mind*, "In its mineral composition, the water in our cells is comparable to that found in the sea" (10). He goes on to explore our evolutionary beginnings and again implicates water in that history: "Our ancient ancestors came out of the water and evolved from swimming to crawling to walking. Human fetuses still have 'gill slit' structures in their early stages of development and we spend our first nine months of life immersed in the 'watery environment' of our mothers' wombs" (10). That our first experience of life is bathed in amniotic water at once highlights humans' intimate connection to water and, concomitantly, maternalizes water: "Water is life's matter and matrix, mother and medium. There is no life without water" (quoted in Nichols). In considering whether other planets in our solar system have water, the marine biologist Sylvia Earle succinctly remarks: "No blue, no life" (quoted in Hitchcock, 98). This life-giving element holds particular currency when considered from an African American historical framework, "since more than any other single event, the Middle Passage—the transit from Africa to America—has come to epitomize the experience of people of African descent throughout the Atlantic world" (Berlin, 14). Read from this prism, the waters of the Atlantic are the amniotic fluid that materializes the fluid boundary between freedom and slavery and thus the birth of African American culture.

In this chapter, I consider water's indelible relationship to life-forms on our planet. After all, Earth is a blue planet. Not only does water make up more than two-thirds of the earth's surface, and our body mass, but as Nichols reminds us, "Ocean plankton provides more than half of our planet's oxygen" (8). Given the interrelationship of ecosystems, it is important to note that water is intimately tied to plant life. Hence this chapter is closely aligned with the green, brown, and orange ecologies I have discussed insofar as "the sea was the proto-soil, where Earth, air, water, and the solar fire met for the first time. It was an inverse soil. . . . But from a certain point of view, all Earth's later history is a consequence of that first mixing. In that sense, life is the story of bodies that learned to contain the sea" (Logan, 11). If, as Logan poetically muses, life-forms on earth carry the sea, it is apt that Morrison so readily turns to water, as she insists on the indelible relationship between human and nonhuman environments, where race is always part of the configuration.

Blue, for all its life-giving associations, is also a melancholy color, a hue of sadness. Reading blue in terms of a "blues" ecology provides a nuanced framework for considering an African diasporic perspective. A blue/blues ecology theorizes survival and trauma, and physical and psychological dislocations, a confluence of water, memory, and resistance that is brought to bear on islands and swamps in *Tar Baby* and shorelines in *Love.*

The fact that "water comprises over 70% of the earth's surface, [but] 95% of those waters have yet to be explored" (Nichols, 8) highlights a mysteriousness around water that Morrison exploits in *Tar Baby. Tar Baby* occupies a peculiar place in the Nobel laureate Toni Morrison's oeuvre. Following the epic *Song of Solomon* and preceding her masterwork, *Beloved*, *Tar Baby* has received comparatively little critical engagement. I posit that the critics' discomfort with *Tar Baby* lies in the fact that the politics of postcolonial resistance in the novel are largely encoded in, and voiced by, the nonhuman world. In setting the novel in the Caribbean, Morrison focuses on the biotic world, and the book is thus in keeping with other Caribbean literature. According to Michael Dash in *Caribbean Discourses*, "The relationship with the land becomes so fundamental in Caribbean discourse that landscape . . . stops being merely decorative or supportive and emerges as a full character. Describing the landscape is not enough. The individual, the community, the land are inextricable in the process of creating history" (quoted in Japtok, 475). While Dash's passage is decidedly earth centered—and I offer a reading of water in *Tar Baby*—the configuration of the natural world and humans as embodiments of history is an apt descriptor of Morrison's novel.

Water, in its many forms, is an inescapable presence in *Tar Baby*, which is set on Isle des Chevaliers, a fictional Caribbean island. The beginning of the novel highlights the creation of the island's swamplands. Swamps, as a particular kind of wetland, are a liminal geography, shifting between land and water, complicating and defying, in their very beings, categories of identification, thus constructing a trope neither of terra firma nor of strict watercourse. William Mitsch and James Gosselink, in a definitive treatment on wetlands, admit that there is considerable difficulty in defining this ecosystem but offer three main characteristics: "Wetlands are distinguished by the presence of water, either at the surface or within the root zone; wetlands often have unique soil conditions that differ from adjacent uplands; they support vegetation adapted to the wet conditions (hydrophytes) and conversely, are characterized by an absence of flooding-intolerant vegetation" (26). The authors, though, quickly problematize this definition based on the considerable variation in these conditions from wetland to wetland. What is most important for my analysis here is that wetlands embody an intermediate zone where elemental distinction dissipates: "Wetlands are often located at the margins between deep water and terrestrial uplands and are influenced by both systems" (Mitsch and Gosselink, 27), or as Jyoti Parikh and Hemant Datye succinctly state in their study of wetlands: "Wetlands represent the interface between land and water" (21).[1]

That both elements—land and water—coexist, layer, and overlap to the point of being indistinguishable engenders a theory of reading geographies, bodies, and texts as resisting hegemonic labeling and classification. As a geographic borderland that morphs from one state to another, wetlands are a space of ambiguity, where there is "constant and languid saturation" (Hurd, 5). Swamps, land masses that are "always wet," refuse to be contained. It is with this complex negotiation of geography in mind that we can read wetlands, "resistant to colonization or agriculture" (Wilson, xiv), as environments of subversion and resistance in *Tar Baby*. Indeed, as Frantz Fanon argues, colonization "is a success when . . . indocile nature has finally been tamed" (quoted in Giblett, 74). In this chapter, I consider swamps and their denizens as untamed bodies of postcolonial resistance in *Tar Baby*.

Swamps are intense locations, evocative of peril, dread, and destruction. The swamp does not offer a "steady reflection" but is a "broken, shattered place, [which] dissolves the moment you lean too close" (Hurd, 39). Beyond the fact that swamps are full of "muck and dead trees and algae," threatening elements abound in swamplands, from alligators to poisonous snakes to "saw grass so razor sharp it can slit a horse's legs" to a host of carnivores (Hurd, 13, 55). It is not just what inhabits the swamps that elicits fear, but that a geography can be so thick and dense that it erases our beings, reducing humans to merely part of the larger ecosystem. In fact, without technological alteration, it is nearly impossible for humans to modify a wetland: "The wetland walker can leave a mark with his or her feet on the blank sheet of the wetlandscape, but usually these are quickly erased and rendered back into the watery 'Nothing'" (Giblett, 16–17). The impenetrability of swampland, with its perceived array of dangers, has turned swamps historically into spaces of sanctuary, a staging ground for escaping slaves and a permanent site of Maroon communities.[2]

Through a geographical prism, "nineteenth-century Americans understood swamplands and other inundated areas to be pestilent places. They came to believe that the South was more 'diseased' than the North, as yellow fever and other epidemics increasingly attacked Southern areas (particularly the cities and hinterlands of Charleston, Savannah, and New Orleans) after 1800" (Nelson, 535). The relationship between geography and health has a much earlier antecedent: "The notion of the influence of climate on civilization has been present in European thought since the age of Enlightenment. Indeed, the notion extended well into the nineteenth century when the genre of medical topography already represented a specialised derivation of the original ideas connecting climate, land and development" (Mathe-Shires, 2). In nineteenth-century America, swamplands, as archetypal landscapes of infection, became a synecdoche of the South and especially the lowlands, conflating race, geography, and malady. Malaria and other illnesses like yellow fever and cholera were "a reality for most Americans living along the South Atlantic coast between 1800–1880" (Nelson, 538), and the primary medical theories put forth for these feverous attacks were known as miasmic or anticontagionist.[3] At the time, physicians argued that "miasm" was a "product of decay or putrefaction of animal or vegetable substances, acting with intense heat and moisture, usually in or near standing water" (Nelson, 536). Miasma, "when it got into the air, would poison the individual's internal system as he or she breathed. Miasma would then poison the body as, based on the ancient equilibrium of four elements of the body, the liquid part—the water—of the body would become unbalanced" (Mathe-Shires, 3).

The indelible relationship among bodies of water is illuminated here, as the swamp's seemingly dangerous liquid merges with and taints the human body's. Likewise, contagion theory located disease in stagnant water, especially in what was deemed unsanitary water areas such as bogs, swamps, and inundated rice fields. The medical establishment strongly advocated the purification of these fluid landscapes through a process of dry culture and swamp drainage (Nelson, 556). The conflation of place, water, and pathology was prevalent in the nineteenth century and led to the destruction of wetlands throughout the American Southeast. Though medical science later discovered that it was mosquitoes bred in swamps that caused malaria, and not the water itself, swamplands retained their deleterious character.[4]

In the nineteenth century, the swamp became a site of death, as various tourist brochures and pamphlets of the period attest. Rotten trees, decayed branches, and putrefying flesh became mainstays of swamp iconography, and that representation continues to permeate our cultural limning of bogs and other wetlands. Given the fear associated with Maroon societies in the white imagination, swamps were also characterized as geographies of blackness, dread, and unsavory activity. The racial implications had intercontinental connotations: "The name malaria was used to describe endemic fevers in the Western part of Africa as early as the 1840s" (Mathe-Shires, 3). Owing to malarial tropical fevers and the high mortality rate for white Europeans who traveled to West Africa, the area became a site of great anxiety: "The image of West Africa in the popular imagination and to some extent in the official British mind of the second half of the nineteenth century can be summarized in the phrase 'white man's grave' or the region of 'deadly climate'" (5). The perception of the tropics in West Africa was mapped onto the American South, merging land, water, and its diseases through the "dangers" of blackness. Race is metaphorically tied to the geopolitical topography.

Vast swamplands, uncultivated and dangerous, turned into the topography in which the body of the Maroon was mapped. This body of water became conflated with the body of the fugitive. Swamplands, and the people who inhabited them either temporarily or permanently, deconstructed plantation hegemony, and the resultant disorder incited social anxiety. Threatening the status quo, the fugitive swamp dweller in effect psychologically reversed the power dynamic, for though few raids were committed by these figures, whites not only feared for their personal safety but also worried about large-scale insurrection.

The belief that wild, defiant communities occupied the swamplands powerfully supported arguments against the "peculiar institution." And, of course, Nat Turner's insurrection, which he plotted, planned, and issued from the swamps, added to the perceived danger of these wetlands. While clearly motivated by different political agendas, all these narratives and incidents coalesced to essentially reinforce swamplands as marginalized, wild terrain. In fact, in some accounts, these marshy watercourses were rendered not merely as threatening topographical spaces but also as haunted: the swamp became the equivalent of a gothic haunted house, and the Maroons became the ghosts dwelling in the spectral landscape (Cowan, 14).

Morrison's *Tar Baby* begins not with swampland but with the sea, whose waters are likewise presented as paradoxical. The fugitive Son, having hidden in a ship, the HMS *Stor Konigsgaarten*, jumps into "soft and warm" waters as the novel opens. Though Morrison's diction suggests comfort and safety, Son's actions belie this tranquility: the sea tosses him into a vortex, and he is prevented from swimming to the pier by a "bracelet of water." Rather than make his way to solid ground, he is "nudged" out to sea by the "water-lady," a Mami Wata, or Mother of Water spirit. Although worshipped throughout Africa, Mami Wata, as her pidgin name implies, is a foreigner, often identified with Europeans and, some conjecture, originating in the Caribbean (Drewal, 160). Her realm lies beneath the sea, and she is an amalgamation of a mermaid and an African water spirit. That she presides over the water provides a context for reading Son's move to the island, as he too is an outsider who throughout the novel is paired with water.

After the "water lady" tosses him farther into the sea, Son locates another boat and hoists himself onto the deck. The terra firma, then, is illusory, a temporary solid footing that is buoyed by water. In fact, the reader comes to realize that this instability is metaphorically tied to the chaotic lives of the characters on the fictional Caribbean island of Isle des Chevaliers. A retired wealthy candy manufacturer, Valerian Street, and his wife Margaret not only build a mansion, L'Arbe de la Croix, on this island but purchase the island itself. Living with and serving them are Sydney and Ondine Childs, the butler and cook, who have worked for the Streets for decades. The relationship between the Streets and the Childses is as contentious as it is intimate, crossing boundaries between homeowner and servant, the possessed and dispossessed. Complicating relationships further, the Streets are patrons of the Childses' niece and surrogate daughter, Jadine, a light-skinned, Sorbonne-educated fashion magazine model residing in Paris. Opening *Tar Baby* with a man poised to jump overboard, Morrison does not begin with fear; rather, "he believed he was safe" (3), foreshadowing the tensions throughout the novel. Yoking freedom to water, this passage also introduces Son, who brings forth the material presence of the water. The fluid interfacing between Son and the elements foreshadows his autonomy within the rigid hierarchy of the Streets' environs. Fleeing his ship, Son inadvertently ends up on Isle des Chevaliers, and his desire for water prompts him to steal away to the Streets' home. Although this home is designed to keep the island in abeyance, Son inserts himself and the island into this inanimate surrounding. Morrison describes Son as part of the "great underclass of undocumented men": "Unbaptized, uncircumcised, minus puberty rites or the formal rites of manhood. Unmarried and undivorced. He had attended no funeral, married in no church, raised no child. Propertyless, homeless, sought for but not after" (165, 166). Unanchored, Son instead dreams of ancestral waters and the knowledge that such an immersion provides: "He used to want to go down in blue water, down, down and then to rise and burst from the waves" (166).[5] It is fitting that Son's surname is Green, for he greens the Streets' world of artifice.

After this cryptic prologue, Morrison begins chapter 1 with the voice of the island, narrating its beauty, its inhabitants and ruin. Building the "collection of magnificent winter houses on Isle des Chevaliers" (*Tar Baby*, 9) signaled the permanent alteration, if not destruction, of the island's ecosystem. The felling of the champion daisy trees, which are "part of a rain forest already two thousand years old and scheduled for eternity" (9), reads as a murder: they were "wild-eyed and yelling," sinking their roots deeper into the ground as the men "gnawed through" them. Sudden death is followed by grieving: "Trees that had been spared dreamed of their comrades for years" (10).[6] Morrison's personification of the trees discloses Valerian's occupation of the island, paralleling the indigenous community with the natural world. Matthew Wynn Sivils, in his analysis of trees in southern literature, argues that "the concepts of human and tree bodies are so related that many trees take on anthropomorphic characteristics. . . . 'Association between . . . sap and blood, leaves and hair, limbs and arms, bark and skin, or trunk and the human body should not be taken as merely analogical, for they establish a kind of identity between signifier and signified'" (90). As such, the trees in *Tar Baby* morph into the indigenous bodies, those who are likewise displaced and cut down, despite roots that run deep in the Caribbean. Here the trees function as connections between the natural world and the human world, characterized, in this instance, by Valerian's power, indifference, and greed as he consumes the island's natural resources and its inhabitants. Rodney James Giblett, who offers a cultural analysis of wetlands, maintains that "colonisation is as much about the colonisation of nature as it is about the colonisation of 'the natives,' and the colonisation of nature is just as much about the colonisation of 'swamps' as the colonisation of 'the bush'" (74).

The condition of the river manifests the devastation wrought by the building of seasonal homes:

> The men had already folded the earth where there had been no fold and hollowed her where there had been no hollow, which explains what happened to the river. It crested, then lost its course, and finally its head. Evicted from the place where it had lived, and forced into unknown turf, it could not form its pools or waterfalls, and ran every which way. The clouds gathered together, stood still and watched the river scuttle around the forest floor, crash headlong into the haunches of hills with no notion of where it was going, until exhausted, ill and grieving, it slowed to a stop just twenty leagues short of the sea. (*Tar Baby*, 9)

In this description, Morrison reveals the devastations associated with gentrification. The river, functioning as both an actual waterway and a metaphorical device, is displaced by the built environment, just as the island people are radically dislocated by the influx of Americans and Europeans.[7] As this passage makes clear, geographical displacement and racism underscore *Tar Baby*. Centralizing place, though, Morrison does not use the river solely as a means of highlighting the travails of the human world; rather, its devastation is rendered in its own right. The natural world, though not indifferent, is powerless, the clouds reduced to merely "watching" the tragedy unfold. And it is a tragedy, as the river's confusion, exhaustion, and grief attest.[8] The reconfiguration of the "poor insulted, brokenhearted river" (10) results in the stagnated water and the creation of the island's noxious swamp: "Now it sat in one place like a grandmother and became a swamp the Haitians called Sein de Vieilles. And witch's tit it was: a shriveled fogbound oval seeping with a thick black substance that even mosquitoes could not live near" (10). That Morrison equates the swamp to a lactating woman indicates that this breast-like body of water that emits tar is not a stagnant watercourse but a life-giving, maternalized ecosystem. Numerous critics have read the title of Morrison's fourth novel in terms of its folkloric resonance—the tar baby, the hare, and the farmer—and others have considered Morrison's metaphoric usage of the expression in terms of Black female authenticity, or what is referred to in *Tar Baby* as the women's "ancient properties"; however, few have gestured toward the materiality of tar, though I believe it underlies the text and, in fact, provides a lens through which to read water as a racialized body.[9]

Morrison gestures in a myriad of ways to Trinidad's Pitch Lake in her rendering of the swamps on Isle des Chevaliers.[10] Pitch Lake is a tar-asphalt pit, a phenomenon that occurs when a substance known as bitumen, a viscous, sticky, black liquid, rises to the surface through fissures in the earth's crust, which, depending on the amount of fluid generated, causes a large puddle, pit, or even lake to form. As the largest asphalt lake in the world, Pitch Lake is a well-known tar pit, attracting thousands of tourists annually to gaze at what is not an aesthetically striking body of water (it is often referred to as one of the ugliest tourist attractions in the Caribbean) but a moving, active, black lake.[11] The lake, a composite of oil, clay, and mud, is impressive in size and approximately 250 feet deep at its center. Signaling the Caribbean thus, Morrison implicitly identifies a relationship between Pitch Lake and her fictional geography.[12]

Before Jadine's experience in Sein de Vieilles (arguably the principal swamp scene in the novel), Morrison introduces the swamp's centrality to the island's history. Therese, a blind island elder, relays a creation narrative to Son: Blind horsemen populate the hills of the island; according to a fisherman's tale, they are descendants of captives who went blind upon seeing

Dominique, men who refused to be enslaved and took to the hills as fugitives. The horsemen couple with the women who live in the swamps, though they are largely invisible to the rest of the island's population. These mythic figures who inhabit the natural world—the hills and the swamps—become part of the island's topography, acting as a foil to the destructive opulence that the Streets' home epitomizes. Here Morrison references actual Maroon communities who "lived in organized bands in the mountains [and] periodically came down to the plains to steal provisions, pillage warehouses, and carry away livestock" (Fouchard, 257). Therese recounts this island legend to Son because she regards him as a symbolic horseman, a Maroon who belongs with this race of men: "'I told you!' said Therese [to Gideon]. 'He's a horseman come down here to get her. He was just skulking around waiting for his chance'" (*Tar Baby*, 107).

Indeed, the novel provides ample evidence for reading Son in terms of marronage. Looking for water, Son goes to the Streets' home not to cause harm but to quench his thirst:

> What he went toward the house for was a drink of water. . . . He tried the door and found it unlocked. He walked in. There in the moonlight was a basket of pineapples, one of which he rammed into his shirt mindless of its prickers. He listened a moment before opening the refrigerator door a crack. . . . Three chicken wings were wrapped in wax paper. He took them all and closed the door. . . . The chicken was incredible. He hadn't tasted flesh since the day he went crazy with homesickness and jumped into the sea. (*Tar Baby*, 135, 137, 138)

Son's physical state mirrors that of fugitive enslaved peoples, whose continuous malnutrition was a primary cause of marronage and "appears to have been the most distressing lot of the slave, representing the most serious and incomprehensive negligence on the part of the colonist. In order to adequately feed himself, the slave had frequently to resort to pillage" (Fouchard, 161). Like Maroons, Son survives by stealing provisions from the nearby "plantation" of L'Arbe de la Croix.

Sidney Mintz offers insight into the relationship between food and slavery: "It was the slaves themselves, who commonly emerged as the major food producers, working in family groups and on their own time, producing the bulk of the food of free people, and their own as well" (41). The ruling class was well provided for and dependent on their cooks to feed them. The tragedy here is that those who were forced to cultivate and prepare food often went without: "We have seen that the slaves were poorly provided for, often half starved. Despite the many laws prescribing cultivation or rations, slaves commonly died of hunger, and a prime reason for marronage—running away—was hunger" (45).[13]

While Maroon societies enjoyed a certain amount of autonomy (some permanent Maroon communities "built homes, maintained families and pursued agriculture" [Price, 152]), many depended on the fraternity of those who were still on plantations for various forms of aid. Therese, the Streets' washerwoman and symbolic field hand, functions as Son's community. Long before she sees him, she senses his desperation: "She caught the scent twelve days ago: the smell of a fasting, or starving, as the case might be, human. . . . A smell they reproduced when they were down to nothing for food. So a hungry man was on the grounds, or, as she said to Gideon [the Streets' gardener], 'Somebody's starving to death round here. . . . A really starving somebody'" (*Tar Baby*, 105). Therese, supplying Son with water and chocolate, purposefully leaves the Streets' house open for this modern-day Maroon to enter.[14]

The term "'maroon' derives, it is believed, from the Spanish *cimarron*, meaning wild, the word itself coming from the name of an Indian people in Panama, the Symarons, who revolted against Spanish domination" (Fouchard, 247). Not only are Son's actions and appearance, with his "wild, aggressive, vicious hair that needed to be put in jail" (*Tar Baby*, 113), in keeping with the etymology of the word, but he is frequently described as "wild" in the novel: Ondine claims that she sees "Wildness. Plain straight-out wildness" in Son's eyes (192); Son's friend cautions that any attempt to control Son "makes him, you know wildlike" (255); and Sydney describes him as a "wild-eyed pervert" (100). These depictions underscore Son's relationship to the Maroons, as well as the uncharted territories they inhabit. Believed to be untamed and uncontrollable, Son is "threatening to the security and property of the privileged" (Fouchard, 257), which he himself recognizes: "They are all frightened, he thought. All but the old man" (*Tar Baby*, 133). Here again, Morrison introduces another trope of Maroon society, namely, desertion. The origin of the term notwithstanding, the word "maroon" has come to mean desertion, which describes Son's actions: he leaves his hometown to avoid serving jail time and subsequently jumps ship: "There are runaways by sea, who flee by small craft or rowboats, braving a thousand dangers in the search for some shore where one might have leisure to be free. Some were picked up clinging to a rock after being shipwrecked. Others, thanks to the winds, were caught off Jamaica shores. As they set out on their venture 'over liquid routes,' none knew for certain where they were headed" (Fouchard, 259).

Beyond these larger intertexts, Morrison nods to Maroon practices with what are seemingly insignificant details from Son's life. For example, in their efforts to secure freedom, fugitives used numerous forms of documentation, including "hand-written passes, legitimate and counterfeit, faked declarations of liberty and enfranchisement, faked baptism papers and certificates of all types" (Fouchard, 263), a practice echoed in Son's life. Jadine pushes Son on his lack of authentic identification, beginning with his name: "'I told you already—everybody calls me Son.' 'I want to know what's on your birth certificate.' 'No birth certificates in Eloe.' 'What about your Social Security card. That says Son?' 'No. That says William Green. . . . One of them anyways. I got another that says Herbert Robinson. And one says Louis Stover. I got a driver's license that says—'" (*Tar Baby*, 173–74). All these textual details catalyze Son as the modern-day Maroon, the heir (or "son") of the blind horsemen who live in the hills and ride the swamps.[15]

Sein de Vieilles, the island's swamp, is not a primary setting in the text, though it is an anchoring geography sounded throughout. Early on, Son reveals to Valerian that he was in the swamps before hiding in his home, and their conversation illuminates the swamp's folkloric significance: "It couldn't have been very comfortable for you there. The local people avoid it entirely. Spirits live there, I'm told" (93). Though Son admits to not seeing any spirits, he nevertheless offers: "In a swamp, I believe" (93). Swamps have long been thought to possess mystical properties: "The American swamp seems a locus of African American magic and spirituality. Often, the plantation conjurer or root doctor was associated with the margins of the community, living in or beside a swamp" (Cowan, 62). Even those who remained on plantations would make temporary journeys into the wilderness. For example, some women, especially "older slave women, possessed highly detailed medical knowledge about various substances" found in the swamplands (Blum, 6). Their knowledge of horticulture was such that they not only knew how to identify plants and herbs in the wilderness but used the botanical world for various homeopathic treatments, as well as nourishment (6). In this way, Son's foray into the swamps before entering the built environment suggests a connection to the natural world and to those who know the healing properties of the land's resources. Transcending temporal constraints, the swamps become a locus of ancestral immersion as Morison implicitly arcs toward the fecundity and regenerative possibilities of the swamplands.[16]

Son's cultivation of ancestral associations on the island is mitigated by Sydney and Ondine Childs and their reinforcement of class and race hierarchy. Speaking with the dominant voice of society, Sydney debases Son as a "wife-raper" (99); Jadine calls him a "river rat" (159); and Margaret, upon finding Son in her closet, can only utter "Black" (79). Jadine reinforces the stereotype of Son as a brute: "You rape me and they'll feed you to the alligators" (121), which discursively resituates Son in the swamplands, as "crocodiles are the archetypal swamp monster" (Giblett, 32), as well as ancient African symbols for water spirits. His dangerous mystique is historically salient, given the reputation of African American males who inhabited the swamp, for they were seen as undeterred by the laws of the antebellum South.[17] Son, too, threatens the neoplantation order that the Streets have created; his presence unravels its hierarchy and dismantles the secrets contained within.

While Son's time in the swamps serves not only as a means of survival but also as a harbinger for his intimacy and alliance with the island and its people (namely, Gideon and Therese), Jadine's swamp experience reinforces her cultural disinheritance. Unlike Son, who uses the swamps as a refuge, Jadine's time in what she calls the "jungle muck" (180) is unplanned and unwanted, as this is, by her own account, the "ugly" part of the island that "she averted her eyes from whenever she drove past. Its solitude was heavy and there was something sly about its silence" (181). Jadine's attitude toward this uncharted terrain reinforces her adoption of Eurocentric values and the hierarchized, racialized order those values imply. Indeed, Helen Tiffin argues that "attitudes to landscape are intimately connected to social values and mores. The disturbing fecundity and decay of tropical vegetation, the debilitating effects of non-European climates on Europeans, necessarily involved attitudes to bodies" (201). The many bodies Jadine finds unseemly (if not altogether fears) are brought together on Caribbean soil.

Throughout this section, Morrison equates the swamps to Pitch Lake: both are oval in size, oozing with a black, thick substance, from which emanates the strong smell of sulfur, a "jungle-rot smell" that deters even mosquitoes (*Tar Baby*, 181). In the swamps-cum-tar-pit, swamp women hang from trees, sway in the wind, and watch Jadine with arrogance in their eyes as she is consumed by the pitch. The presence of the swamp women is fitting, as there is "room for the erratic and irrational" in swamplands (Hurd, 106). Like Pitch Lake, which is capable of slowly devouring even heavy objects in its thick tar, Sein de Vieilles begins to consume Jadine. Sinking up to her knees in the tar, Jadine saves herself by shinnying up a tree, in a scene replete with a sexualized idiom of dance:

> Just count. Don't sweat or you'll lose your partner, the tree. Cleave together like lovers. Press together like man and wife. Cling to your partner, hang on to him and never let him go. Creep up on him a millimeter at a time, slower than the slime and cover him like moss.

> Caress his bark and finger his ridges. Sway when he sways and shiver with him too. . . . Love him and trust him with your life because you are up to your kneecaps in rot. (*Tar Baby*, 182–83)

Rhetorically, Jadine's survival is aestheticized; beautiful diction jarringly harmonizes her struggle for freedom.

Morrison advances this association as the tar seems to pull Jadine slowly into itself, perhaps in a parallel gesture of intimacy and absorption, which Jadine nonetheless experiences as a kind of death, a reaction befitting the geography: the wetland is "a place of death. . . . But it is also a place of life. . . . They are living black waters where . . . the intermingling of life and death takes place. . . . In the midst of death and decay in wetlands, we are in the midst of new life being reborn" (Giblett, 128). Despite the swamp women's indifference to Jadine's apparent suffocation in the swamp, the "mudhole" is active, endeavoring to christen Jadine into its "ancient properties," suggestive of new life. Though critics have generally noted that various female characters in *Tar Baby* act as ambassadors of these ancient properties—namely, the woman in yellow with "skin like tar" (45), the swamp women, the night women, and even Jadine's Aunt Ondine—I believe it is the natural world, crystallized by the swamps, that first and foremost embodies ancient properties. Morrison gives voice to place, and it is place that endeavors to give Jadine voice. As Morrison explains in an interview with Tom LeClair:

> I found that there is a tar lady in African mythology. I started thinking about tar. At one time, a tar pit was a holy place, at least an important place, because tar was used to build things. It came naturally out of the earth; it held together things like Moses's little boat and the pyramids. For me, the tar baby came to mean the black woman who can hold things together. (122)

Morrison's circular movement from the African tar lady to tangible tar pits and back to the human embodiment of tar suggests that tar is multilayered in the novel, with strata of literal and metaphoric import.

The swamp's tar, alternately describe as oily, mossy, and gelatinous, defies a clear elemental designation. As Jadine expresses to Margaret: "Mud I guess, but it felt like jelly while I was in it. But it doesn't come off like jelly. It's drying and sticky" (*Tar Baby*, 184). In this way, the "pitch" (184), an apparent reference to race and place, represents the contradictions and tensions of the swampland in African American letters: "Mud runs the whole geological gamut, from mountain to silt to sedimentary rock buried below the surface. It's the one substance we can hold in our hands, smear on our faces, that embodies both birth and death. That can blend the wet grains of both creation and destruction into one matter" (Hurd, 20). Despite Jadine's fear of suffocating in the swamps, an attentive reading of the scene reveals an interesting subtext of sexuality and creation. Jadine's insistence on reading the tree as a male partner establishes the sexuality of the swamps. In fact, Jadine's swamp dance is foreshadowed by her romantic outing with Son. Like the swamps, which are filled with dangers, it is at this picnic that Son tells Jadine that he murdered his philandering wife in a moment of rage, a pairing of sexuality and violence that serves as a context for Jadine's experience in the swamps. Hurd sheds light on the swamp as a sexualized body of water: "soaked with danger—its insidious, murky, sexual wet nature always about to leak through the tight barriers of morality and hard work of anyone who goes there" (105). Giblett notes that the swamp, conflated with the "nether regions of the body," is regarded in terms of aberrant sexuality—filthy and grotesque—which Margaret's reaction to Jadine epitomizes. Jadine's body, covered in tar, becomes a site of projection for Margaret, who is horrified by this apparent defilement, a dirtiness that is clearly imbricated with racial bodies, both human and geographic. Interestingly, though, Jadine defies Margaret's tirade against Son: "Margaret, I fell in, not you. And it was my fault, not his" (186). Jadine chooses to describe this incident as falling into the mud, which linguistically parallels falling in love, a pairing that is furthered by the description of her legs "burning" long after the confrontation with the swamp. Finally, Jadine's description of the gelatinous tar can also be read as seminal in nature, returning the reader to the underlying "body" of Margaret and Jadine's discourse, namely, Son, who throughout the text is conflated with dangerous sexuality and uncultivated geographies.[18]

Margaret is not the only character who maps herself onto Jadine; Son attempts to imprint himself and his culture onto her: "He had thought hard during those times in order to manipulate her dreams, to insert his own dreams into her. . . . Oh, he thought hard, very hard during those times to press his dreams of icehouses into hers" (119). Son's slumber-time interlude illuminates his desire to immerse Jadine in a rural, Black, southern consciousness, which is later materialized as he takes her to his hometown of Eloe, Florida, a trip that results in the dismantling of their relationship. Florida is a significant setting in *Tar Baby*, because the "South houses the greatest concentration of wetlands in America. . . . [and] Louisiana and Florida fall into the highest category of concentration, with 50 to 55% of their total land mass composed of wetlands" (Wilson, xiii). Place is again implicated in the gulf between Son and Jadine. Son, from the all-Black town of Eloe, announces his culture through nostalgic community imagery, epitomized for him by "yellow houses with white doors which women opened and shouted Come on in, you honey you! And the fat black ladies in white dresses minding the pie table in the basement of the church and white wet sheets flapping on a line, and the sound of a six-string guitar plucked after supper while children scooped walnuts up off the ground" (119).

Jadine, by contrast, is an "orphan," a familial state reflected in her nomadic existence, as she lives alternately in Baltimore, Philadelphia, New York, Paris, and Isle des Chevaliers. In fact, Mary Beth Pringle argues that Jadine "turns placelessness—a seat in an airplane far above the sites on earth that would entrap her—into a home of sorts" (37), and Marilyn Sanders Mobley maintains: "While [Son] values the nurturing aspects of home and fraternity, [Jadine] is rootless and places greater value on what she can own" (289). Son's nighttime visits to Jadine in the Streets' Caribbean home are akin to the swamp's gesticulations, as both he and the mud want to initiate Jadine into her ancient properties; he "assumes the role of ancestor, instructive and protective" (Paquet, 510). Despite his intentions, Son cannot remedy Jadine's lack of grounding in physical and cultural place.

Though Morrison does not pathologize Jadine and, in fact, reveals that Son's construction of his hometown is highly romanticized, Jadine's reaction to Eloe bespeaks her racial sensibilities, which again are communicated through a discourse of the geophysical world: she "looked out at the blackest nothing that she ever saw. Blacker and bleaker than Isle des Chevaliers, and loud. Loud with the presence of plants and field life. If she was wanting air there wasn't any. It's not possible, she thought, for anything to be this black. . . . She might as well have been in a cave, a grave, the dark womb of the earth, suffocating with the sound of plant life moving, but deprived of its sight" (*Tar Baby*, 251).[19] Morrison ties locale to lineage. Just as Jadine fears being buried in the mud and muck of the Caribbean swamp, so too does she find the rural South suffocating. Jadine's disparaging remarks about the climate, plant life, and people are encoded in a racialized discourse, suggesting an interplay between her rejection of Eloe and her disavowal of blackness.

Son's body is signaled throughout the novel as a sign of blackness, as his conflation with the racialized body of the swamplands attests, and much of his relationship with Jadine consists of his aborted attempts to "blacken" her, understood here as another swamp reenactment. Read from this prism, the recurring motif of scent is illuminated. Son, the fugitive swamp dweller, is initially odiferous, an aspersion that Jadine flails at him after an altercation: "I know you're an animal because I smell you" (121), to which Son unexpectedly responds, "'I smell you too' . . . and pressed his loins as far as he could into the muted print of her Madeira skirt. 'I smell you, too'" (122).[20] Jadine's threat to tell Valerian is met by Son's loaded response, "Leave out one thing. Don't tell him that I smelled you" (122). While Son repeatedly makes indecent remarks about Jadine's smell, we can read scent within a larger framework of smell on the island. Mingling with the pleasant horticultural aromas permeating the Caribbean, there is Trinidad's Pitch Lake. The sulfuric odor of this living body is omnipresent and unmistakable, with visitors and residents equating the scent to rotten eggs. Ironically, though, the elemental sulfur, toxic to many bacteria, may be the source of the lake's healing properties. Indeed, legend suggests that Pitch Lake, and the rainwater that collects on its surface, can cure a range of maladies. Breathing into a sleeping Jadine "the smell of tar and its shiny consistency" (120), Son is symbolically returning to the tar pit–swamplands, with their connotative range of race, sexuality, and healing. Deliberately destabilizing Son as merely crude and hypersexualized, Morrison connects these various bodies on the island as multilayered sites of cultural identity. In addition to the scent of Pitch Lake, intense smell is also associated with swamplands. Son knew he was in a swamp because of its "foul smell" (134): "Miasma, they called the swamp air, meaning poisonous vapor. Today the word also suggests a funk" (Hurd, 103).

As discussed in chapter 1, funk is Morrison's overarching metaphor for cultural heritage and resistance to dominant societal norms, "an intrusion of the past into the present" (Willis, 325). As Willis in "Eruptions of Funk" notes:

> Morrison's aim in writing is very often to disrupt alienation with what she calls eruptions of "funk." Dismayed by the tremendous influence of bourgeois society on young black women newly arrived from the deep South cities like "Meridian, Mobile, Aiken and Baton Rouge," Morrison describes the women's loss of spontaneity and sensuality. They learn "how to behave. The careful development of thrift, patience, high morals, and good manners. In short, how to get rid of the funkiness. The dreadful funkiness of passion, the funkiness of nature, the funkiness of the wide range of human emotions." (310)

For Morrison, cultural repression is closely tied to the denial of the body and the natural world, and thus Son's acceptance—if not embodiment—of the funk stands in stark contradistinction to Valerian and the plantation order he resituates on Isle des Chevaliers, an island undergirded by histories of slavery, the African diaspora, forced plantation labor, and colonial practices. Morrison does not retreat from the materiality and exigencies of the somatic; both human and geographic bodies are, in fact, funky, epitomized in her description of the "whole island . . . vomiting up color like a drunk" (*Tar Baby*, 187), and the sea, "away from the tourist shops, away from the restaurants and offices . . . [throwing] up what it could not digest" (293).

Jadine similarly perceives the island in terms of excess: "The island exaggerated everything. Too much light. Too much shadow. Too much rain. Too much foliage and much too much sleep" (68).[21] Jadine's adoption of Western values is epitomized by her regard of the island's unseemliness, for as Tiffin argues, there is "a reevaluation of the local" through Euro-American perceptions (201). It is because the island's vegetation is as beautiful as it is uncontrollable that Valerian prefers his greenhouse, complete with transplanted North American flora, temperate climates, and European classical music. Valerian's desire to contain horticulture is in keeping with the attitudes of Euro-American expatriates, who found the "tropics, with their emphasis on the somatic. . . . dangerous to English reason and control" (201). Indeed, the Caribbean "was often perceived as richly but degenerately tropical, frightening, fecund, even pathological" (201). It is apt that Son would literally shake up Valerian's greenhouse, a microcosm of the main house. Valerian's cyclamens refuse to bloom, and Son explains that the plants need chaos: "Shake it. . . . They just need jacking up."[22] "Flick[ing] the stems hard," Son is met by Valerian's threat, "If they die I'll have Sydney chase you back into the sea" (*Tar Baby*, 148). Though seemingly jocular, Valerian's language returns Son not only to the ship he abandons but on a larger historical scale paints him, a Black man, as a mere commodity, less valuable than Valerian's greenhouse flora. Morrison's prose refers subtly to the commerce of the transatlantic slave trade, as Son's body is deemed disposable, threatened with drowning for a minor infraction. Such language notwithstanding, Son's stealth, both in the Streets' home and in Valerian's greenhouse, indicates that he is not under Valerian's dominion. Despite Valerian's illusion of control over "his" tropical paradise, the island, though colonized, resists in myriad ways, fighting against the artifice of the seasonal homes at every turn.

Morrison seizes on fog, another registry of water, to foreground the natural world as resisting hegemonic control: it is nearly invisible, yet uncontainable and omnipresent. The aggressive destruction of the river and the trees marks Valerian's most dramatic disturbance of the island, but he manifests his disdain for its ecosystem in myriad ways: Valerian has "mongooses shipped to the island to get rid of snakes and rats" (*Tar Baby*, 39), an eradication that has historic parallel; as the Caribbean writer Jamaica Kincaid explains, "Antigua is empty of much wildlife natural to it. When snakes proved a problem for the planters, they imported the mongoose from India" (329).[23] Despite Valerian's colonization of the island, the fog prevails.

Though Valerian wants to create his tropical island home in his own image, he cannot deny that L'Arbe de la Croix, positioned, as it is, "on a hill high enough to watch the sea from three sides" (11), is "situated in the pure sea air" (68) and thus shrouded in fog. The omnipresence of fog within the Streets' mansion is lyrically presented. Fog, liminal, ghostlike, and eerie, is feminized as the hair of maiden aunts:

> Hair so thin and pale it went unnoticed until masses of it gathered around the house and threw back one's own reflection from the window. The sixty-four bulbs in the dining room chandelier were no more than a rhinestone clip in the hair of the maiden aunts. The gray of it, the soil and the swirl of it, was right in the room, moistening the table linen and clouding the wine. Salt crystals clung to each other. Oysters uncurled their fringes and sank to the bottom of the tureen. Patience was difficult to come by in that fuzzy caul and breathing harder still. It was then that the word "island" had meaning. (*Tar Baby*, 62)

One could conjecture that these water figures are another iteration of Mami Wata, which Morrison subtly calls on at the opening of the novel. After all, Mami Wata is known for her flowing hair and, despite her appellation, is childless and participates in a shared mermaid mythology. However, the maiden aunts do not conform to female sirens with sensuous, flowing hair, as Morrison refuses to hypersexualize them. Fog is personified as the maiden aunt's hair—wispy and gray—which counsels against a reading of eroticized sea creatures. Instead Morrison's maternalizes the water as "diaspora mothers" (288) who issue forth African Atlantic history, seething though unvoiced on the island. In this way, fog is the metaphor for what is felt and experienced, ubiquitous but mostly unseen.

Since fog is a cloud of minute water droplets that exists at ground level, it once again presences the water that circumscribes the Caribbean island. What is particularly useful for this reading is the merging of water and air; when air can no longer absorb water, fog forms. Hence it is not an inconspicuous conflation but a fusion of water and air that creates another entity. Fog surfaces as a layered metaphor with multiple referents. Within the Streets' home, fog can be read as the water's refusal to be contained. Despite the alteration of the river into a stagnant swamp, the island's water remains agentic, permeating even the built environment. Given the opulent chandelier's reduction to a mere clip in the hair of the maiden aunts, fog does not simply enter the mansion but presides over it, perpetually making its presence known: "Jadine and Margaret touched their cheeks and temples to dry the places the maiden aunts were kissing"; "The maiden aunts stroked her cheek and she wiped away the dampness their fingers left" (62). Among the many permutations of water, fog is its most ethereal, and its lingering presence haunts the home as it becomes synonymous with bodily moisture.

The fog's corporeal inscription is furthered by Morrison's metaphor of hair. Hair, an image of connectivity, serves to link the human to the nonhuman world and forms a recurring trope of race in *Tar Baby*: Therese disparages Ondine as "machete hair" (104); Jadine's hair, overcome with humidity, is described as a "rain cloud" (64); and the young woman on the island, Alma Estee, is obsessed with an artificial red wig, a white aesthetic commodity that mirrors the blue eyes that murdered Pecola in *The Bluest Eye*: "her sweet face, her midnight skin mocked and destroyed by the pile of synthetic dried blood on her head" (299). Son's hair, a sign of blackness that frightens Jadine, is antithetical to Alma Estee's wig: "His hair looked overpowering—physically overpowering, like bundles of long whips or lashes that could grab her and beat her to jelly. And would. Wild, aggressive, vicious hair that needed to be put in jail. Uncivilized, reform-school hair. Mau Mau, Attica, chain-gang hair" (113). The man "with living hair" is understandably horrified by Alma Estee's wig: "'Oh, baby baby baby baby,' he said, and went to her to take off the wig, to lift it, tear it, throw it far from her midnight skin and antelope eyes. But she jumped back, howled and resecured it on her head with clenched fingers" (299). Hair is a metaphor for ancestral roots, and in this case Alma's hair is literally rootless, unattached to her body and thus to her race.[24] Alma Estee's body is the site of colonization; though physically placed in the Caribbean, she is psychologically displaced.

Juliette Harris and Pamela Johnson begin their anthology *Tenderheaded* with a similar semiotics of African American hair as a symbol of displacement, colonization, and rootlessness:

> Our hair speaks with a voice as soft as cotton. If you listen closely—put your ear right up to it—it will tell you its secrets. Like the soothing peace it knew before being yanked out of Africa. Like the neglect that it endured sweating under rags in the sun-lashed fields of the South. And even today, it speaks of its restless quest for home; a place that must be somewhere between Africa and America, between rambunctious and restrained, and between personally pleasing and socially "acceptable." (xv)

In her attempt to replicate whiteness, Alma Estee falls victim to white consumer culture, which Jadine's body services. The tension that Morrison advances resides in her description of Alma Estee's hair of dried blood competing with her "antelope eyes." Above all, hair constitutes a recurring link between the island's elements—water, flora, trees, and creatures—conveying a complex interweaving of humans and the natural world. Son's hair, rooted and decolonized, is, like the swamp, a matrix of ancestry. Just as the ecoculture of the swamp is resistant to colonization, so Son, the temporary swamp denizen, resists cultural assimilation, as his lifestyle, body aesthetic, and relationships attest.

Son carefully places himself in his surrounding ecosystem: humans, animals, plants, rocks, and water all coalesce in the novel's final pages. Intertwining ecology with culture, and landscape with race, Morrison employs fog, the trope of interconnectivity, in the conclusion. While the ending of the novel has engendered numerous interpretations, many of which center on Jadine and Son's future, it is not the fate of this couple's relationship that is important to my analysis. Rather, the final boat ride—which Peter Erickson avers is "a reenactment of the prologue," in which Therese "guides him through water to the island" (303)—has currency for the textured examination of water, place, and identity that Morrison advances in *Tar Baby*. Son, who believes Therese is taking him to L'Arbe de la Croix to reunite with Jadine, is being led to the hills to join the blind horsemen. Morrison not surprisingly uses water imagery to catalyze his baptism into marronage. Near blind, Therese, the "archetypal earth mother" (Paquet, 508), implores Son to feel the ancestral knowledge that the water offers: "The feel of the current was what she went by" (*Tar Baby*, 303). The sea mist, coupled with the light rain on the rocking boat, puts Son in a trancelike state, "tranquil, dozing, weakly fighting sleep" (304). Commingling water with the embodied self, Son is on the borderland, as his state of consciousness evinces. Like wetlands that straddle earth and water, Son's final destiny cannot be mapped or represented in this concluding scene.

Mobley argues that in the end Son abandons the quest for Jadine and chooses instead a life of marronage: "He ultimately yields to the maternal powers of nature and joins the blind horsemen in the tree-covered hills" (287). Given the legend of the Maroon community on Isle des Chevaliers, it is reasonable to conclude that Son, the temporary swamp dweller, would join this race of men, whose very embodiment is a site of cultural remembering. However, the ending for me remains ambiguous. It is useful to consider that water crossings bracket the novel, and in both instances, Son physically enters water. If we want to read this state of fluidity as an objective correlative of his future, then it is not the fixity and groundedness of the hills that ultimately beckon Son, whose complexion, notably, is "riverbed darkness" (*Tar Baby*,

114). Borderless, water carries evidence of human history; thus Son experiences not merely a baptism of purification in these water crossings but an immersion into cultural pasts.

Reading from this prism, we can reasonably conclude that Son's water journeys portend further voyages, as his cultural knowledge is interwoven with the cycles of water. In this concluding moment, Son's integration with the natural world is such that the trees recognize and honor him: after he leaves the boat, "the mist lifted and the trees stepped back a bit as if to make the way easier" (306). In the novel's final pages, we are immersed in blue: the rain, the ocean, and Son's personal blues, which Therese places inside the larger traumas on the island, imploring Son to resist by joining the horsemen. Water, holding the memory of people, place, displacement, and resistance, is an echo of the transatlantic slave trade, the fundamental sorrow or blues in Morrison's blue ecology.

Like *Tar Baby*, *Love* traffics in liminality. Morrison's eighth novel is set in an East Coast beach town with a resort that, in the first half of the twentieth century, catered to wealthy African Americans. Integration, the civil rights movement, the smell of the nearby cannery, and a hurricane are the many reasons Morrison cites for the closure of Bill Cosey's Hotel and Resort, so that by the 1990s, when the novel takes place, this seaside hotel, while still standing, is long deserted. The nearby town of Up Beach, owing to the hurricane, is "drowned . . . twenty feet underwater" (*Love*, 9), and before the storm, the town was beset by a drought, which left mothers "pumping mud from their spigots" (9). The proprietor of the resort, the self-made millionaire Bill Cosey, is deceased but remains "eerily present" (Mueller, 95) and, arguably, is the novel's central character. Moving between the past and the present, a temporal fracturing bespeaks the novel's overall fluidity. Or, as Stefanie Mueller in *The Presence of the Past in the Novels of Toni Morrison* argues, the "past has come alive" in *Love* (97). That Morrison sets *Love* in a seaside town underscores the ecotonal aspects of place where aquatic and terrestrial frontiers encounter and integrate. This ecosystem becomes an objective correlative of the many ontological collapses in the novel, as *Love* troubles the boundary between past and present, water and land, and brown and blue.

The ecotone is sounded through the repeated tropes of sand and shells. As the authors of *The World's Beaches: A Global Guide to the Science of the Shoreline* explain: "Seashells are . . . important components of the ecosystems of beaches, and the remnants of their skeletons often make up a large part of the sand that is moved about in nature's most dynamic environment. Almost all seashells are made up of calcium carbonate ($CaCO_3$) that has been extracted from seawater" (Pilkey et al., 185). Moreover, the authors of *The Secrets of Sand* elucidate the creation of sand:

> Every grain of sand is a snapshot in time: each originated somewhere and is headed somewhere else. Once mountains are formed, they begin to slowly erode into increasingly smaller fragments due to the forces of the environment. Biogenic sands contain fragments of the hard tissues from marine organisms such as shells, corals, sponges, sea urchins, forams, marine plants, and bryozoans. When these organisms die, the hard tissues that are left behind erode into some of the most spectacular grains of sand imaginable. (Greenberg, Kiely, and Clover, 7)

Seashells—made up, in part, of seawater and biogenic sand containing the remnants of marine organisms—mediate life and death, the terrestrial and the aquatic. Sand and shells are not just confined to the beaches and shorelines in *Love* but scattered throughout the town, underscoring the impossibility of segregating aspects of the natural world. That skeletal remains of shells make up a large part of beach sand allows for a reading of these elements as memory in fossilized form.

L, the mysterious narrator of *Love*, is a spectral presence who muses on the history of place and its inhabitants: It is "odd what oceanfront can do to empty buildings. You can find the prettiest shells right up on the steps, like scattered petals or cameos from a Sunday dress, and you wonder how they got there, so far from the oceans. Hills of sand piling in porch corners and between banister railings are whiter than the beach, and smoother, like twice-sifted flour" (7). The evocative metaphors that Morrison advances in this passage—flour-like sand and shells as delicate as vintage brooches—underscore that these treasures from the ocean are not confined to the beach but are as intimate as domestic wares, woven into the lives of the beachfront community. Indeed, that these elements travel from the shoreline to the doorsteps furthers the connection between natural and built environments and indicates that the beach is not merely adjacent to the homes of the residents but imbricated in their lives.

Using the discourse of color, L, the former cook at Cosey's Hotel and Resort, voices the complex and dynamic environment of the seashore:

> Pale mornings fade into white noons, then by three o'clock the colors are savage enough to scare you. Jade and sapphire waves fight each

> other, kicking up enough foam to wash sheets in. An evening sky behaves as though it's from another planet—one without rules, where the sun can be plum purple if it wants to and clouds can be red as poppies. . . . Foxglove grows waist high around the gazebo, and roses, which all the time hate our soil, rage here, with more thorns than blackberries and weeks of beet red blossoms. (*Love*, 7–8)

The chromatic intensity of the natural world paired with the death of the resort is a stark juxtaposition, especially as L's opening monologue reads more like a lament than an introduction, a narrative gesture reminiscent of *Sula*, where the opening of the novel chronicles a once thriving neighborhood, a kind of community in memoriam. Morrison again draws attention to color, and thus the vegetation in this seaside town is startling, growing heartily in unsuitable conditions, adding to the deep chroma of the landscape and vivifying the juxtaposition of life and decay.

Love is graphic in its representation of sexuality and brutality as Morrison limns human relationships as jarringly as she does the nonhuman world. As the novel opens, two elderly women, childhood friends, but now sworn enemies, are cohabiting in Bill Cosey's mansion, though he has been dead for over twenty years. They occupy the home because each believes that she is the sole inheritor of the estate. Christine is Cosey's granddaughter, and Heed the Night is his widow. Cosey wed Heed when she, the best friend of his granddaughter, was only eleven years old, and the marriage caused the dissolution of the girls' friendship. Time has not softened these enmities, and much of the novel surrounds the complicated dynamics of Heed and Christine's relationship. The will, written on an old hotel menu, bequeathed the house to my "sweet Cosey child," and since Heed called her husband "Papa," the "child" could refer either to his wife or to his granddaughter. The novel is set in motion when a streetwise Junior Viviane answers a job advertisement to perform secretarial work for Heed, which is later revealed to be the forging of a new will to secure control of Cosey's estate. Her presence in the home unearths buried secrets and shared traumas.

When Junior first enters Cosey's decaying mansion, "a marine odor hovered" in the air (*Love*, 19) owing to Christine's preparation of shrimp. Christine's multiple rings "snatched the light from the ceiling fixtures and seemed to elevate her task from drudgery to sorcery" (20), while the "tick of shrimp shell" provides the acoustic backdrop to Junior and Christine's meeting. At this moment, Christine recalls the shore "when the beach was the color of cream but glittery and the sucking waves reached out from water so blue you had to turn away lest it hurt your eyes" (23). The scent of the sea in the domestic space, coupled with the rings as glittery as the ocean waves, unmistakably elides the home and the shore. Morrison highlights the transcorporeal exchange between the beach and the residents: "The crash of the sea is sounding in Christine's ear. She is not close enough to the shore to hear it, so this must be heightened blood pressure" (169). Even small details, such as Heed's small, arthritic hands that resemble "fins" (28), evoke the sea and its creatures.

Just as the shore permeates bodies and domestic spaces, so the specter of Cosey is omnipresent and haunts the home on Monarch Street. Cosey is a complex character, a pedophile who is yet admired by his family and members of his community. The prepubescent Heed comes from an impoverished family: she is a "girl without a nightgown or bathing suit. Who had never used two pieces of flatware to eat. Never knew food to be separated on special plates. Who slept on the floor and bathed on Saturday in a washtub full of the murky water left by her sisters" (75). Cosey's wealth, coupled with Heed's family's ignorance and poverty, allowed him to practically purchase this child bride. Yet Heed, throughout most of the novel, narrates their marriage as a fairy tale and her husband as a savior figure.

Morrison, notably, turns to water to sketch the contours of Cosey and Heed's marriage. An aged Heed, while bathing in the tub, mourns the loss of "skin memory, the body's recollection of pleasure. Of her wedding night, for instance, submerged in water in his arms. Creeping away from the uncomfortable reception, out the back door into the dark, rushing in tuxedo and way-too-big bridal gown across sea grass to powdery sand. Undressing. No penetration. No blood. No eeks of pain or discomfort. Just this man stroking, nursing, bathing her. She arched. He stood behind her, placed his hands behind her knees, and opened her legs to the surf" (*Love*, 76–77). Heed fondly recalls this "bathing," yet a close reading of the scene reveals that what Heed finds pleasurable is not sexual intimacy with her husband but her elision with seawater—waves, wind, and sand:

> Waves are the pulse of the ocean. They are generated by the transfer of energy from the atmosphere to the water, by wind moving over the water's surface toward the shore. The size of a wave depends on how far, how fast, and how long the wind blows. Gentle winds produce ripples and light waves; strong and steady winds blowing over large stretches of open water create chop and large waves. As waves approach the shoreline the waves break and crash, and the friction sets sand grains in motion. This is called the surf zone. (Greenberg, Kiely, and Clover, 61)

Heed attributes the pleasure she receives from the surf zone—the pulse and friction of the waves—to Cosey, but in truth, it is her body's union with the water that is responsible for her wedding night bliss.

The prepubescent Heed participates in a feminized ritual initiating her into the power of the maternal body: "For the ocean currents," according to the pioneering environmentalist Rachel Carson, "are not merely a movement of water; they are a stream of life, carrying always the eggs and young of countless sea creatures" (189). Beyond the current, Morrison situates Heed's ritual in a fecund area, as the biodiversity of this ecotone where two ecosystems meet is "crowded with plants and animals" (Carson, 1). In *The Sea around Us*, Carson elucidates the shoreline's hidden fertility:

> In this difficult world of the shore, life displays its enormous toughness and vitality by occupying almost every conceivable niche. Visibly, it carpets the intertidal rocks; or half hidden, it descends into fissures and crevices, or hides under boulders or lurks in the wet gloom of sea caves. Invisibly, where the casual observer would say there is no life, it lies deep in the sand, in the burrows and tubes and passageways. It tunnels into solid rock and bores into peat and clay. (2)

Human observers may not recognize this generative space, but microscopic and macroscopic life is quietly pulsating throughout the shoreline.

Riding the surf, Heed is in touch with the moon, as this celestial body—along with the sun—is responsible for the rising and falling of tides. The moon, too, has long been associated with women and, specifically, menstrual cycles: "Our word menstruation signifies 'moon change,' *mens* being 'moon.' German peasants call the menstrual period simply 'the moon.' . . . The Mandingo use the word *carro* for both moon and menstruation; in the Congo *njonde* has a similar double meaning" (Harding, 55). Even "Darwin, observing that both moon and menstrual cycles were of twenty-eight days' duration, actually theorized that menstruation was directly related to the action of the moon on the tides and began when we were all sea creatures" (Delaney, Lupton, and Toth, 165). Morrison's association of Heed with the tide on her wedding night arcs toward ancient beliefs casting the moon as an archetypal female symbol, indispensable for growth and imbued with fertilizing power. In fact, folklore insists that the moon's fertility outstrips human intercourse, which only served to create a space for the moonbeams to impregnate women (Harding, 23). It follows, then, that in this moment Heed does not solidify her connection to Cosey but instead recognizes the erotic energy of her own body through its organic relationship to the natural

Shoreline. Credit: Gerry Bishop / Shutterstock.com.

world. Morrison provides additional evidence for this claim as the dying Heed admits to Christine that she wished that she, her best friend, had accompanied her on her honeymoon.

Morrison further signifies on the moon with Celestial, Cosey's longtime lover and the woman to whom he in truth bequeathed all his earthly possessions. Like L, Celestial is a posthumous figure in the novel, and her name is discursively used by a young Heed and Christine as a secret shorthand. The girlfriends are taken by this "sporting woman," whose profile was "etched against the seascape." In their first encounter with Celestial, she does not acknowledge a man's catcall of "Hey Celestial" but turns her gaze to the young girls and "winked at them making their toes clench and curl with happiness" (*Love*, 188). The girls recognize the sexual power of Celestial and incorporate her name into their private idiom. Their refrain of "Hey Celestial" is an acknowledgment of "a particularly bold, smart, risky thing" (*Love*, 188). This phrase, echoed throughout the novel, establishes Morrison's ecofeminist politics, offering a complex layering of the female body, sexuality, the moon, and the seashore.

Heed's connection to the shore—her openness to seawater—can also be read intertextually with Cee's healing ritual in *Home*. As discussed in chapter 2, Cee, in an effort to complete her curative treatment, submits to a "sun smacking," allowing the sun to enter her body. Though initially hesitant, Cee, like Heed, comes to find this union enjoyable. In both instances, Morrison highlights a transcorporeal exchange between elements of the natural world and wounded female bodies, which engenders feelings of pleasure and well-being for the women outside of heterosexual coupling. Interestingly, neither Cee nor Heed ever becomes a mother, or as L elucidates in distinctly aquatic diction: "Heed never gave Cosey a tadpole" (*Love*, 105). Yet their bodies, in these moments, are maternalized, their wombs touched by the more-than-human world. Read from this prism, the first line of *Love*—"The women's legs are spread wide open, so I hum" (3)—takes on additional meaning. L begins her monologue with a lament about the changing sexual mores, yet seen from the angle of Heed's wedding night, it is reasonable to read the women as transcorporeal beings absorbing their environment, sexually and otherwise.

The complex relationship that Morrison advances between Cosey and Heed is, aptly, situated along the shore. The shoreline does not have a static boundary but is drawn and redrawn throughout the day and night. As shifting and changing geographies, shorelines enact the liminality that pervades *Love.* Carson muses on this meeting of marine and terrestrial ecosystems:

> The edge of the sea is a strange and beautiful place. All through the long history of Earth it has been an area of unrest where waves have broken heavily against the land, where the tides have pressed forward over the continents, receded, and then returned. For no two successive days is the shore line precisely the same. . . . Today a little more land may belong to the sea, tomorrow a little less. Always the edge of the sea remains an elusive and indefinable boundary. (1)

Carson's language deftly renders the shoreline, a transition zone that is fluid and shifting, creating an atmosphere of beauty and mystery. In fact, as Drew Hubbell and John Ryan in "Scholarly Ecotones in the Information Landscape" explain: "The term *ecotone*, first used by the plant ecologists Burton Edward Livingston in 1903 and Frederic Clements in 1905, combines two Greek words: *oikos*—meaning 'home' or 'household' and *tonos*—meaning 'tension.'. . . Livingston identifies a 'zone of tension' between biotic communities in his pioneering early twentieth-century writings on plant ecology and physiology" (Hubbell and Ryan, 9).

This zone of tension is an apt descriptor for *Love*, for of all Morrison's novels, *Love* offers, arguably, the most uncomfortable treatment of a character. Bill Cosey is, like the ecotone, rife with paradoxes. In this way, Morrison uses the shoreline not merely as setting but as a metaphor for Cosey and the many lives he touched. He is an enigmatic character who embodied many roles, articulated by the chapter titles: "Portrait," "Friend," "Stranger," "Benefactor," "Lover," "Husband," "Guardian," "Father," and "Phantom." While these are the identifications bestowed on the patriarch, as readers, we bear witness to the nuances, the complexities, and all that is not articulated by these designations. Cosey is as indefinable as the shore, changing with each tide, storm, and relationship, or as L rightly asserts: "You could call him a good bad man, or a bad good man. Depends on what you hold dear—the what or the why. I tend to mix them" (200).

L, too, occupies a liminal world; she straddles the spiritual and the material and is profitably read through the shoreline and its inhabitants. Again I turn to Rachel Carson: "Whenever I go down to this magical zone of the low water of the spring tides, I look for the most delicately beautiful of all the shore's inhabitants—flowers that are not plant but animal, blooming on the threshold of the deeper sea" (3–4). Carson goes on to discuss a type of hydroid that is related to jellyfish, a sea creature whose appearance bestrides flora and fauna. What is useful for my analysis here is the ambiguity of life-forms at the water's edge, their appearance belying their species.

L, in fact, is closely associated with water. Her parents, as she explains, delivered her in a downpour:

> You could say going from womb water straight into rain marked me. It's noteworthy, I suppose, that the first time I saw Mr. Cosey, he was standing in the sea, holding Julia, his wife, in his arms. I was five; he was twenty-four and I'd never seen anything like that. Her eyes were closed, head bobbling; her light blue swimming dress ballooned or flattened out depending on the waves and his strength. She lifted an arm, touched his shoulder. He turned her to his chest and carried her ashore. I believed then it was the sunlight that brought those tears to my eyes—not the sight of all that tenderness coming out of the sea. Nine years later, when I heard he was looking for house help, I ran all the way to his door. (64)

The origin story of L's birth and career begins with water, and notably, she is the character whose voice begins and concludes the novel. Seamlessly moving from L's emergence into the world amid a downpour to her five-year-old self watching Cosey and Julia's intimate immersion in seawater, Morrison eroticizes water. Cynthia Barnett in *Rain* identifies rain as a "love story" inspiring "excitement, longing, and heartbreak" and historicizes the association between rainwater and fertility: "Some cultures made a more literal link between rain and semen; farming couples took to making love in the fields to induce rain. Others sent nude women into the crops to song ribald songs to the rain" (56–57). Pairing L's birth story with her first glimpse of intimate coupling reinforces the elision of water and fecundity. L "believes" it was the sunlight and not the "tenderness coming out of the sea" that is responsible for her connection to Cosey. Morrison elides human activity with the natural world, as L cannot readily discern the source of her emotional reactivity.

What we do know is that she pledges her allegiance to Cosey, working for him throughout her life, yet the last pages of the novel reveal that she is responsible for Cosey's death and the alterations to his will, arguably the two major events around which the story is structured.

L's murder of Cosey is not based on vengeance, jealousy, or hate but couched in a discourse of concern for the women in Cosey's life: "I wasn't going to let him put his family out in the street" (201), referencing the fact that the patriarch had bequeathed all his possessions, save for a fishing boat, to Celestial. L's unexpected murder of Cosey is morally vexing; she commits a crime but does so to protect Heed and Christine. Perhaps not surprisingly, L stopped Cosey's heart with an element of the natural world, foxglove, a plant that continues to grow waist high around the boarded-up hotel.[25]

By the novel's end, Heed and Christine review their past traumas. These aged women end up together in the dark, crowded attic of Cosey's boarded-up hotel. Surrounded by artifacts from the past, they inhabit a space of memory. In this way, Heed and Christine, facing the beachfront, wade through the flotsam and jetsam of their past. The women come to understand that Cosey was the shipwreck in their lives. Before Heed dies,[26] the friends speak with interchangeable voices: "He took all my childhood away from me, girl. He took all of you away from me" (194). After these admissions, the women retreat to fond remembrances of their youth, which centers on the beach; they reminisce about the sky, sun, and sand, a narrative moment that provides relief for the dying Heed.

Morrison begins and ends *Love* with a reference to L's humming; it is the background noise that haunts the novel. L's wordless singing marks an interesting parallel to the acoustics of the beach in a seaside town; the perpetual cadence is often overshadowed by more prominent sounds. L's humming is layered with the music of the sea; after all, there are no boundaries in an ecotone and no barriers or strict lines in the ecological world. L elides with the ocean and is the screen through which *Love* unfolds. An ecotonal reading of *Love* not only provides a paradigm for reimagining place but allows for a rethinking of the politics of boundaries and labels. The ecotone blurs the line between earth and water, and the ecological and the cultural, which is nowhere more evident than in the "See there, what did I tell you?" things that happened on the beach (5). Morrison distills the elusiveness of the shore into the Police-heads, dirty, hat-wearing sea creatures who emerge from the ocean to "harm loose women and eat disobedient children" (5).[27] These ghostlike creatures are looming beach figures that mitigate against reading the sea as merely a safe space for women. While these Police-heads are not gendered as such, that their punishment is only meted out on women and children masculinizes the creatures as regulating patriarchal forces that "police" behavior. With the introduction of the Police-heads, Morrison refuses to pacify readers with a romanticized vision of the sea as solely curative for female characters; rather, the ocean-shore margin remains a vexed space. It is a negotiated area, rife with paradoxes. The edge of the sea, which at first glance appears to function as mere backdrop to *Love*, is an analogue of the liminality that structures and gives meaning to Morrison's blue ecology.

A BLACK AND WHITE ECOLOGY

Plantations and Race Formation in *A Mercy* and *Jazz*

A Mercy, Morrison's ninth novel, occupies an important place in her canon. Set at the close of seventeenth-century colonial America, at the dawn of the slave trade when race was not yet rhetorically constructed as an absolute category, *A Mercy* links nation building to the plantation economy and the creation of race. According to Morrison, she wrote *A Mercy* to explore a time before slavery was identified with race, and thus, as readers, we bear witness to the origins of a black and white racial binary. In turning her attention to the colonies, Morrison examines the artifice of race and in so doing lays bare the myriad ways in which racial categorization is foundational to the building of America. "The deployment of 'race' has virtually always been in service to political agendas" (62), according to Lucius Outlaw in "Towards a Critical Theory of 'Race,'" and so, in the book's conclusion, I bring a black and white ecology to bear, as these colors have become defining categories of identity laden with social and political meanings. In *A Mercy*, Morrison reaches the apotheosis of her environmental vision; this novel offers an ecosystem where people and nature encounter each other, where the origin story of the nation meets America environmentalism. Therefore a black and white ecology is juxtaposed against a polychromatic living world.

Important for this ecocritical analysis, Morrison positions the reader inside a small working farm in Virginia owned by an Anglo-Dutch farmer and landowner, Jacob Vaark, and his mail-order bride from England, Rebekka. Working on the farm are three women of color—Lina, Sorrow, and Florens—and two white male indentured servants, Willard and Scully. Not only does Morrison highlight the instability of race as a category of identity, but she withholds background information about one of the main characters, Sorrow. Sorrow's phenotypical characteristics are provided—skin color and hair texture—but no general label is foisted on her, save for being "mongrelized" (120). Her story gestures to the transatlantic slave trade, as she is associated with the Atlantic Ocean and is the last survivor on a foundering ship, but again, Morrison discloses no information about her nationhood. Florens's skin color is highlighted, especially when she leaves the farm to seek medical assistance for Rebekka. She is confronted by white Puritans who read her skin color as a sign of otherness and malevolence: "Naked under their examination I watch for what is in their eyes. No hate is there or scare or disgust but they are looking at me my body across distances without recognition. Swine look at me with more connection when they raise their heads from the trough" (133). The transcorporeal link between humans and animals is brought to the fore. Morrison speaks back to the rhetoric that dehumanized African Americans by equating people to livestock and instead juxtaposes the swine's sentience with the Puritan community who refuse to regard Florens as a fellow human. In this scene, Florens's skin—not her slave status—is in question: "One woman speaks saying I have never seen any human this black. . . . It is true then says another. The Black Man is among us. This is his minion" (131). This contrasts to Jacob, who early on in the novel takes comfort in the "relative safety of his skin" while traveling at night (11). A black and white ecology is foundational to the New World; it determines social identity and the ability to claim space and agency. Readers in the twenty-first century confront *A Mercy* with full knowledge that the racial binary will soon become codified in language, laws, and customs. After more than two hundred years of the slave trade in the nation, the legacy of a black and white ecology will remain. Outlaw explains: "'Race' continues to function as a critical yardstick for the rank-ordering of racial groups both 'scientifically' and socio-politically, the latter with support from the former. At bottom, then, 'race'—sometimes explicitly, quite often implicitly—continues to be a major fulcrum of struggles over the distribution and exercise of power" (67).

While Vaark's farm is not a plantation per se, the social dynamics and hierarchies of the farm are a microcosm of plantation life: Florens, Sorrow, and Lina are "owned" by Rebekka and Jacob and, as such, are at the mercy of their owners' whims and changing attitudes. In addition to farming, Jacob increases his wealth by lending money. In fact, it is Jacob's collection of the debt owed to him by the Portuguese plantation owner Senhor D'Ortega at the outset of the novel that is the catalyst for his participation in the slave trade. D'Ortega cannot discharge his debt unless Jacob accepts an enslaved person on his plantation. Jacob initially rejects this offer, for he purportedly disdains the slave trade and is repulsed by D'Ortega's life. And yet Jacob is seduced by the grandeur of the estate:

> In spite of himself, [he] envied the house, the gate, the fence. . . . So mighten it be nice to have such a fence to enclose the headstones in his own meadow? And one day, not too far away, to build a house that size on his own property? . . . Not as ornate as D'Ortega's. None of that pagan excess, of course, but fair. And pure, noble even, because it would not be compromised as Jublio [the Ortega plantation] was. (27)

This event shapes the novel in two important ways. It is at this dinner that Jacob agrees to take Florens—notably, at her mother's request—as "payment" for D'Ortega's debt.[1] Further, Jacob's jealousy of D'Ortega's plantation fuels his desire for a plantation house of his own, which is financed by his investment in a Barbadian sugarcane plantation.

Since the "plantation has become synonymous with slavery" (Mack, 1), Morrison turns to this symbol to highlight that the nation's great wealth was achieved, in large part, on the backs of the enslaved. The relationship between nation building and plantations is made explicit in the frontispiece of *A Mercy*, which features a 1690 Virginia map, and in this way, we read the novel through the lens of colonial landownership. In fact, at the outset, Jacob remarks on the settler's appropriation of land and power in the colonies: "In short, 1682 and Virginia was still a mess. Who could keep up with the pitched battles for God, king and land?" (*A Mercy*, 11).

Jacob seeks legitimacy through his plantation home, yet he will occupy this dream home only in death. He contracts smallpox during the construction of the estate, and on his deathbed he asks to die in his newly constructed home: "They hauled him through a cold spring rain. Skirts dragging in mud, shawls asunder, the caps on their head drenched through to the scalp. There was trouble at the gate. They had to lay him in mud while two undid the hinges and then unbolted the door to the house. As rain poured over his face, Rebekka tried to shelter it with her own" (89). The contrast between the grand home, a supposed reflection of Jacob's station, and his final state, filthy and immobile, lays bare the brutality underlying the opulent estate and offers an allegory of the nation itself.

Jacob's participation in the rum trade enables the construction of the home, and yet he insists on maintaining a distance from transatlantic slavery, arguing that "there was a profound difference between the intimacy of slave bodies at Jublio and a remote labor force in Barbados. Right? Right" (35). Jacob's rhetorical question is an attempt to disassociate himself from slave masters like D'Ortega, but the truth is otherwise. Morrison also signals his participation in the slave trade as a violation of the natural world: "That third and presumably final house that Sir insisted on building distorted sunlight and required the death of fifty trees" (43). The distorted sunlight confirms that the large house, built on the back of slavery, violates the natural environment. Given his colloquy with Rebekka, who implores him to rethink the construction, it is clear that his house is not intended to be a home, or a place of family. Morrison inextricably links Jacob's untimely death with his clear-cutting of the forest: "Killing trees in that number, without asking their permission, of course his efforts would stir up malfortune. Sure enough, when the house was close to completion he fell sick with nothing else on his mind" (44). Jacob has lost his connection to the natural world and regards it only as a resource for building his wealth.

Jacob's death after the loss of the trees indicates what may be considered the primary environmental principle, sounded in various ecological treatises, namely, all living organisms are interrelated and interconnected. "Through metaphors such as the biotic pyramid or the Web of Life, ecology has brought us relational categories to understand our connections to others and to the natural world. . . . All living things (and dead things, too) are interwoven into innumerable ecological communities" (Allister, 20). After all, felling that many trees results in the reduction of biodiversity and habitat loss.

Lina, the Native American servant on Vaark's farm, is an environmental steward. As an indigenous person, she is an inheritor of the land: "Other than certain natives, to whom it all belonged, from one year to another any stretch might be claimed by a church, controlled by a Company or become the private property of a royal's gift to a son or a favorite. Since land claims were always fluid, except for notations on bills of sale, he paid scant attention to old or new names of town or forts" (*A Mercy*, 13). In this way, Morrison positions Lina, who "cawed with birds, chatted with plants, spoke to squirrels, sang to the cow and opened her mouth to rain" (48–49), to speak on behalf of the nation and the land. Lina's critique of the plantation home echoes her earlier admonition of the Europeans' desecration of the earth:

> They would forever fence land, ship whole trees to faraway countries, take any woman for quick pleasure, ruin soil, befoul sacred places and worship a dull, unimaginative god. They let their hogs browse the ocean shore turning it into dunes of sand where nothing green can ever grow again. Cut loose from the earth's soul, they insisted on purchase of its soil, and like all orphans they were insatiable. (54)

After this scathing critique, Lina tempers her sweeping admonition of the colonists, excepting Jacob and Rebekka, who initially attempt to live harmoniously with the land. Jacob's land ethics are compromised by his desire for the plantation home. In fact, Jacob, a colonist in the making, articulates his power and his whiteness—that is, his privilege—through his involvement in the plantation, both as investment and as domicile.

In "Blind Memory and Old Resentments: The Plantation Imagination," Michael Harris sheds light on the ongoing national trauma that is embodied in the symbol of the plantation:

> The reality of American life is that the plantation was, and remains, an open sore. It continues to sting and stain the society in which it grew. In 1860 more than forty-six thousand plantations stretched across the South, about twenty-three hundred of which had enslaved workforces of more than one hundred people. Whites in both the North and South were enriched by them; African Americans today cannot separate themselves from them. The term *plantation* encompasses contradictory visions and competing views that are still in contention. (140)

Morrison turns to the plantation as a powerful symbol of the nation and its brutal history. Lina's assessment that Jacob's estate is a "profane monument to himself" (*A Mercy*, 44) is revelatory of plantations, which were modeled on the plantation home as the epicenter of power and control. Plantations stand as reminders of white privilege, the slave trade, and unsustainable farming practices. As discussed in chapter 2, plantations trafficked in monocrop farming of cash crops—sugarcane, cotton, indigo, coffee—a practice that exhausts the soil, leaving it weak and unsustainable for healthy plant growth.

Morrison also gives voice to the plantation in *Jazz*, evocatively presenting a black and white ecology in the early stages of Joe and Violet's relationship. The two meet in Virginia under a black walnut tree: Violet takes shelter under the tree at night, and Joe sleeps in its branches. Joe falls from the tree near Violet, and thus begins their courtship: "Violet always believed that because their first conversation began in the dark (when neither could see much more of the other than silhouette) and ended in a green-and-white dawn, nighttime was never the same for her" (104). Shades of darkness surround the couple—the dark of the night sky, the shadowed outlines of forms, and their own silhouettes—which give way to the white of dawn, an illumination that, aptly, reveals the white borders of their nighttime shelter in the forest to be acres of cotton. Indeed, Joe and Violet wake to "dazzling acres of white cotton against the gash of a ruby horizon" (105). Morrison presents the plant as dominating the physical and social landscape of Palestine, Virginia:

> Three double seasons in a row of bad weather had ruined all expectations and then came the day when the blossoms jumped out fat and creamy. Everybody held his breath while the landowner squinted his eyes and spat. His two black laborers walked the rows, touching the tender flowers, fingering the soil and trying to puzzle out the sky. Then one day of light, fresh rain, four dry, hot and clear, and all of Palestine was downy with the cleanest cotton they'd ever seen. Softer than silk, and out so fast the weevils, having abandoned the fields years ago, had no time to get back. Three weeks. It all had to be done in three weeks or less. Everybody with fingers in a twenty-mile radius showed up and was hired on the spot. (*Jazz*, 102)

I quote this passage at some length because it illustrates the ways in which the human sphere is inextricably linked to the ecological world. The community's livelihood depends on the plant's survival and success. It is not the plantation owner who reads the land, the cotton flowers, and the weather, but the "black laborers" who walk the rows, touch the soil, and puzzle out the sky. In short, the plantation owner recognizes the botanical knowledge of these Black male horticulturalists, who, though not named as such, have deep agricultural acumen. Even with this ecological wisdom, they cannot fully control the plant's success; Morrison goes on to describe the ideal weather conditions that make cultivation of the cotton crop possible, showing, again, humans' relationship to the living world.

Finally, though this incident took place in the early 1900s, more than three decades after the Emancipation Proclamation, Morrison's inclusion of cotton in a novel that primarily engages with the cityscape of New York in the 1920s gestures to slavery and the plant's enormous role in altering Black lives, a reality that continues to affect Joe and Violet. Though the rise of cotton came in the later years of the slave trade, it changed the landscape of the nation, both ecologically and socially. According to Gates, cotton plantations were created from Georgia to New Mexico, and given Great Britain's desire for textiles and Eli Whitney's invention of the cotton gin, the need for labor increased greatly. As a result, hordes of enslaved African Americans were pressed into the service of cotton. People were sold in droves to meet this increased agricultural need, and thus cotton is layered with trauma. It should be noted, too, that, as in *A Mercy*, Native American villages were destroyed,

Cotton field. Credit: Megan Betteridge / Shutterstock.com.

and forests were decimated and replaced with more and more cotton plantations, as there were enormous profits to be made. Therefore Morrison's description of the "county erupt[ing] in fat white cotton balls" (175) speaks to the transmogrification of the nation's landscape, a history that undergirds a black and white ecology.

According to Michael Harris, "For many African Americans in the twentieth century, cotton, plantations, lynching, the Klan, and segregation seemed to overlap as a series of related tropes signifying oppression and exclusion" (144). Indeed, Professor Emeritus John E. Dowell's 2018 exhibit *Cotton: The Soft, Dangerous Beauty of the Past* at the African American Museum in Philadelphia sheds light on the plantation as a site where slavery, agriculture, beauty, and the ongoing trauma of racism converge, and thus elucidates Morrison's evocation of the plantation in *A Mercy* and *Jazz*. Dowell's exhibit, consisting of photography, printmaking, and interactive installations, showcases panoramic shots of cotton fields, images of cotton superimposed onto unexplored sites of African American history, and an "altarpiece" that includes baskets of cotton bolls for visitors to handle, allowing a tangible engagement with the plant. Dowell's exhibit offers a powerful aesthetic presentation of the tenets of African American material ecocriticism insofar as cotton, a crop that legions of enslaved peoples worked, is "a symbol for the black body and the actual places [black bodies occupied]" (quoted in

Glasper), an elision of people, place, and plants that provides another registry of a black and white ecology.

In turning to such large-scale images of cotton, Dowell surrounds visitors in whiteness. The photos are hung at eye level, immersing viewers in cotton. This white-dominated color palette creates an overwhelming visceral experience that gestures toward the enormity of King Cotton in the American landscape, an engine of our economy, on which the nation was built. It also has particular resonance for the artist. Dowell recounts a story about his grandmother, who, as a young child, became lost in cotton fields and, by the time she found her way out, was bloodied by the plant's sharp edges and brittle leaves.

Red, then, becomes part of this black and white schema, since "trying to pluck the soft bolls quickly from their pointy, sharp-edged shells inevitably bloodies fingers, hands, and arms" (Forsythe), a clear metonym of the wounds of slavery. In this exhibit, Dowell powerfully explicates that the cotton plant is history, is the Black body, is the plantation, and is our past. Indeed, according to Carney in *In the Shadow of Slavery: Africa's Botanical Legacy in the Atlantic World*, "agriculture shaped the lives of the majority of Africans in America" (81)

Morrison likewise regards the plantation as a loaded symbol of history, and at the end of *A Mercy*, she stages an intervention in the plantation narrative. The white male homeowner is dead, having never lived in the plantation house, and the three women of color inhabit the home, despite protests from Rebekka. This is not an easy cohabitation; after all, Lina "finds horror in this house" (*A Mercy*, 161), yet Florens claims the home not only as shelter but as a text on which to inscribe her trauma.

That Florens writes with a nail—a metaphorical instrument of home and nation building—suggests an alternative mapping of space and place. According to Lindsay Christopher in "The Geographical Imagination in Toni Morrison's *Paradise*," "The term geography itself means earth writing or earth describing, a practice many literary critics are beginning to recognize as a rhetorical cousin to writing" (89). Florens's cartography is a refutation of imperial maps, which, in effect, authorized the world to be divided and claimed: "During the Age of Discovery, new lands were drawn as unoccupied, unowned property waiting to be made productive" (Christopher, 90). Home is contested terrain in *A Mercy*, with landownership marked by power and violence. Lina's story of the eagle is an allegory of the colonist's desire to reshape and rename geography by violently claiming dominion over land. The eagle builds a nest to lay her eggs far from the harm of natural predators, but there is "one thing she cannot defend against: the evil thoughts of man" (62). The "traveler" who comes to this country claims ownership over the land, saying, "This is perfect. This is mine" (62). The echo of the traveler's words, "Mine. Mine. Mine" (62), reverberates across the land. Such ownership is confounding; the traveler's words are "strange, meaningless [and] incomprehensible." The destruction of life is both immediate—the eggs "quiver" and "crack," and the eagle is beaten by the traveler's stick—and long term, as Lina explains that the injured mother eagle continues to scream in her suffering: "she is falling forever" (62). The implications of the traveler's story are such that Morrison presents a colonial nation defined by property ownership. On his way to the D'Ortega plantation, Jacob muses about colonial power and land control:

> He knew the landscape intimately from years ago when it was still the old Swedish Nation and, later, when he was an agent for the Company. Still later when the Dutch took control. During and after that contest, there had never been much point in knowing who claimed this or that terrain; this or another outpost. . . . In such ad hoc territory, Jacob simply knew that when he came out of that forest of pine skirting the marshes, he was, at last, in Maryland which, at the moment, belonged to the king. Entirely. (12–13)

Colonies are rendered not as self-governed but rather as an extension of the land claims of the controlling colonial power. In this way, the land and those who inhabit it are not autonomous but subject to imperial rule, tenuous, and contested. Indeed, Lina's story features not a resident but merely a traveler.

Florens's narrative, sprawling, spiraling, defying geographic borders and boundaries, is a metaphor for the establishment of home for those who were denied property rights, landownership, and even citizenship. Through Florens, Morrison imagines other narratives, other maps in spaces that have been claimed, made explicit in Jacob's plantation home.

RACE, ASH, AND RAINBOWS: A CODA

Florens's words fashion a "talking room" (161), engraved, as they are, on the walls and floorboards. They are not stagnant in the plantation home but enter the ecological world: "Perhaps these words need the air that is out in the world. Need to fly up then fall, fall like ash over acres of primrose and mallow. Over a turquoise lake, beyond the eternal hemlocks, through clouds cut by rainbow and flavor the soil of the earth" (*A Mercy*, 161). The imagery

Morrison turns to in the closing pages of *A Mercy*—soil, ash, and rainbows—encapsulates her ecocritical vision. "Flavoring the soil," Florens's words are embedded in the dirt; they are the bedrock of America's origin story and the terra firma of our nation. Morrison insists that American environmentalism must take into account genocide and slavery; the soil, after all, is redolent with these narratives. Indeed, even as Florens writes this story, she knows that she will soon be "sold."

These counternarratives of the New World inscribed in the earth merge with the rainbow, thereby complicating a black and white ecology. In fact, the color spectrum is a productive site of inquiry into Morrison's fiction. As I discussed in the introduction, Pilate conceives of blackness as a rainbow, a multihued richness that is evocative of St. Clair's description of black as "expansive and capacious . . . and complicated" (261). Morrison also turns to the rainbow to limn Pauline and Cholly's relationship in *The Bluest Eye*. Lest the reader believe that Morrison only paints a dynamic chromatic picture of the couple's courtship, she returns to the same discourse to describe their marriage, before their relationship dissolves, before they are inculcated into destructive ideologies of whiteness in Lorain, Ohio. The omniscient narrator proclaims simply and without hesitation that "Pauline and Cholly loved each other" (115) and depicts that sensuality through a rhetoric of color and the natural world. In describing her sexual activity with Cholly, Pauline muses: "I begin to feel those little bits of color floating up into me—deep in me. That streak of green from the june-bug light, the purple from the berries trickling along my thighs, Mama's lemonade yellow runs sweet in me. Then I feel like I'm laughing between my legs, and the laughing gets all mixed up with the colors. . . . It be rainbow all inside" (131). Later, after the dissolution of their marriage, Pauline, who claims that she "don't care 'bout it no more," submits that the "only thing I miss sometimes is that rainbow" (131). Morrison's description of Pauline as a body infused with color is resonant with the wildlife ecologist J. Drew Lanham's description of the self in *The Home Place: Memoirs of a Colored Man's Love Affair with Nature*. Identifying as a "man of color," Lanham begins by describing his racial and ethnic origins (African American, Native American, British, Irish, etc.), but he quickly elucidates that his multihued identity largely consists of the natural world: "But that's only part of the whole. There is also the red of miry clay, plowed up and planted to pass a legacy forward. There is the brown of spring floods rushing over a Savannah River shoal. There is the gold of ripening tobacco drying in the heat of summer's last breath. There are endless rows of cotton's cloudy white. My plumage is a kaleidoscopic rainbow of an eternal hope and the deepest blue of despair and darkness. All of these hues are me: I am, in the deepest sense,

Double rainbow and a field of dandelions. Credit: Aleksandr Ozerov / Shutterstock.com.

colored" (4). Lanham's poetic description of the self as a richly saturated canvas of colors drawn from the human and the more-than-human world provides a paradigm for reading Pauline's prismatic identity. Both Lanham and Morrison draw deeply from the exigencies of their African American heritage but complicate pigmentation as the sole maker of meaning. They disclose the many ways in which they are imprinted with the living world, resulting in a polychromatic selfhood, or, in Lanham's words, a "kaleidoscopic rainbow."

Jeffrey Cohen, in "Ecology's Rainbow," sheds light on this meteorological phenomenon involving a spectrum of light and human visual perception:

> This ethereal spectrum shimmers when a tumble of raindrops refracts and reflects daylight back to an observer at an angle of 42 degrees. For the sun's white brilliance to separate into its constituent colors, its rays must arrive from directly behind the perceiver. . . . The celestial band of hues shimmers through a particular biology without which it cannot exist. A rainbow forms when the organic and inorganic, eye and sunlight, matter and energy are brought into a sudden relation that changes the quality of light itself. (xxv, xxvi)

Put simply, Philip Fisher in *Wonder, the Rainbow, and the Aesthetics of Rare Experiences* maintains that "without observers there are no rainbows" (quoted in Cohen, xxvi). That humans, refracted light, and water work in tandem to produce a rainbow's ethereal colors bespeaks the tenets of material ecocriticism. In aligning the evanescent beauty of this phenomenon with her characters, Morrison negotiates the terrain of the living world. Whether in Pilate's philosophical treatise on blackness, "You think dark is just one color, but it ain't. . . . May as well be a rainbow" (40), or in Pauline's poetic musing on her body's sensuality, "It be rainbow all inside," or in *A Mercy*, where the rainbow is inflected by a Black woman's story, Morrison turns to this spectrum of light to convey her polychromatic environmental vision. Material ecocriticism maintains that the boundaries of the body are not closed but porous and open to the nonhuman world. Thus Morrison's characters do not merely perceive this arc of color from a distance; rather, they are materially enmeshed with the rainbow. After all, Pauline carries the rainbow inside her body, and the rainbow holds Florens's pain. Such racial and ecological entanglements are endemic to Morrison's canon.

In *Jazz*, Morrison again pairs the rainbow with race. Golden Gray, who is biracial, journeys to locate his African American father, Henry Lestory. Finding an empty home, Golden Gray waits for his arrival. A neighbor, Honor, recalls the incident thus:

> It rained all morning. Sheets of it made afternoon rainbows everywhere. Later he told his mother that the whole cabin was rainbowed and when the man came out the door, and Honor looked at his wet yellow hair and creamy skin, he thought a ghost had taken over the place. Then he realized that he was looking at a whiteman and never believed otherwise, even though he saw Mr. Henry's face when the whiteman told him he was his son. (168)

This scene is chromatically rich, as Honor beholds a white man with the face of a Black man and does so through the lens of the rainbow. To highlight the instability of race and color, Morrison explains that there were "rainbows everywhere," and even the cabin was "rainbowed," indicating that prismatic colors are not confined to the heavens—or even to the ecological world—but enter the home and change its complexion, a multihued coloring related to this temporary inhabitant. In fact, his name discloses his ambiguous coloring: he is both gold and gray, being neither "black" nor "white," descriptors that, in reality, do not adequately match skin pigmentation but only serve power and social hierarchy.

Though the spectrum of light comes from nature—it is materially present—its divisions are artificial, bringing into relief the constructedness of sight. The way we observe the rainbow and name it is culturally mediated, thus providing a salient metaphor for Morrison's environmental and racial politics. In *A Mercy*, the boundary between the human and the nonhuman dissolves as the multihued beauty of this optical phenomenon merges with the ash: Lina's burned village, the colonization of America, and the trans-atlantic slave trade. The interdependence between people and the natural world is such that throughout Morrison's canon, the author directs our gaze to the primrose fields, the turquoise lake, and the eternal hemlock trees, that is, to the beauty that surrounds us. Yet such splendor is inseparable from the history of the African diaspora, as mapped onto the living world. In that way, Morrison insists that black is always a color of the rainbow.

NOTES

PREFACE

1. Bennett Graves, email correspondence with the author, August 30, 2019.
2. Chloe Bell, email correspondence with the author, August 9, 2019.

INTRODUCTION. "ALL OF THEM COLORS WAS IN ME": EMBODIMENT AND MATERIAL ECOCRITICISM

1. Although few, there have been important ecocritical studies of African American literature. One of the earliest and most significant works that considers the African American environmental imagination is Melvin Dixon's *Ride Out the Wilderness*. Examining the intractable relationship between geography and identity performance, Dixon considers culturally salient tropes of the biotic world—wilderness, valleys, mountains—that frequently recur in spirituals and literary texts. More recently Kimberly Ruffin in *Black on Earth* argues that African Americans were ecological agents before the beginning of the American nature writing tradition. Further, Camille Dungy's recently edited collection, *Black Nature: Four Centuries of African American Nature Poetry*, showcases the long history of African American writers' engagement with the living world.

2. This spurious natural discourse that held that racial features were malleable and had to be kept in check does not mean that skin color, from an evolutionary standpoint, was disconnected from place. Melanin is linked to geography. According to Jablonski in *Skin: A Natural History*, "This exquisite sepia rainbow shades from darkest near the equator to the lightest near the poles. This range forms a natural cline, or gradient, that is related primarily to the intensity of the ultraviolet radiation (UVR) that falls on the different latitudes of the earth's surface" (3).

1. BROWN ECOLOGY AND FERTILITY: SKIN, DIRT, AND COMPOST IN *PARADISE* AND *THE BLUEST EYE*

1. Morrison maintains that *Paradise* is a meditation on the love of God, and thus an environmental approach may seem tangential to the larger themes; however, the words

of Lone, the novel's midwife, give credence to such a reading: "You need what we all need: earth, air, water. Don't separate God from His elements. He created it all. You stuck on dividing Him from His works. Don't unbalance His world" (244). Lone explains that God *is* the biotic world embodied in—and materialized through—the elements of earth, air, and water, and thus an ecocritical reading of *Paradise* offers a nuanced examination of spirituality and the biophysical world.

2. This chapter builds on previous scholarly work on *Paradise*, such as Melanie Anderson's *Spectrality in the Novels of Toni Morrison*, in which she reads the Convent and its spiritual mother as "situated on the border between life and death and past and present" (88). Reading as an ecocritic, I too am interested in troubling the borderland in *Paradise*, but specifically in terms of understanding the transmogrification of dead material into new life, hence my focus on compost.

3. Some residents claim that the couple is not heterosexual but "two women making love in the dirt," again eliding women with soil.

4. Though Gigi never locates the rock couple, she meets a man on the bus who tells her about embracing trees that, unlike the rock couple that engages in its own sexual fulfillment, provide human ecstasy: "He once heard about a place where there was a lake in the middle of a wheat field. And that near this lake two trees grew in each other's arms. And if you squeezed in between them in just the right way, well you would feel an ecstasy no human could invent or duplicate" (66). While we have no confirmation that the rock couple exists, the intertwined fig trees are mentioned in Deek and Connie's affair. In this instance, the couple's sexual fulfillment is mirrored in the biotic world, highlighting the erotic nature of biota. After all, all living species reproduce.

5. A secondary usage of root cellars is to warehouse wine and other alcoholic beverages, which are also housed in the Convent's basement.

6. According to Westmacott in *African-American Gardens and Yards in the Rural South*, "Almost all the gardeners felt that rainfall was God's will and that He would send it in His own good time" (95).

7. Louis Pasteur finally disproved the theory of spontaneous generation in 1859.

8. This is not the first time Morrison's portmortem characters grow and age. The crawling- already baby in *Beloved* does not stay a baby but matures in death, taking on the shape of a young woman, and later transforms into a pregnant woman.

9. Haraway defines human exceptionalism as "the premise that humanity alone is not a spatial and temporal web of interspecies dependencies" (11).

10. That Morrison employs seasons as a rhetorical device in *The Bluest Eye* is apt, because the word "season" comes from the Latin word "to sow," which underscores the importance of human engagement with plants throughout the novel.

11. Pecola repeatedly tries to escape her body and "disappear." After she is bullied by the children at school, Pecola "tucked her head in. . . . A kind of hunching of the shoulders, pulling in of the neck, as though she wanted to cover her ears" (72); she later "folded into herself, like a pleated wing," and after her encounter with Geraldine, she backs slowly out of the room, with her "head down against the cold" (93).

12. Mrs. MacTeer takes pity on Pecola because her father "burned up his house, gone upside on his wife's head, and everybody, as a result, was outdoors" (17). Cholly burned down the family's domestic space, destroying even the veneer of home, for it was merely a

shell in which the family replayed societal traumas, enacting wounds that foreclosed the ability to experience a safe interior space.

13. Although Soaphead Church acquires his nickname based on the texture of his hair, it is reasonable to conclude that the name also underscores his obsession with cleanliness; in metaphorically "cleaning" his hair, he attempts to eradicate a racial phenotype.

14. This is not to suggest that the natural world is an environmental refuge for the children in the novel. As Claudia remarks, "Even now spring for me is shot through with the remembered ache of switchings, and forsythia holds no cheer." As a child, Claudia learns to associate springtime with a change in the style of whipping, for in place of the "dull pain of a winter strap" or "the firm but honest slap of a hairbrush" comes the sting of the new green switches, a sting that lasts "long after" the whipping is over (97). The seasons are manipulated by the adult world, used, as they are, for brutal enactments against the children. The girls see themselves as part of the more-than-human world and the living world as part of society.

15. The pairing of garbage workers and the violation of African Americans' human rights is seared in our national consciousness, as Martin Luther King Jr. was killed while supporting the sanitation workers' strike in Memphis, Tennessee, in 1968. The unsafe working conditions were brutally illustrated when two men were crushed by garbage packing machinery. In recognizing that sanitation workers were equated with the garbage that they hauled, the workers went on strike, bearing signs that read "I Am a Man." Fighting against dangerous work conditions, the workers were fighting to be seen as more than trash.

16. Milkweed was used to treat asthma and suppress coughs.

2. GREEN ECOLOGY AND HEALING: BOTANICAL LIFE IN *BELOVED*, *HOME*, AND *SONG OF SOLOMON*

1. From a chromatic perspective, chlorophyll is not really "green"; rather, it absorbs the light most strongly in the blue and red portions of the electromagnetic spectrum but does not absorb green. This is another example of subtractive color, which I discussed in the introduction.

2. Our breath, though invisible, has material consequences. Take, for example, the Lascaux cave paintings in France, which were painted at the end of the Ice Age and depict "horses and stags, bison, and even a bear. And in the center, on the ceiling . . . was a huge bull, 17 feet long. These paintings were so real, they almost seemed to be breathing" (Finlay, *Brilliant History*, 11). Once the cave opened for public viewing, the colors that had been preserved for "so many thousands of years became almost invisible in just 20," largely owing to the breath of the visitors (9). Estimates suggest that nearly 400,000 visitors arrived annually to see the cave art. As Finlay remarks, "This is another element of the history of colors in art: they are there, and then they go. They do not stay the same, and when you look at a painting, you're always, in a tiny way, changing it" (11). The interaction of breath, color, and plant material suggests the porosity of the physical world and sheds light on the ways in which we are always interacting with and altering our environment.

3. Linnaeus, who cataloged life-forms, also established an ethnocentric categorization of humans into races and paved the way for scientific racism.

4. The exception here is the scholarship that has been done on trees in *Beloved*. Reading as an ecocritic, I build on this insightful work by considering trees not only metaphorically but materially as part of the ecosystem.

5. It is likely that Ma'am used herbal abortifacients, highlighting again her connection to the plant world.

6. Without the mother to provide the steady heartbeat—through the body and her agricultural work—Sethe is motherless, a condition she will not allow her children to endure.

7. While plants do not have sight as humans do, they have the same photoreceptor proteins all over their bodies that people have in the back of their retinas.

8. There is a current trend for trees to move westward. Since 1980, about three-fourths of trees species found in eastern forests have shifted their populations to the West. More than half are also moving north. Climate change and wetter conditions are the main hypothesis to explain this shift (Meyer). While trees are incapable of uprooting and migrating, their saplings are moving, which suggests that plants are not stationary but agentic, living entities.

9. Sethe's sycamore could be labeled a "witness tree," because it witnessed historical events from the nation's past and can therefore be read as a historical text. This is especially poignant of the sycamore tree, which is known for its longevity. A number of trees still stand as a testament to our nation's tragic past, and often they are the only living witness to that past.

10. In this way, *Beloved* is a refutation of "plant blindness," which is defined as the inability to see or notice the plants in one's own environment, leading to the inability to recognize the importance of plants in the biosphere and in human affairs. Whether biological or social, the floral world often does not occupy the same level of human concern as the faunal world. In fact, although 57 percent of the endangered species in the United States are plants, they receive less than 4 percent of endangered-species funding. *Conservation: The Source for Environmental Intelligence*, August 31, 2016, http://www.conservationmagazine.org/2016/08/plant-blindness.

11. This evocative scene has rightly engendered important critical conversations. Most important among them is Michele Bonnet's "To Take the Sin Out of Slicing Trees," which offers an insightful analysis of trees as symbols of life, regeneration, and religion in *Beloved*.

12. Deforestation continues to provoke major environmental crises and drive climate change. Nearly 80 percent of land animals and plants live in the forest, and thus the loss of these habitats is threatening life on Earth. According to *Dirt! The Movie*, 100 million trees are felled annually and turned into twenty billion mail order catalogs.

13. It is also important to note that species diversification is essential to forest health. Forests regenerate when a diversity of species, genes, and genotypes is present.

14. While Bonnet is right to assert that Morrison only uses the term "sin" to describe the sawyer's work, and not, for example, Sethe's infanticide, it is important to note the myriad associations Morrison makes between logging and Sethe's murder of the crawling-already baby. Sethe believes that she and her children will be "cut down" by

Schoolteacher, that is, returned to Sweet Home plantation, and thus she takes her children to the woodshed, cuts her daughter's throat with a saw, and her boys, catatonic, lie bleeding in the sawdust (149). Here Morrison's arboreal imagery invites a parallel reading of the sawyer and Sethe.

15. Bonnet reminds the reader that "trees, and in particular sacred groves, play a crucial role in African religion, where they are considered as intermediaries between God and man—they are even worshiped by some tribes as God himself" (42).

16. The first flowering plant is believed to be the *Archaefructus sinensis*, and the fossil slabs that contained these flowers also contained the fossils of small fish, leading researchers to believe that these plants may have been aquatic or semiaquatic, "growing in shallow lakes, extending their leaves, thin stems, and flowers above the water's surface" (Buchmann, 26). That Morrison analogizes Sethe's birth to the spores of the bluefern hovering in the water nods to the history of flowering plants and their growth in water, an origin story of flowers and humans.

17. Ferns belong to an ancient group of plants that developed before flowering plants, and they do not produce flowers and therefore do not produce seeds. They reproduce, instead, by spores. This group of seedless plants, known as cryptogams, also includes mosses, algae, fungi, and lichens.

18. The geobiologist Hope Jahren explains that seeds are "just food to sustain a waiting embryo. The embryo is a collection of only a few hundred cells, but it is a working blueprint for a real plant with root and shoot already formed" (70). Jahren's language brings to the fore the fertility of this scene, but given that the vast majority of seeds will not survive ("Of the many million seeds dropped on every acre of the Earth's surface each year, less than 5 percent will begin to grow. Of those, only 5 percent will survive to their first birthday" [Jahren, 500]), it follows that the bluefern's survival in the Ohio River is unlikely.

19. Crawford's insistence on claiming home is in keeping with a worldview shared by many African Americans. A Freedman Bureau official who worked in the postbellum plantation districts remarked that African Americans were a "remarkably permanent people. They love to stay in one place, where they have always lived, where they were born and where their children are buried" (M. Stewart, 16–17). This sentiment points to a vision of the land that is sacralized by those who have lived there and those who are interred in the soil.

20. Although Guitar is the perpetrator in this scene of violence, he and his family (recent southern migrants) are marked throughout the novel as victims of racial and economic oppression. Traumatized by the heinous death of his father, Guitar's entire life is constructed in response to this crime. His manic desire for the gold is motivated largely by his work in the Seven Days. He also expresses his desire to purchase a headstone for his father's grave. While the two acts are seemingly disparate, it is useful to recall Guitar's earlier explanation of the Seven Days to Milkman: "What I'm doing ain't about hating white people. It's about loving us. About loving you. My whole life is love" (*Song*, 159). Although his work in the Seven Days may be considered a misguided response to racism, and his desire to mark his father's life a more obvious show of love and honor, Morrison conflates these acts as Guitar's homage to his father's memory.

21. Here I borrow from Derek Walcott's poem "The Sea Is History."

3. ORANGE ECOLOGY, DEATH, AND RENEWAL: FIRE, ASH, AND IMMOLATION IN *GOD HELP THE CHILD* AND *SULA*

1. In Morrison's fiction, it is young girls who are marked as "other" by their darker complexion. This societal punishment is fruitfully read alongside scientific discoveries that have found that women, in all societies, tend to have lighter skin than men. Scientists have proposed many hypotheses for this biological difference. Some have speculated that childbearing women need to absorb more vitamin D in their diets. Others believe that women's fairer skin is based on an evolutionary need for women to mimic babies to garner some of the same protection afforded to the young in a given society (Jablonski, 88). Regardless of the veracity of these claims, the fact that females tend to be lighter provides another layer of context for the virulent forms of racialized abuse that both Pecola and Bride suffer. In other words, their maltreatment occurs at the nexus of race and gender.

2. On the one hand, we see markers of an ecologically sound disposal of Queen's body; on the other, the Environmental Protection Agency has "has raised concerns about air pollution from cremations" (Stowe, Vernon-Schmidt, and Green, 1817).

3. That Booker could not find a color that matches the fading radiance of the sun is in line with many visual artists who claim that synthetic paints are incapable of capturing the depth and breadth of our multihued natural world. The mycologist and botanical illustrator Mary Banning, for example, in referencing the glowing colors of fungi, remarked: "I invite the careful observation of the skeptical and they will find that their paint boxes hardly afford pigments bright enough to sketch those beauties of the woods" (quoted in Eckstut and Eckstut, 139).

4. One of the chapter titles in *Sula* is "1921."

4. BLUE ECOLOGY AND RESISTANCE: ISLANDS, SWAMPS, AND ECOTONES IN *TAR BABY* AND *LOVE*

1. It is the edge or margin of the swamp that is particularly elusive. In fact, the "government's guide to finding the edge of a swamp is fifty pages long, complete with graphs and soil maps you need a magnifying glass to decipher" (Hurd, 69). After enrolling in a weeklong seminar to learn to delineate wetlands, Hurd comes to the realization that "a liquid landscape cannot be nailed down with maps and charts, any more than love can be understood as the biochemical action of pheromones" (69).

2. The majority of narratives use the terms "swamps" and "the woods" to signify uncharted landscapes in which African Americans retreated for safety; bayous are occasionally used in similar ways.

3. As Mathe-Shires explains, "The name malaria, meaning bad air, originated in Italy. The term's first usage dates back to the 1740s when the English traveler, Horace Walpole, was describing some fever-like incident around Rome" (3).

4. It is difficult to overstate the import of wetlands as an ecosystem: "Wetlands are sometimes described as the 'kidneys of the landscape,' because they function as the downstream receivers of water and waste from both natural and human sources. They

stabilize water supplies, thus ameliorating both floods and drought. They have been found to cleanse polluted water, protect shorelines, and recharge groundwater aquifers" (Mitsch and Gosselink, 3).

5. Significantly, Ondine spends her nights dreaming of water: "Ondine dreaming of sliding into water, frightened that her heavy legs and swollen ankles will sink her" (61). Ondine's water dream is apt, given the Streets' complicated positioning in the home. She dreams of the water, and the succor it offers, but because she is steeped in the Streets' ideology, she does not give herself over to ancestral waters, believing she would drown in their current.

6. Morrison's embodiment of trees as a critique of colonization recalls Charles Chesnutt's short story "Po' Sandy," in which Sandy, enslaved, is turned into a pine tree so that he may stay near to his wife, Tenie. However, the tree is eventually felled, and Myers argues, "the sound of the tree's 'sweekin', en moanin', and groaning' is a living cry of outrage over the devastation wreaked on the bodies of slaves and the body of nature" (16). Likewise, Alice Walker describes logging in the hills of California as a death: "Each day on the highway, as I went to buy groceries or to the river to swim, I saw the loggers' trucks, like enormous hearses, carrying the battered bodies of the old sisters and brothers, as I thought of them, down to the lumberyards in the valley" (*Living by the Word*, 141).

7. As Tiffin reminds us, it is a misnomer to claim that island residents are indigenous: "In the Caribbean, with the exception of the Caribs and Arawaks, all present-day populations are to some degree in ancestral exile, whether they be descendants of European settlers, Africans kidnapped into slavery, or the Chinese and Indian indentured laborers who followed slavery's abolition in the 1830s" (199). I am using the term loosely to differentiate between residents whose ancestry is tied to the island for centuries (like the race of blind horsemen) and the Euro-American newcomers, like the Streets. The Streets, as their name implies, are conflated with the man-made world, a built environment that they carry with them and impose on this island community.

8. Ryan asserts that *Tar Baby* offers an ecological critique of the "European/Euro-American capitalist apparatus that has unleashed a cycle of destruction on nature which we have only now come to acknowledge, amid the life-threatening realities of acid rain, ozone depletion, toxic waste, the contamination of lakes, rivers and oceans, etc." (73). Throughout, we find a lament on the state of the environment. Water crises are one of Michael's long-standing social complaints (*Tar Baby*, 77), but the most trenchant critique of environmental destruction is voiced by Son, the man who regards the sky as "holy": "From Micronesia to Liverpool, from Kentucky to Dresden, they killed everything they touched including their own coastlines, their own hills and forests" (*Tar Baby*, 269).

9. Morrison gestures toward tar in the conclusion of *Song of Solomon* as Milkman's shout to his "brother man" Guitar echoes through the hills: "tar, tar, tar" (337).

10. Pitch Lake is not classified as a swamp; rather, the swamps on Isle des Chevaliers, Sein de Vieilles, share properties that are in keeping with this famous tar pit.

11. Despite its reputation, one can find much beauty in Pitch Lake. In fact, a variety of trees ring the lake, and lilies and birds of paradise actually grow out of the muck. Further, it is a natural source of revenue; the country routinely exports pitch to more than fifty countries.

12. Pitch Lake is one of only three natural asphalt lakes in the world; the others are in California (the famous La Brea tar pits) and Venezuela.

13. Some enslaved people were granted the opportunity to grow subsistence gardens, the yield of which could stave off hunger. These gardens were tended to during midday respites or in the darkness of night. However, they did not provide a reliable source of food, largely because of inadequate water supplies: "It has been noted that, whenever the subsistence gardens were ravaged by prolonged drought, first to be affected were the slave gardens, for which water could be provided only by rainfall or when stolen from the master . . . the resulting scarcity of food would bring on an increase in marronage" (Fouchard, 162).

14. That Valerian is known as the "Candy King" encodes Morrison's critique of Valerian's occupation of Isle des Chevaliers. His move to this predominate site of sugar-cane production reinforces his colonial power and his commodification of landscape and people. Symbolic of a nineteenth-century plantation owner, Valerian "accepted the proposition that nature should be dominated, brought under control, and used for profit" (Blum, 2).

15. In lieu of Michael, the son who never materializes, Son appears. Son's conversation with Margaret highlights that the two men are to be read as doppelgängers: "'How old are you?' 'About as old as your son.' 'My son is twenty-nine going on thirty.' 'Okay. Almost as old as your son'" (198). Interestingly, Son refers to Michael only as "son."

16. While the liberty afforded by these uncultivated landscapes is unmistakable, plantation labor was not entirely removed from swamplands. In fact, one of the most lucrative of all plantation crops, rice, was cultivated in low-country coastal swamplands. Although historians give more attention to cotton and cane plantations, rice plantations were a major site of forced labor: by 1850, for example, "fifty-eight thousand slaves lived on tidal rice plantations," and another "two thousand domestic slaves were attached to the urban residences of rice planters in Charleston and Savannah" (Dusinberre, 389). Further, rice plantations were huge, rivaling the vastness of Caribbean estates: "The majority of the South's truly rich antebellum slave masters derived their fortunes from rice—not from cotton, tobacco, or sugar" (6). Rice was initially, in the seventeenth century, grown on dry land, but it quickly became cultivated on swampland, which in turn highlighted the travail of this plantation economy as the entire cultivation of rice became tied to strenuous labor in muddy and swampy environments.

17. Though women were certainly part of escaped slave communities, marronage was encoded as a male activity, for women, often caring for small children, "ran away permanently far less often than men" (Blum, 3). Moreover, the seclusion of the woods engendered violent acts against women, such as rapes and beatings, which also reduced the number of female fugitives.

18. Son is not presented merely as a threatening sexual being in the novel; he is also a site of beauty, female desire, and charm. In a detailed shower scene, Son carefully bathes, washing the detritus of the sea and swamp from his body, a physical alteration that causes a change of heart for Jadine and Margaret: "They stayed in their rooms all afternoon, and the next time they saw the stranger he was so beautiful they forgot all about their plans" (*Tar Baby*, 130). Here again, water is implicated in another, albeit not as significant, transformation.

19. While Jadine critiques the natural world, she is comfortable dominating it, as evidenced by her relationship to the sealskin coat. Like Valerian, who purchases the island and begins dismantling it, the ninety baby seals were dismembered for Jadine's pleasure. Her erotic relationship to the coat is enacted through a position of dominance: "She went to the bed where the skins of the ninety baby seals sprawled. She lay on top of them and ran her fingertips through the fur. How black. How shiny. Smooth. She pressed her thighs deep into its dark luxury. Then she lifted herself up a little and let her nipples brush the black hairs, back and forth, back and forth" (91). Highlighting the blackness of the coat, a near match to Jadine's own hair, Morrison draws attention to Jadine's complex positionality. She shares a racial alliance to the island and its people, yet her actions with the fur coat bespeak her political alliance with European culture and desire.

20. The wetland is a place that "assaults the sense of smell" (Giblett, 13), and this passage suggests that Son carries swamp effluvia with him.

21. Jadine's fear is foreshadowed at the supermarket in Paris where she meets the woman in yellow, whose dark complexion and Africanized presence undermine Jadine's Anglo beauty. The woman, with skin like tar, whose only purchase is three eggs, is a site of both beauty and maternity. Jadine's critique of the island's excesses echoes her disparaging remarks of the woman in yellow: "There was too much hip, too much bust" (*Tar Baby*, 45). Thus race and place are elided.

22. Son analogizes the shaking up of plant life to his treatment of women, who he claims need to be "jacked up" every once in a while to make them "act nice," a problematic remark that he follows with what promises to be a sexist and racist joke about "three colored whores who went to heaven" (*Tar Baby*, 148). Despite Son's connection to the natural/ancestral world, he, like Jadine, is a flawed character, as his racial essentialism and phallocentric bonding with Valerian reveal.

23. Kincaid points out the irony of exporting animals from one colony to tame another.

24. In *Song of Solomon*, Morrison used the metaphor of hair as a sign of racial connectivity, as Pilate tries in vain to convince her dying granddaughter that Milkman's rejection of her hair is a disavowal of himself and his race: "Pilate put her hand on Hagar's head and trailed her fingers through her granddaughter's soft damp wool. 'How can he not love your hair? It's the same hair that grows out of his own armpits. The same hair that crawls up out his crotch on up his stomach. All over his chest. The very same. . . . It's his hair too. He got to love it'" (315). The relationship Morrison draws between hair and liberation is likewise sounded in Alice Walker's "Oppressed Hair Puts a Ceiling on the Brain," in which she argues that her hair was a barrier to spiritual growth. Quickly pointing out that it was not her natural hair that betrayed her, Walker describes the joy she experienced in her "friend hair": "I found it to be springy, soft, almost sensually responsive to moisture. As the little braids spun off in all directions but the ones I tried to encourage them to go, I discovered my hair's willfulness, so like my own! I saw that my friend hair, given its own life, had a sense of humor. I discovered I liked it" (286). Concluding with a botanical metaphor ("The ceiling at the top of my brain lifted. . . . The plant was above ground!"), Walker, like Morrison, affirms the relationship between hair and the natural world.

25. Even posthumously, L is aligned with the natural world, claiming an intimacy with the sea: "The ocean is my man now. He knows when to rear and hump his back, when to

be quiet and simply watch a woman. He can be devious, but he's not a false-hearted man" (*Love*, 100). Echoing earlier scenes, L's eroticism is played out against the ocean. The sea, her "man," is full of mystery, but steadfast, another oxymoronic description that follows the logic of the novel.

26. Given the context clues, I believe that Heed dies, but Morrison's diction is ambiguous as to which of the women dies in the attic.

27. Employing a presentist lens, Police-heads evoke a thoughtful meditation on environmental degradation and exploitation of the biotic world. The creatures that haunt the beachside community are symbols of marine and terrestrial degradation. The health of our oceans—and thus our planet—is suffering from garbage, especially plastics, overfishing, offshore drilling, acidification, and rising temperatures. Given the ecotonal reading I have advanced in this chapter, one can profitably read the Police-heads as an embodiment of marine destruction, as well as a lesser-known environmental crisis, namely, sand extraction. While seemingly inconsequential, sand, from an environmental perspective, is, according to Vince Beiser in *The World in a Grain: The Story of Sand and How It Changed Civilizations*, the most important solid substance in the world. It is the "literal foundation of modern civilization" (1). He elucidates that concrete is made of sand; hence it is the building block of our modern cities, buildings, homes, roads, and even glass. Given the population explosion in cities, humans are extracting massive amounts of sand and, in so doing, damaging the ecological world. Miners are stripping riverbeds and beaches bare and ripping out farmlands and forests to extract the sand underneath. Beiser explains that dredging sand from the bottoms of lakes and rivers leads to annihilation of habitats, destroying species of fish, birds, and plants. The desperate need for sand is catalyzing criminal activity and violence. Illegal sand miners have stolen entire beaches, and people have lost their lives. Therefore, from an environmental perspective, Police-heads stand as a metonym of these ecological crises, marine and terrestrial.

CONCLUSION. A BLACK AND WHITE ECOLOGY: PLANTATIONS AND RACE FORMATION IN *A MERCY* AND *JAZZ*

1. Florens's mother makes the heartbreaking decision to save her daughter from D'Ortega's sexual predation. Florens never learns of her mother's protective gesture and instead believes that her mother rejects her in favor of her younger brother.

BIBLIOGRAPHY

Adler, Jonathan. "Foreword." In *Life in Color: National Geographic Photographs*. Washington, DC: National Geographic Society, 2014.

Agee, James K. "Ecological Effects of Fire." *Science*, n.s., 217, no. 4566 (1982): 1244.

Aguiar, Sarah Appleton. "'Passing on' Death: Stealing Life in Toni Morrison's *Paradise*." *African American Review* 38, no. 3 (Fall 2004): 513–19.

Alaimo, Stacy. *Bodily Natures: Science, Environment, and the Material Self*. Bloomington: Indiana University Press, 2010.

Alexandre, Sandy. "From the Same Tree: Gender and Iconography in Representations of Violence in Beloved." *Signs: Journal of Women in Culture and Society* 36, no. 4 (Summer 2011): 915–40.

Allen, Valerie. "Mineral Virtue." In *Animal, Mineral, Vegetable: Ethics and Objects*, edited by Jeffrey Jerome Cohen, 123–52. Washington, DC: Oliphaunt Books, 2012.

Allister, Mark. *Refiguring the Map of Sorrow: Nature Writing and Autobiography*. Charlottesville: University Press of Virginia, 2001.

Anderson, Melanie R. *Spectrality in the Novels of Toni Morrison*. Knoxville: University of Tennessee Press, 2013.

Anthony, Carl. "Reflections on African American Environmental History." In *To Love the Wind and the Rain*, edited by Dianne D. Glave and Mark Stoll, 200–210. Pittsburgh: University of Pittsburgh Press, 2005.

Bachelard, Gaston. *The Psychoanalysis of Fire*. Boston: Beacon Press, 1964.

Backer, Dana M., Sarah E. Jensen, and Guy R. McPherson. "Impact of Fire Suppression Activities on Natural Communities." *Conservation Biology* 18, no. 4 (2004): 937–46.

Ball, Philip. *Bright Earth: Art and the Invention of Color*. Chicago: University of Chicago Press, 2011.

Baluška, František, Stefano Mancuso, Dieter Volkmann, and Peter W. Barlow. "The 'Root-Brain' Hypothesis of Charles and Francis Darwin: Revival after More Than 125 Years." *Plant Signaling and Behavior* 4, no. 12 (2009), https://www.ncbi.nlm.nih.gov/pmc/articles/PMC2819436.

Barnett, Cynthia. *Rain: A Natural and Cultural History*. New York: Crown, 2015.

Beiser, Vince. *The World in a Grain: The Story of Sand and How It Transformed Civilization*. New York: Riverhead Books, 2018.

Benn, James A. "Written in Flames: Self-Immolation in Sixth-Century Sichuan." *T'oung Pao: Revue Internationale de Sinologie / International Journal of Chinese Studies*, 2nd ser., 92, nos. 4–5 (2006): 410–65.

Bennett, Jane. *Vibrant Matter: A Political Ecology of Things*. Durham, NC: Duke University Press, 2010.

Berlin, Ira. *The Making of African America: The Four Great Migrations*. New York: Penguin, 2010.

Blum, Elizabeth D. "Power, Danger, and Control: Slave Women's Perceptions of Wilderness in the Nineteenth Century." *Women's Studies: An Interdisciplinary Journal* 31, no. 2 (March–April 2002): 247–65.

Bonnet, Michele. "To Take the Sin Out of Slicing Trees: The Law of the Tree in *Beloved*." *African American Review* 31, no. 1 (1997): 41–54.

Bouson, J. Brooks. *Quiet as It's Kept: Shame, Trauma, and Race in the Novels of Toni Morrison*. Albany: State University of New York Press, 2000.

Braziel, Jana Evans, and Annita Mannur. "Nation, Migration, Globalization: Points of Connection in Diaspora Studies." In *Theorizing Diaspora: A Reader*, edited by Jana Evans Braziel and Annita Mannur, 1–22. Malden, MA: Blackwell, 2003.

Buchmann, Stephen. *The Reason for Flowers: Their History, Culture, Biology, and How They Changed Our Lives*. New York: Scribner, 2015.

Burnside, Madeleine. *Spirits of the Passage: The Transatlantic Slave Trade in the Seventeenth Century*. Edited by Rosemarie Robotham. New York: Simon and Shuster, 1997.

Cann, Candi K. *Virtual Afterlives: Grieving the Dead in the Twenty-First Century*. Lexington: University Press of Kentucky, 2014.

Carney, Judith. *Black Rice: The African Origins of Rice Cultivation in the Americas*. Cambridge, MA: Harvard University Press, 2001.

Carney, Judith. "Out of Africa: Colonial Rice History in the Black Atlantic." In *Colonial Botany: Science, Commerce, and Politics in the Early Modern World*, edited by Londa Schiebinger and Claudia Swan, 204–22. Philadelphia: University of Pennsylvania Press, 2005.

Carney, Judith A., and Richard Nicholas Rosomoff. *In the Shadow of Slavery: Africa's Botanical Legacy in the Atlantic World*. Berkeley: University of California Press, 2011.

Carson, Rachel. *The Sea around Us*. New York: Oxford, 1950.

Chamovitz, Daniel. *What a Plant Knows: A Field Guide to the Senses*. New York: Farrar, Straus and Giroux, 2012.

Chen, Sharon. "Professor Spotlight: Carolyn Finney on Leaving Cal." Student Environmental Resource Center, University of California Berkeley, June 10, 2015. https://serc.berkeley.edu/professor-spotlight-carolyn-finney-on-leaving-cal.

Chiles, Katy L. *Transformable Race: Surprising Metamorphoses in the Literature of Early America*. New York: Oxford University Press, 2014.

Christopher, Lindsay M. "The Geographical Imagination in Toni Morrison's *Paradise*." *Rocky Mountain Review* 63, no. 1 (2009): 89–95.

Clark-Lewis, Elizabeth. *Living In, Living Out: African American Domestics and the Great Migration*. New York: Kodansha, 1996.

Cohen, Jeffrey Jerome. "Introduction: All Things." In *Animal, Mineral, Vegetable: Ethics and Objects*, edited by Jeffrey Jerome Cohen, 1–8. Washington, DC: Oliphaunt Books, 2012.

Cohen, Jeffrey Jerome. "Introduction: Ecology's Rainbow." In *Prismatic Ecology: Ecotheory beyond Green*, edited by Jeffrey Jerome Cohen. Minneapolis: University of Minnesota Press, 2014.

Couric, Katie. "The Blood of Lynching Victims Is in This Soil." *National Geographic*, March 12, 2018. https://www.nationalgeographic.com/magazine/2018/04/race-lynching-museum-katie-couric-alabama.

Cowan, William Tynes. *The Slave in the Swamp: Disrupting the Plantation Narrative*. New York: Routledge, 2005.

Damrosch, Barbara. "Volcanoes Provide a Boom for Gardeners." *Washington Post*, May 20, 2010. http://www.washingtonpost.com/wp-dyn/content/article/2010/05/18/AR2010051804093.html?noredirect=on.

Dash, Michael. Preface to *Caribbean Discourse: Selected Essays*, by Édouard Glissant, v–xliii. Charlottesville: University Press of Virginia, 1989.

Delaney, Janice, Mary Jane Lupton, and Emily Toth. *The Curse: A Cultural History of Menstruation*. New York: E. P. Dutton, 1976.

DellaSala, Dominick A., and Chad T. Hanson. *The Ecological Importance of Mixed-Severity Fires: Nature's Phoenix*. Waltham, MA: Elsevier Press, 2015.

Dirt! The Movie. Directed by Gene Rosow and Bill Beneson. Common Ground Media, 2009.

Dixon, Melvin. *Ride Out the Wilderness: Geography and Identity in Afro-American Literature*. Urbana: University of Illinois Press, 1987.

Dobbs, Cynthia. "Diasporic Designs of House, Home, and Haven in Toni Morrison's *Paradise*." *MELUS* 36, no. 2 (Summer 2011): 109–26.

Douglas, Christopher. "What *The Bluest Eye* Knows about Them: Culture, Race, Identity." *American Literature: A Journal of Literary History, Criticism and Bibliography* 78, no. 1 (March 2006): 141–68.

Draper, Jan. "Blurring, Moving and Broken Boundaries: Men's Encounter with the Pregnant Body." *Sociology of Health and Illness* 25, no. 7 (November 2003): 743–67.

Drewal, Henry John. "Performing the Other: Mami Wata Worship in Africa." *Drama Review: A Journal of Performance Studies* 32, no. 2 (Summer 1988): 160–85.

Dungy, Camille T. "Introduction: The Nature of African American Poetry." In *Black Nature: Four Centuries of African American Nature Poetry*, xix–xxxv. Athens: University of Georgia Press, 2009.

Dungy, Camille T. "Tales from a Black Girl on Fire, or Why I Hate to Walk Outside and See Things Burning." In *The Colors of Nature: Culture, Identity, and the Natural World*, edited by Alison Deming and Lauret E. Savoy, 28–32. Minneapolis: Milkweed Editions, 2011.

Dusinberre, William. *Them Dark Days: Slavery in the American Rice Swamp*. New York: Oxford, 1996.

"The Ecological Importance of Forest Fires." Greentumble, April 20, 2016. https://greentumble.com/the-ecological-importance-of-forest-fires.

Eckstut, Joann, and Arielle Eckstut. *The Secret Language of Color: Science, Nature, History, Culture, Beauty of Red, Orange, Yellow, Green, Blue, and Violet*. New York: Workman Publishing Company, 2013.

Engelsiepen, Jane. "Trees Communicate." July 10, 2019. https://www.positivenewsus.org/trees-communicate-with-each-other.html.

Erickson, Peter B. "Images of Nurturance in *Tar Baby*." 1984. In *Toni Morrison: Critical Perspectives, Past and Present*, edited by Henry Louis Gates Jr. and K. A. Appiah, 293–307. New York: Amistad, 1993.

Evans, Shari. "Programmed Space, Themed Space, and the Ethics of Home in Toni Morrison's *Paradise*." *African American Review* 46, nos. 2–3 (Summer–Fall 2013): 381–96.

Evernden, Neil. "Beyond Ecology: Self, Place, and the Pathetic Fallacy." In *The Ecocriticism Reader: Landmarks in Literary Ecology*, edited by Cheryl Glotfelty and Harold Fromm, 92–104. Atlanta: University of Georgia Press, 1996.

Feerick, Jean E., and Vin Nardizzi. "Swervings: On Human Indistinction." Introduction to *The Indistinct Human in Renaissance Literature*, edited by Vin Nardizzi and Jean E. Feerick. New York: Palgrave, 2012.

Feldman, Mark. "Inside the Sanitation System: Mierle Ukeles, Urban Ecology and the Social Circulation of Garbage." *Iowa Journal of Cultural Studies* 10 (2009): 42–56.

Finlay, Victoria. *The Brilliant History of Color in Art*. Los Angeles: J. Paul Getty Museum, 2014.

Finlay, Victoria. *Color: A Natural History of the Palette*. New York: Random House, 2002.

Finney, Carolyn. *Black Faces, White Spaces: Reimagining the Relationship of African Americans to the Great Outdoors*. Chapel Hill: University of North Carolina Press, 2014.

Forsythe, Pamela J. "The Fabric of Enslaved Lives." *Broad Street Review*, September 25, 2018. https://www.broadstreetreview.com/film/aamp-presents-john-dowell-cotton-the-soft-dangerous-beauty-of-the-past.

Fouchard, Jean. *The Haitian Maroons: Liberty or Death*. Trans. A. Faulkner Watts. Preface by C. L. R. James. 1972. Reprint, New York: Edward W. Blyden Press, 1981.

Franklin, John Hope, and Alfred A. Moss Jr. *From Slavery to Freedom: A History of African Americans*. 7th ed. New York: McGraw-Hill, 1994.

Fricker, Donna. "The Louisiana Lumber Boom c. 1880–1925." Fricker Historic Preservation Services LLC. https://www.crt.state.la.us/Assets/OCD/hp/nationalregister/historic_contexts/The_Louisiana_Lumber_Boom_c1880-1925.pdf.

Fulton, Lorie Watkins. "Hiding Fire and Brimstone in Lacy Groves: The Twinned Trees of *Beloved*." *African American Review* 39, nos. 1–2 (Spring–Summer 2005): 189–99.

Gagliano, Monica. "Seeing Green: The Re-discovery of Plants and Nature's Wisdom." In *The Green Thread: Dialogues with the Vegetal World*, edited by Patricia Vieira, Monica Gagliano, and John Ryan, 19–35. New York: Lexington Books, 2016.

Garrard, Greg. *Ecocriticism*. New York: Routledge, 2004.

Gates, Henry Louis, Jr. "The Cotton Economy and Slavery." PBS, n.d. http://www.pbs.org/wnet/african-americans-many-rivers-to-cross/video/the-cotton-economy-and-slavery.

Giblett, Rodney James. *Postmodern Wetlands: Culture, History, Ecology*. Edinburgh: Edinburgh University Press, 1996.

Glasper, Janyce Denise. "John Dowell Spins Redemption from Cotton's Painful History at the African American Museum of Philadelphia." *Artblog*, November 8, 2018. https://

www.theartblog.org/2018/11/john-dowell-spins-redemption-from-cottons-painful-history-at-the-african-american-museum-of-philadelphia.

Glave, Dianne D. *Rooted in the Earth: Reclaiming the African American Environmental Heritage*. Chicago: Lawrence Hill Books, 2010.

Greenberg, Gary, Carol Kiley, and Kate Clover. *The Secrets of Sand: A Journey into the Amazing Microscopic World of Sand*. Beverly, MA: Voyageur Press, 2015.

Grier, William H., and Price M. Cobbs. *Black Rage*. 1968. Reprint, New York: Basic Books / HarperCollins, 1992.

Haraway, Donna. *When Species Meet*. Minneapolis: University of Minnesota Press, 2007.

Harding, M. Esther. *Woman's Mysteries: Ancient and Modern*. New York: Harper & Row, 1971.

Harris, Anne. "Pyromena: Fire's Doing." In *Elemental Ecocriticism: Thinking with Earth, Air, Water, and Fire*, edited by Jeffrey Jerome Cohen and Lowell Duckerts, 27–54. Minneapolis: University of Minnesota Press, 2015.

Harris, Juliette, and Pamela Johnson. "Ms. Strand Calls a Press Conference." In *Tenderheaded: A Comb-Bending Collection of Hair Stories*, edited by Juliette Harris and Pamela Johnson, xv. New York: Washington Square Press, 2002.

Harris, Michael. "Blind Memory and Old Resentments: The Plantation Imagination." In *Landscape of Slavery: The Plantation in American Art*, edited by Angela D. Mack and Stephen G. Hoffius, 140–58. Columbia: University of South Carolina Press, 2008.

Hatch, Peter J. "African-American Gardens at Monticello." Thomas Jefferson Monticello, January 2001. https://www.monticello.org/house-gardens/center-for-historic-plants/twinleaf-journal-online/african-american-gardens-at-monticello.

Hempton, Gordon. "Super Soul Original Short: One Man's Mission to Record the Earth's Rarest Sounds." *Super Soul Sunday*, June 1, 2015. http://www.oprah.com/own-super-soul-sunday/super-soul-original-short-acoustic-ecologist-gordon-hempton-video.

Herzogenrath, Bernd. "White." In *Prismatic Ecology: Ecotheory beyond Green*, edited by Jeffrey Jerome Cohen, 1–21. Minneapolis: University of Minnesota Press, 2014.

Hitchcock, Susan Tyler. *Life in Color: National Geographic Photographs*. Washington, DC: National Geographic, 2012.

Hobhouse, Henry. *Seeds of Change: Five Plants That Transformed Mankind*. New York: Harper & Row, 1985.

Holloway, Karla. *Passed On: African American Mourning Stories*. Durham, NC: Duke University Press, 2002.

hooks, bell. *Belonging: A Culture of Place*. New York: Routledge, 2009.

Hubbell, Drew, and John Ryan. "Scholarly Ecotones in the Information Landscape." *Landscapes: The Journal of the International Centre for Landscape and Language* 7, no. 1 (2016).

"Humans Are Blind to Plants: Can We Get Over It?" *Conservation: The Source for Environmental Intelligence*, August 31, 2016. http://www.conservationmagazine.org/2016/08/plant-blindness.

Hurd, Barbara. *Stirring the Mud: On Swamps, Bogs, and Human Imagination*. Boston: Beacon Press, 2001.

Iovino, Serenella, and Serpil Oppermann, eds. *Material Ecocriticism*. Bloomington: Indiana University Press, 2014.

Jablonski, Nina G. *Skin: A Natural History*. Berkeley: University of California Press, 2006.

Jackson, Chuck. "'A Headless Display': *Sula*, Soldiers, and Lynching." *Modern Fiction Studies* 52, no. 2 (2006): 374–92.

Jahren, Hope. *Lab Girl*. New York: Knopf, 2016.

Japtok, Martin. "Sugarcane as History in Paule Marshall's 'To Da-Duh in Memoriam.'" *African American Review* 34, no. 3 (2000): 475–82.

Jenkins, Virginia. *The Lawn: A History of an American Obsession*. Washington, DC: Smithsonian Institution, 1994.

Jones, Lauren. "U.Va. Undergraduate Researcher Studies Sunflowers' Power to Clean Up Soil." *UVA Today*, July 9, 2014. https://news.virginia.edu/content/uva-undergraduate-researcher-studies-sunflowers-power-clean-soil.

Kincaid, Jamaica. *My Garden (Book)*. New York: Farrar, Straus and Giroux, 1991.

Kowalski, Philip J. "No Excuses for Our Dirt: Booker T. Washington and a 'New Negro' Middle Class." In *Post-bellum, Pre-Harlem: African American Literature and Culture, 1877–1919*, edited by Barbara McCaskill and Caroline Gebhard, 181–96. New York: New York University Press, 2006.

Landy, Joshua, and Michael Saler. "Introduction: The Varieties of Modern Enchantment." In *The Re-enchantment of the World: Secular Magic in a Rational Age*, edited by Joshua Landy and Michael Saler. Stanford, CA: Stanford University Press, 2009.

Lanham, J. Drew. *The Home Place: Memoirs of a Colored Man's Love Affair with Nature*. Minneapolis: Milkweed Editions, 2016.

Lee, Valerie. *Granny Midwives and Black Women Writers: Double-Dutched Readings*. New York: Routledge, 1996.

Li, Qing. "Effect of Forest Bathing Trips on Human Immune Function." *Environmental Health and Preventive Medicine* 15, no. 1 (January 2010): 9–17.

Logan, William Bryant. *Dirt: The Ecstatic Skin of the Earth*. New York: W. W. Norton, 1995.

Louv, Richard. *Last Child in the Woods: Saving Our Children from Nature-Deficit Disorder*. Chapel Hill, NC: Algonquin Books, 2008.

Mack, Angela D. Introduction to *Landscape of Slavery: The Plantation in American Art*, edited by Angela D. Mack and Stephen G. Hoffius, 1–15. Columbia: University of South Carolina Press, 2008.

Marder, Michael. *Plant-Thinking: A Philosophy of Vegetal Life*. New York: Columbia University Press, 2013.

Marder, Michael. "What's Planted in the Event? On the Secret Life of a Philosophical Concept." In *The Green Thread: Dialogues with the Vegetal World*, edited by Patricia Vieira, Monica Gagliano, and John Ryan, 3–17. New York: Lexington Books, 2016.

Mathe-Shires, Laszlo. "Imperial Nightmares: The British Image of 'the Deadly Climate' of West Africa, c. 1840–74." *European Review of History* 8, no. 2 (August 2001): 137–56.

Mentz, Steve. "Phlogiston." In *Elemental Ecocriticism: Thinking with Earth, Air, Water, and Fire*, edited by Jeffrey Jerome Cohen and Lowell Duckerts, 55–76. Minneapolis: University of Minnesota Press, 2015.

Meyer, Robinson. "American Trees Are Moving West, and No One Knows Why." *The Atlantic*, May 17, 2017. https://www.theatlantic.com/science/archive/2017/05/go-west-my-sap/526899.

Mintz, Sidney W. *Tasting Food, Tasting Freedom: Excursions into Eating, Culture, and the Past*. Boston: Beacon, 1996.

Mitsch, William J., and James G. Gosselink. *Wetlands*. 2nd ed. New York: Van Nostrand Reinhold, 1993.

Mobley, Marilyn Sanders. "Narrative Dilemma: Jadine as Cultural Orphan in *Tar Baby*." 1987. In *Toni Morrison: Critical Perspectives, Past and Present*, edited by Henry Louis Gates Jr. and K. A. Appiah, 284–93. New York: Amistad, 1993.

Montgomery, David R. *Dirt: The Erosion of Civilizations*. Berkeley: University of California Press, 2007.

Morrison, Toni. *A Mercy*. New York: Knopf, 2008.

Morrison, Toni. "The Art of Fiction." Interview with Elissa Schappell and Claudia Brodsky Lacour. *Paris Review*, no. 128 (Fall 1993). https://www.theparisreview.org/interviews/1888/toni-morrison-the-art-of-fiction-no-134-toni-morrison.

Morrison, Toni. *Beloved*. New York: Plume, 1987.

Morrison, Toni. "A Bench by the Road." *World Journal of the Unitarian Universalist Association* 3, no. 1 (January–February 1989): 4–5, 37–41.

Morrison, Toni. "Blacks, Modernism, and the American South: An Interview with Toni Morrison." In *Toni Morrison: Conversations*, edited by Carolyn Denard, 178–205. Jackson: University Press of Mississippi, 2008.

Morrison, Toni. *The Bluest Eye*. 1970. Reprint, New York: Plume, 1993.

Morrison, Toni. "Chloe Wofford Talks about Toni Morrison." Interview by Claudia Dreifus. *New York Times Magazine*, September 11, 1994.

Morrison, Toni. "Conversation: Toni Morrison." Interview with Elizabeth Farnsworth. In *Toni Morrison: Conversations*, edited by Carolyn Denard, 155–58. Jackson: University Press of Mississippi, 2008.

Morrison, Toni. *God Help the Child*. New York: Knopf, 2015.

Morrison, Toni. *Home*. New York: Knopf, 2012.

Morrison, Toni. "'I Regret Everything': Toni Morrison Looks Back on Her Personal Life." Interview with Terry Gross. *NPR Books*, August 24, 2015. https://www.npr.org/2015/08/24/434132724/i-regret-everything-toni-morrison-looks-back-on-her-personal-life.

Morrison, Toni. *Jazz*. New York: Plume, 1992.

Morrison, Toni. "The Language Must Not Sweat: A Conversation with Toni Morrison." Interview with Thomas LeClair. 1981. In *Conversations with Toni Morrison*, edited by Danielle Taylor-Guthrie, 119–28. Jackson: University Press of Mississippi, 1994.

Morrison, Toni. *Love*. New York: Knopf, 2003.

Morrison, Toni. *Paradise*. New York: Knopf, 1998.

Morrison, Toni. "Predicting the Past." Interview with Susanna Rustin. *The Guardian*, October 31, 2008. https://www.theguardian.com/books/2008/nov/01/toni-morrison.

Morrison, Toni. *Song of Solomon*. New York: Penguin, 1977.

Morrison, Toni. *Sula*. New York: Knopf, 1973.

Morrison, Toni. *Tar Baby*. New York: Knopf, 1981.

Morrison, Toni. "Unspeakable Things Unspoken: The Afro-American Presence in American Literature." In *Within the Circle: An Anthology of African American Literary*

Criticism from the Harlem Renaissance to the Present, edited by Angelyn Mitchell, 368–400. Durham, NC: Duke University Press, 1994.

Morton, Timothy. *The Ecological Thought*. Cambridge, MA: Harvard University Press, 2012.

Mueller, Stefanie. *The Presence of the Past in the Novels of Toni Morrison*. Heidelberg: University of Heidelberg, 2013.

Myers, Jeffrey. "Other Nature: Resistance to Ecological Hegemony in Charles W. Chesnutt's *The Conjure Woman*." *African American Review* 37, no. 1 (Spring 2003): 5–20.

NAACP. *Burning at the Stake in the United States: A Record of the Public Burning by Mobs of Five Men, during the First Five Months of 1919 in the States of Arkansas, Florida, Georgia, Mississippi, Texas*. 1919. Baltimore, MD: Black Classic Press, 1986.

Nelson, Megan Kate. "The Landscape of Disease: Swamps and Medical Discourse of the American Southeast, 1800–1880." *Mississippi Quarterly: The Journal of Southern Cultures* 55, no. 4 (2002): 535–67.

Nichols, Wallace J. *Blue Mind: The Surprising Science That Shows How Being near, in, on, or under Water Can Make You Happier, Healthier, More Connected and Better at What You Do*. New York: Little, Brown, 2014.

Novak, Phillip. "'Circles and Circles of Sorrow': In the Wake of Toni Morrison's *Sula*." *PMLA* 114, no. 2 (1999): 184–93.

Oladipo, Jennifer. "Porphyrin Rings." In *The Colors of Nature: Culture, Identity, and the Natural World*, edited by Alison Deming and Lauret E. Savoy, 263–68. Minneapolis: Milkweed Editions, 2011.

Oppermann, Serpil. "Nature's Colors: A Prismatic Materiality in the Natural/Cultural Realms." In *Ecocritical Aesthetics: Language, Beauty, and the Environment*. Bloomington: Indiana University Press, 2018.

Oppermann, Serpil, and Serenella Iovino. "Coda: Wandering Elements and Natures to Come." In *Elemental Ecocriticism: Thinking with Earth, Air, Water, and Fire*, edited by Jeffrey Jerome Cohen and Lowell Duckerts, 310–17. Minneapolis: University of Minnesota Press, 2015.

O'Reilly, Andrea. *Toni Morrison and Motherhood: A Politics of the Heart*. Albany: State University of New York Press, 2004.

Outka, Paul. *Race and Nature: From Transcendentalism to the Harlem Renaissance*. New York: Palgrave, 2008.

Outlaw, Lucius. "Towards a Critical Theory of 'Race.'" In *Anatomy of Racism*, edited by David Theo Goldberg, 58–82. Minneapolis: University of Minnesota Press, 1990.

Painter, Nell Irvin. "Long Divisions." *New Republic*, October 11, 2017. https://newrepublic.com/article/144972/toni-morrisons-radical-vision-otherness-history-racism-exclusion-whiteness.

Paquet, Sandra Pouchet. "The Ancestor as Foundation in *Their Eyes Were Watching God* and *Tar Baby*." *Callaloo* 13, no. 3 (Summer 1990): 499–515.

Parikh, Jyoti, and Hemant Datye. *Sustainable Management of Wetlands: Biodiversity and Beyond*. Thousand Oaks, CA: Sage Publications, 2003.

Patterson, Orlando. *Slavery and Social Death: A Comparative Study*. Cambridge, MA: Harvard University Press, 1982.

Patton, Kimberley C. *The Sea Can Wash Away All Evils: Modern Marine Pollution and the Ancient Cathartic Ocean*. New York: Columbia University Press, 2007.

Phillips, Dana, and Heather I. Sullivan. "Material Ecocriticism: Dirt, Waste, Bodies, Food, and Other Matter." *ISLE* 19, no. 3 (Summer 2012): 445–57.

"Phytoremediation: An Environmentally Sound Technology for Pollution Prevention, Control and Remediation." United Nations Environment Programme. Division of Technology, Industry and Economics. March 31, 2017.

Pilkey, Orrin H., William J. Neal, James Andrew Graham Cooper, and Joseph T. Kelley. *The World's Beaches: A Global Guide to the Science of the Shoreline*. Berkeley: University of California Press, 2011.

Potter, Jennifer. *Seven Flowers and How They Shaped Our World*. New York: Overlook Press, 2013.

Price, Richard. *Maroon Societies: Rebel Slave Communities in the Americas*. Garden City, NY: Anchor Press, 1973.

Pringle, Mary Beth. "On a Jet Plane: Jadine's Search for Identity through Place in Toni Morrison's *Tar Baby*." *Midwestern Miscellany* 24 (1996): 37–50.

Pyne, Stephen. "The Ecology of Fire." *Nature Education Knowledge* 3, no. 10 (2010): 30.

Read, Alan. "The English Garden Effect: Phyto-Performance, Abandoned Practices, and Endangered Uses." In *The Green Thread: Dialogues with the Vegetal World*, edited by Patricia Vieira, Monica Gagliano, and John Ryan, 255–79. New York: Lexington Books, 2016.

Rich, Adrienne. *Of Woman Born: Motherhood as Experience and Institution*. New York: W. W. Norton, 1995.

Roberts, Diane. *The Myth of Aunt Jemima: White Women Representing Black Women*. New York: Routledge, 1994.

Robertson, Kellie. "Exemplary Rocks." In *Animal, Mineral, Vegetable: Ethics and Objects*, edited by Jeffrey Jerome Cohen, 91–122. Washington, DC: Oliphaunt Books, 2012.

Rosenberg, Matt. "Geophagy—Eating Dirt: A Traditional Practice Which Provides Nutrients to the Body." ThoughtCo., October 24, 2020. https://www.thoughtco.com/geophagy-eating-dirt-1433451.

Ruffin, Kimberly. *Black on Earth: African American Ecoliterary Traditions*. Athens: University of Georgia Press, 2010.

Ryan, Katy. "Revolutionary Suicide in Toni Morrison's Fiction." *African American Review* 34, no. 3 (2000): 389–412.

Sanders, Scott Russell. "Staying Put." In *Earth Works: Selected Essays*. Bloomington: Indiana University Press, 2012.

Savoy, Lauret. *Trace: Memory, History, Race, and the American Landscape*. Berkeley, CA: Counterpoint, 2016.

Savoy, Lauret E., and Alison H. Deming. "Widening the Frame." In *The Colors of Nature: Culture, Identity, and the Natural World*, edited by Alison Deming and Lauret E. Savoy, 28–32. Minneapolis: Milkweed Editions, 2011.

Schell, Jennifer. "Preserving Plants in an Era of Extinction: Sentimental and Scientific Discourse in Mary Thacher Higginson's 'A Dying Race.'" In *The Green Thread:*

Dialogues with the Vegetal World, edited by Patricia Vieira, Monica Gagliano, and John Ryan, 109–27. New York: Lexington Books, 2016.

Schiebinger, Londa. *Plants and Empire: Colonial Bioprospecting in the Atlantic World*. Cambridge, MA: Harvard University Press, 2004.

Shiva, Vandana. *Monocultures of the Mind: Perspectives of Biodiversity and Biotechnology*. London: Zed Books, 1993.

Simard, Suzanne. "How Trees Talk to Each Other." TEDSummit, June 2016. https://www.ted.com/talks/suzanne_simard_how_trees_talk_to_each_other?language=en.

Sivils, Matthew Wynn. "Reading Trees in Southern Literature." *Southern Quarterly: A Journal of the Arts in the South* 44, no. 1 (2006): 88–102.

Slicer, Deborah. "The Body as Bioregion." In *Reading the Earth: New Directions in the Study of Literature and Environment*, 107–16. Moscow: University of Idaho Press, 1998.

Smitherman, Geneva. *Talkin and Testifyin: The Language of Black America*. Detroit: Wayne State University Press, 1977.

Sommerer, Christa, Laurent Mignonneau, and Florian Weil. "The Art of Human to Plant Interaction." In *The Green Thread: Dialogues with the Vegetal World*, edited by Patricia Vieira, Monica Gagliano, and John Ryan, 233–54. New York: Lexington Books, 2016.

Squier, Susan Merrill. *Poultry Science, Chicken Culture: A Partial Alphabet*. New Brunswick, NJ: Rutgers University Press, 2011.

Stafford, Fiona. *The Long, Long Life of Trees*. New Haven, CT: Yale University Press, 2016.

Stave, Shirley A., and Justine Tally. Introduction to *Toni Morrison's "A Mercy": Critical Approaches*, 1–8. New York: Cambridge Scholars Publishing, 2011.

St. Clair, Kassia. *The Secret Lives of Color*. New York: Penguin, 2017.

Steingraber, Sandra. *Having Faith: An Ecologist's Journey to Motherhood*. Cambridge, MA: Perseus, 2001.

Stewart, Jude. *Roy G. Biv: An Exceedingly Surprising Book about Color*. New York: Bloomsbury, 2013.

Stewart, Mart A. "Slavery and the Origins of African American Environmentalism." In *To Love the Wind and Rain*, edited by Dianne D. Glave and Mark Stoll, 9–20. Pittsburgh: University of Pittsburgh Press, 2006.

Stinson, Elizabeth. "Turn Your Dead Grandma into a Tree through Technology." *Wired*, July 29, 2017. https://www.wired.com/story/turn-your-dead-grandma-into-a-tree-with-this-smart-planter.

Stowe, Johnny P., Elise Vernon-Schmidt, and Deborah Green. "Toxic Burials: The Final Insult." *Conservation Biology* 15, no. 6 (December 2001): 1817–19.

Stuart, Andrea. *Sugar in the Blood: A Family's Story of Slavery and Empire*. New York: Vintage, 2013.

Sullivan, Heather I. "Dirt Theory and Material Ecocriticism." *ISLE* 19, no. 3 (December 2012): 515–31.

Sullivan, Heather I. "The Ecology of Colors: Goethe's Materialist Optics and the Ecological Posthumanism." In *Material Ecocriticism*, edited by Serenella Iovino and Serpil Oppermann, 97–113. Bloomington: Indiana University Press, 2014.

Tiffin, Helen. "Man Fitting the Landscape: Nature, Culture, and Colonialism." In *Caribbean Literature and the Environment: Between Nature and Culture*, edited by Elizabeth M. DeLoughrey, Renee K. Gosson, and George B. Handley, 199–212. Charlottesville: University of Virginia Press, 2005.

Tomich, Dale W. *Slavery in the Circuit of Sugar: Martinique and the World Economy.* Baltimore, MD: Johns Hopkins University Press, 1990.

Wagner-Martin, Linda. *Toni Morrison and the Maternal: From "The Bluest Eye" to "Home."* New York: Peter Lang, 2014.

Walker, Alice. *Living by the Word: Selected Writings, 1973–1987.* New York: Harcourt Brace, 1989.

Walker, Alice. "Oppressed Hair Puts a Ceiling on the Brain." In *Tenderheaded: A Comb-Bending Collection of Hair Stories*, edited by Juliette Harris and Pamela Johnson, 283–87. New York: Washington Square Press, 2002.

Westmacott, Richard Noble. *African-American Gardens and Yards in the Rural South.* Knoxville: University of Tennessee Press, 1992.

White, Evelyn C. "Black Women and the Wilderness." In *The Stories That Shape Us: Contemporary Women Write about the West*, edited by Teresa Jordan and James R. Hepworth, 376–83. New York: Norton, 1995.

Wilentz, Gay. "Civilizations Underneath: African Heritage as Cultural Discourse in Toni Morrison's *Song of Solomon*." In *Toni Morrison's Fiction: Contemporary Criticism*, edited by David L. Middleton, 109–33. New York: Garland, 1997.

Willis, Susan. "Eruptions of Funk: Historicizing Toni Morrison." 1987. In *Toni Morrison: Critical Perspectives, Past and Present*, edited by Henry Louis Gates Jr. and K. A. Appiah, 308–29. New York: Amistad, 1993.

Wilson, Anthony. *Shadow and Shelter: The Swamp in Southern Culture.* Jackson: University Press of Mississippi, 2006.

Wohlleben, Peter. *The Hidden Life of Trees: Why They Feel, How They Communicate—Discoveries from a Secret World.* Vancouver: Greystone Books, 2016.

Yaeger, Patricia. *Dirt and Desire: Reconstructing Southern Women's Writing, 1930–1990.* Chicago: University of Chicago Press, 2000.

INDEX

ABOUT THE AUTHOR

Photo by Malcolm Kurtz

Anissa Janine Wardi is professor of English and African American literature at Chatham University in Pittsburgh, Pennsylvania. Her research is at the nexus of African American literature and ecocritical theory. She is the author of *Water and African American Memory: An Ecocritical Perspective* and *Death and the Arc of Mourning in African American Literature* and has been a contributor to journals such as *African American Review*, *Callaloo*, *ISLE*, and *MELUS*.

CPSIA information can be obtained
at www.ICGtesting.com
Printed in the USA
BVHW071529220521
607915BV00001B/4